Forty Acres and a Mule

Forty Acres

and

a Mule

The Freedmen's Bureau

and Black Land Ownership

CLAUDE F. OUBRE

LOUISIANA STATE UNIVERSITY PRESS

Baton Rouge and London

Designer: Albert Crochet
Type face: VIP Caledonia
Typesetter: The Composing Room of Michigan, Inc., Grand Rapids, Michigan
Printer and Binder: Kingsport Press, Kingsport, Tennessee

973. 714
O 93 f

LIBRARY OF CONGRESS CATALOGING IN PUBLICATION DATA

Oubre, Claude F   1936–
    Forty acres and a mule.

    Bibliography: p.
    Includes index.
    1. Freedmen. 2. United States. Bureau of
Refugees, Freedmen, and Abandoned Lands.
3. Reconstruction. 4. Land reform—Southern
states. I. Title.
E185.2.09   973.7'14   78-2687
ISBN 0-8071-0298-9

199076

To Patricia, Michael, and Karen
without whose love, encouragement, and patience
this work would not have been possible

Contents

Maps

Tables

Preface

RECONSTRUCTION HISTORIANS have generally agreed that one of the great tragedies of emancipation and Reconstruction was the failure to provide economic security for the former slaves, principally by failing to provide them land. During two hundred years of slavery the blacks were closely tied to the land. Slave laborers provided the muscle to clear a wilderness and make the land productive. The newly freed blacks realized that without land of their own they were still subject to the will of their former owners. Many believed that the benevolent government which emancipated them would provide a small tract of land for each family. During the first months after emancipation the actions and statements of high-ranking government and military officials convinced many of the former bondsmen that the government shared their belief and would provide them with "forty acres and a mule."

Historians, while lamenting the insufficient assistance provided the former slaves, have not provided an analysis of the freedmen's failure to become landowners. Instead, they have generally concentrated either on the development of the share-tenant system of agriculture, or on efforts to provide the freedmen with education. Of the few writers who have actually discussed land, some, like LaWanda Cox, have questioned whether Congress ever promised land to the freedmen. Others, like Martin Abbott, have argued that it was of little consequence whether Congress intended to give or sell land to the freedmen because President Johnson's restoration policy effectively nullified any land reform programs. Howard Ashley White argued that the failure of the "Freedmen's Bureau to provide an economic base for the advancement of Negroes was the failure of Congress and of the nation."[1] The purpose of this study, therefore, is to delve into the problem and discover, if possible, whether any concerted efforts were made to secure land for the freedmen.[2]

Initial experiments in land reform began during the Civil War as military commanders and congressional leaders faced the problem of providing for the blacks who sought freedom in the Union military camps. Through a series of confiscation measures, which included a colonization plan, President Lincoln and Congress provided the executive and legislative measures which military commanders administered to provide for the immediate needs of some newly freed bondsmen.

These early experiments led to the creation of the Bureau of Refugees, Freedmen, and Abandoned Lands, which was charged with the responsibility for assisting the newly freed slaves to make the transition from slavery to freedom. In order to fulfill this obligation, Congress authorized the bureau to pro-

1. LaWanda Cox, "The Promise of Land for the Freedmen," *Mississippi Valley Historical Review*, XLV (1958), 413–40; Martin Abbott, "Free Land, Free Labor, and the Freedmen's Bureau," *Agricultural History*, XXX (1956), 150–56; Howard Ashley White, *The Freedmen's Bureau in Louisiana* (Baton Rouge: Louisiana State University Press, 1970), 63.

2. Historical works which have touched briefly upon the subject of land for the freedmen include Paul W. Gates, "Federal Land Policy in the South, 1866–1888," *Journal of Southern History*, VI (1940), 303–360; Joel Williamson, *After Slavery: The Negro in South Carolina During Reconstruction, 1861–1877* (Chapel Hill: University of North Carolina Press, 1965); Martin Abbott, *The Freedmen's Bureau in South Carolina, 1865–1872* (Chapel Hill: University of North Carolina Press, 1967); Elizabeth Bethel, "The Freedmen's Bureau in Alabama," *Journal of Southern History*, XIX (1948), 49–92; John and LaWanda Cox, "General O. O. Howard and the 'Misrepresented Bureau,'" *Journal of Southern History*, XIX (1953), 427–56; Edwin D. Hoffman, "From Slavery to Self Reliance," *Journal of Negro History*, XLI (1956), 8–42.

vide emergency rations to destitute refugees and freedmen and gave it control over abandoned and confiscated lands. The act creating the bureau directed that these lands first be subdivided into forty-acre plots, then rented or sold to freedmen.

Oliver Otis Howard, who earned the reputation of being a "Christian General" during the war, was selected by Lincoln and appointed by Johnson to serve as bureau commissioner. Historians who have studied the bureau, while disagreeing over its worth, seem to agree that the choice of Howard was a wise one. Howard, realizing the enormity of his task, set a course calculated to achieve the greatest good. Since Congress failed to provide an appropriation, all activities had to be self-supporting. Howard instructed his subordinates to rent land to the freedmen and use the rents thus generated to pay for the rations, clothing, medical supplies, and shelter that were provided for the destitute. During the entire first year of the bureau's activities, therefore, the freedmen, through their labor, paid for the care of many who were unable to work.[3]

Howard believed that the freedmen should have land and that the South could be reconstructed only if it became a land of small farms rather than a land dominated by the "rebel land aristocrats."[4] He firmly believed that freedmen should earn land and not receive it as a gift. He therefore encouraged freedmen to work and save money in order to purchase land. When southerners, who lacked the finances to plant all their land, refused to sell to the freedmen, Howard recommended that northerners, including bureau agents, purchase or lease farms to provide work for the freedmen.

3. Freedmen received considerable assistance from various benevolent societies throughout the nation as well as in England. This assistance was generally in the form of clothing and educational material.

4. E. Whittlesey for O. O. Howard to H. Wilson, July 14, 1868, Selected Series of Records, Issued by the Commissioner of the Bureau of Refugees, Freedmen and Abandoned Lands (BRFAL), 1865–1872, in Record Group 105, National Archives, Microcopy 742, Roll 4, p. 293.

Unfortunately, before the bureau could fully organize its activities, President Johnson's amnesty proclamation rendered permanent tenure of abandoned and confiscated land improbable. Consequently, bureau agents were compelled to seek alternate means of providing land. Howard forwarded their recommendations to Congress, which passed the Southern Homestead Act restricting the public land of the South to homesteading for actual settlement. This act made available approximately forty-six million acres of public lands and therefore should have been beneficial to the freedmen who desired land. Howard even viewed his efforts under this act as another method of acquiring land by individual purchase since the homestead fees were approximately the same as the cost of the land under earlier public laws.

The act creating the bureau did not specify the actual powers of the commissioner. Howard interpreted the clause giving him control of "all subjects relating to refugees and freedmen"[5] in as broad a manner as possible. He decided that the bureau should actively supervise the labor system of the South to assure that the freedmen received fair wages. When southern courts denied freedmen equality before the law, he instituted a system of bureau courts to protect the freedmen. He also cooperated with various freedmen aid societies in providing education and relief for the freedmen. Under a program which was this comprehensive, Howard hoped that freedmen would easily make the transition from slavery to freedom.

Unfortunately, although Congress through its confiscation legislation and the Southern Homestead Act provided land, freedmen experienced considerable difficulty in acquiring land. In general, southern whites, realizing that land carried status, opposed any program to provide land for the freedmen. Some northern whites, on the other hand, agreed with Howard that

5. U.S., *Statutes at Large*, XII, 507

the freedmen should have land (provided they remain in the South); yet, most northerners were unwilling to provide the necessary assistance.

As a result, when Reconstruction ended, the Negro who owned his own land in the South was the exception rather than the rule. Somehow, during those first critical years of freedom, he failed to secure ownership of land. Therefore, the questions must be asked: Did the Freedmen's Bureau fail to fulfill its obligation to help the freedmen secure land? If so, wherein did it fail? If not, why were the majority of freedmen not land owners by 1870? These are the major questions to which this study is devoted. The study concentrates on the Freedmen's Bureau as the agency most directly concerned with the land programs. However, the actions of Congress, the military, Presidents Lincoln and Johnson, as well as the actions of northern and southern whites also affected the success or failure of efforts to assist the freedmen. Consequently these actions are also investigated.

Acknowledgments

ALTHOUGH IT IS IMPOSSIBLE for me to recognize all who helped in this endeavor, some individuals rendered assistance above and beyond what would normally be considered duty. I wish, therefore, to thank Lawrence D. Rice of the University of Southwestern Louisiana who planted the seed of this work in his seminar on Reconstruction, and then, as my major professor and mentor, guided my research through a thesis and a dissertation. As I continued the research and expanded the work, his interest, suggestions, and assistance made the tedious research more enjoyable.

Special recognition also goes to the staff of Dupre Library, particularly Dennis Gibson, who secured the microfilmed records which made it possible for me to complete much of the research while I continued my employment as a high school history teacher.

A portion of Chapter VI appeared as an article in *Louisiana History*, XVII (Spring 1976), pp. 143–58. I wish to thank the editor, Glenn Conrad, for permission to use material from the article in this work.

Finally, I wish to acknowledge the timely assistance and professional skill of Brice Palmer, who prepared the maps.

Forty Acres and a Mule

I

Wartime Efforts
Toward Economic Security
for Blacks

IN THE CRUCIBLE of war, situations frequently arise which compel men to take actions which they might hesitate to take under other conditions. Such was the case with the various measures which brought freedom to nearly four million southern slaves. In an effort to make the war costly to the South, Congress enacted a series of confiscation acts and levied a direct tax on property. President Lincoln, Congress, and private individuals experimented with colonization schemes, and military commanders and direct tax commissioners grappled with the problems of confiscating land and providing for the freedmen. All these activities indicate that those directly concerned with emancipation recognized that economic security through land ownership was a basic need of the newly freed slave.

Thaddeus Stevens of Pennsylvania proposed to remake the South through massive confiscation of the lands of slave owners and redistribution of those lands to former slaves. He championed, and Congress enacted, the first confiscation act, of August 6, 1861, giving the president power to seize property used in aid of rebellion and freeing slaves employed either in arms or labor against the United States.[1] Although the act promised much, enforcement depended on Lincoln. Since the state gov-

1. U.S., *Statutes at Large*, XIII, 352.

1

ernments were in rebellion, he could have interpreted the act to include not only the property actually used in waging war but also all of the public lands belonging to the states. Because of the necessity of keeping the border states in the Union, however, Lincoln interpreted the act conservatively. Consequently, relatively few slaves were freed and little land confiscated. In fact, when General John C. Fremont in Missouri, on August 30, 1861, issued a proclamation placing the state under martial law and declaring forfeited the land and slaves of those who supported the Confederacy, President Lincoln countermanded his proclamation and instructed him to issue orders more in conformity with the first confiscation act.[2] Fremont refused to comply and was relieved of command.

Although President Lincoln did not actively press confiscation and emancipation under the first confiscation act, he proposed in his annual message to Congress on December 3, 1861, that Congress free slaves actually seized under the act. He further recommended that steps be taken for colonizing them "at some place, or places, in a climate congenial to them."[3] Over the next six months Lyman Trumbull in the Senate and Thomas D. Elliot in the House led the fight for passage of a new confiscation act which would embody Lincoln's recommendation. The second confiscation act, approved on July 17, 1862, provided for the confiscation of property of five different classes of persons guilty of disloyalty to the Union. The act also provided that the slaves of persons who engaged in or gave aid to rebellion would be forever freed whenever the area in which they resided came under control of the United States military. Congress also included in the act President Lincoln's recommendation that pro-

2. Roy P. Basler (ed.), *The Collected Works of Abraham Lincoln* (8 vols; New Brunswick, New Jersey: Rutgers University Press, 1953), IV, 506.

3. *Ibid.*, V, 48. In addition to his proposal to colonize the slaves freed by confiscation, Lincoln also recommended: "It might be well to consider too, —whether the free colored people already in the United States could not, so far as individuals may desire, be included in such colonization."

visions be made for colonization of slaves freed through confiscation.[4]

Although the act incorporated some of Lincoln's recommendations, he voiced concern that it placed punishment on persons, whereas Congress had directed the first act against property itself. In response, he prepared a veto message based on the principle that the confiscation portion was a bill of attainder, since such confiscation was permanent. Subsequently Congress passed a joint explanatory resolution limiting the effect of confiscation to the life of the guilty party.[5] The second confiscation act, under which most of the actual confiscation later occurred, did not give the government clear title to the land, thus rendered impractical any future efforts to assign these lands to the freedmen and guarantee permanent possession. Other means were required to provide for the thousands of slaves freed by the act.

Colonization of the liberated slaves in Liberia, Haiti, Central America, and Santo Domingo became a frequent topic in and out of Congress.[6] As early as October, 1861, Lincoln proposed colonizing Negroes on the Chiriqui Improvement Company grant in the district of Panama.[7] In 1855 the company had gained control of several hundred thousand acres of rich coal land on the Isthmus of Panama. During the war the company contracted

4. U.S., *Statutes at Large*, XII, 589–92.

5. Although Lincoln signed the second confiscation act and the joint explanatory resolution, he transmitted his veto message to Congress. J. D. Richardson (comp.), *A Compilation of the Messages and Papers of the Presidents, 1789–1902* (10 vols.: Washington: Government Printing Office, 1896–1907), VI, 85.

6. One proposal which Lincoln appears to have considered was made by General B. F. Butler, who proposed that the Negro troops serving the United States (about 150,000) be sent to Colombia and set to work digging a canal across the Isthmus of Darien. He further proposed to transport the wives and children of these soldiers as well as any other Negroes who wished to emigrate. This would enable the United States to establish a large Negro colony which would aid the freedmen while at the same time protect the proposed canal and serve the economic interests of the United States. William P. Pickett, *The Negro Problem: Abraham Lincoln's Solution* (New York: G.P. Putnam's Sons, 1909), 327.

7. Basler (ed.), *The Collected Works of Abraham Lincoln*, IV, 561.

to provide the Navy Department with coal at one half the cost in the United States. In order to meet the demands of the Department of the Navy the company needed laborers for its coal mines. The Chiriqui project received much attention from Congress during the period from mid-July to mid-October of 1862. Senator Samuel C. Pomeroy was appointed to coordinate the efforts of the government. Blacks who immigrated were to be provided with employment in the company coal mines and each head of family would be granted forty acres of land. Pomeroy requested and received authorization to draw $25,000 from the treasury to pay the cost of transportation and supplies for the colony. He stated that he had received 13,700 applications from blacks and had selected 500 for the first party.[8] By October, 1862, the project floundered due to the opposition of Latin American states which viewed the venture as an imperialistic move on the part of the United States. Futhermore, the Clayton-Bulwer Treaty prohibited either colonization or fortification of the area.[9]

Pomeroy, in accounting for the expenses incurred, reported that he had purchased lumber, window frames, plows, axes, hoes, yokes, carpenter's and blacksmith's tools, wagons, saddles, office furniture, foodstuffs, medicine, garden seeds, and ten mules for the Chiriqui colonists. However, although he received $25,000 he only provided vouchers for about $9,000.

As the Chiriqui project came under increasingly heavy fire from Latin American diplomats, the secretary of the interior sought other areas for colonization. Bernard Kock, the American lessor of Ile a Vache, a small island off the coast of Haiti, proposed to colonize the freedmen on that island. He promised to employ the colonists at standard wages and provide a house and

8. S. C. Pomeroy to J. Doolittle, Oct. 20, 1862, in James R. Doolittle Papers, Library of Congress.

9. Willis Boyd, "Negro Colonization in the National Crisi : 1860–1870" (Ph.D. dissertation, University of California at Los Angeles, 1953), 174. This source should be examined for further information on colonization.

garden for each family. At the end of ten years, when his lease expired, the government of Haiti would give full title to eight acres for each single male and sixteen acres for every head of family. Kock claimed that the only assistance needed was transportation and funds to purchase supplies for the first few months.[10]

After careful investigation the government decided that Kock was untrustworthy. The project should have ended there. However, two New York businessmen, Paul Forbes and Charles Tuckerman, contracted to colonize five hundred blacks on Ile a Vache. The government agreed to pay fifty dollars for each person colonized. One group, numbering 453, sailed from Fortress Monroe, Virginia, for Ile a Vache. Secretary of State William Seward became quite concerned when he learned that Bernard Kock was actually in charge of the expedition. Consequently, the government refused to pay Forbes and Tuckerman until a thorough investigation of the project could be carried out. After over a year of investigation, in which contradictory reports were submitted by various investigators, the government finally decided to end the project and bring the colonists "home." By February 1, 1865, only 292 of the 453 emigrants were still on Ile a Vache. About 73 others had moved to Aux Cayes on the main island, while the remainder had either died or wandered off. Although Congress expended $33,174.04 by March 9, 1964, on various colonization efforts, relatively few Negroes established successful colonies. In July, 1864, because of the unfavorable publicity which the Ile a Vache project received and because of the increasing demand for black labor by the military, Congress repealed the colonization clause of the 1862 confiscation act.[11]

Private efforts to promote emigration were meager but more successful than those of the government. The most successful attempts were those sponsored by the American Colonization

10. *Ibid.*, 181.
11. *Ibid.*, 186–98.

Society. During the Civil War the society was responsible for settling 168 Negroes in Liberia, and between the end of the war and 1870 it settled an additional 2,492.[12] In these ventures the society received some aid from the government. The Freedmen's Bureau provided some emigrants with transportation and rations to Charleston and other points of embarkation. The society furnished the remainder of the passage to Liberia. On March 26, 1868, the society requested transportation for 618 adults and 145 children to either Baltimore or Savannah where they could board the *Golconda* for the trip to Liberia. Agents of the Freedmen's Bureau estimated the cost of transportation to these ports at $6,290. Although the bureau had previously furnished such transportation, General Howard denied their request: "There are so many worthy objects pressing their claim, that it is not deemed just to expend so large a sum of money for transportation as this request calls for."[13] Thus ended government support for one method whereby the freed slaves might obtain economic security. Possibly the most important reason for the failure of colonization lies in the opposition of the blacks. A convention of Negroes in Virginia in August, 1865, resolved: "That as natives of American soil we claim the right to remain upon it, and that any attempt to remove, expatriate, or colonize us in any other land against our will is unjust, for here we were born, and for this country our fathers and brothers have fought, and we hope to remain here in the full enjoyment of enfranchised manhood and its dignities."[14]

12. *Ibid.*, 343.
13. W. McLain to O. O. Howard, October 23, 1867, Registers and Letters Received by the Bureau of Refugees, Freedmen, and Abandoned Lands (BRFAL), 1865–1872, in Record Group 105, National Archives, Microcopy 752, Roll 49, p. 804; W. McLain to O. O. Howard, March 26, 1868, Roll 52, pp. 221, 225. Although the bureau declined to furnish the above transportation, the society did manage to settle 453 Negroes in Liberia in 1868 and an additional 160 in 1869; Boyd, "Negro Colonization in the National Crisis," 343.
14. "Resolution of Convention of Negroes in Virginia," in Record Group 105, National Archives, Microcopy 752, Roll 23, p. 574.

It appears, however, that some blacks may have favored colonization as a means of separating the races. A call was issued for a national colonization convention to meet in New York on October 4, 1864, to discuss several possible colonization programs. One scheme involved a request to Congress to "obtain a grant of land . . . upon which they are to be gathered together and become a people." The New Orleans *Era* on September 20, 1864, reported on two meetings of blacks to select representatives to the national convention. The *Era* stated that the plan could not be successful because "colonization schemes generally prove failures . . . [but] we do not see, however, that the negroes will lose by agitating the matter."[15]

Commenting on the colonization movement, the New Orleans *Tribune*, a black newspaper, reported on September 22, 1864, that no one had been selected by the blacks of Louisiana to represent them at the National Colonization Convention, but rather that some men had designated themselves as delegates to the convention. The *Tribune* denied that these pseudo-delegates had the right to speak for the free persons of color of New Orleans, much less for all of Louisiana. The *Tribune*'s reasons for opposing colonization were virtually identical to those put forth by the Virginia convention a year later, and the *Tribune* raised this question: "But supposing the proud Anglo-Saxons could try to do without them, and would induce them, through deception, to colonize, do they suppose that the negroes could be treated like the Indians have been treated, and that five millions could be 'gathered' into any section of the country without preparing troubles for a future generation—a war of races[?]"

The *Tribune* pointed out further that should an attempt be made to establish a large black colony in any of the unsettled regions of the West, "Maximilian and Napoleon will not look

15. New Orleans *Era*, September 20, 1864.

upon the movement without drawing the advantage which they could on such occasion. They would tender the hand of friendship to the negroes, would hold out to them advantages enjoyed by their citizens, and, as a matter of course, the negroes will prefer to go to Mexico, which is already settled, than going to any new section of this country." [16]

Fortunately for the freedmen, Congress did not confine its efforts to colonization. In addition to the confiscation acts, Congress levied a direct tax on property throughout the United States, including those sections in rebellion. After the Union regained control of the Sea Islands of South Carolina in 1862, the federal courts seized 76,775 acres of land for non-payment of the direct tax. Lincoln, on February 10, 1863, appointed General Rufus Saxton and General David Hunter as members of a commission of five to determine what lands the government should reserve for "charitable, educational, or police purposes." [17] The choice of Hunter as a member of the commission is noteworthy. When Lincoln relieved Fremont of command in Missouri in October, 1861, he chose Hunter as the replacement. Yet in May, 1862, General Hunter, as commander of Union forces in the Sea Islands, issued an order declaring: "the persons in these states—Georgia, Florida, and South Carolina—heretofore held as slaves, are therefore declared forever free." [18] Lincoln, on May 19, 1862, revoked Hunter's order and reserved the responsibility for freeing slaves to himself as chief executive. Consequently, his choice of Hunter as a member of the commission to set apart land in order to provide for the freedmen demonstrated that Lincoln, by this time, associated freedom with the need for land.

Subsequently, the commission reserved 60,296 acres, but offered the remaining 16,479 acres for sale. At the first tax sale,

16. New Orleans *Tribune*, September 22, 1864.
17. Basler (ed.), *The Collected Works of Abraham Lincoln*, VI, 98.
18. *Ibid.*, V, 222.

held in late February and March of 1863, the government disposed of approximately ten thousand acres of land, most of it at less than one dollar per acre. Edward Philbrick bought eight thousand acres for a group of Bostonians at seven thousand dollars and leased two more plantations from the government. Negroes who saved enough money purchased approximately two thousand acres.[19]

In September, 1863, Lincoln instructed the direct tax commissioners for the District of South Carolina to survey and place on sale at public auction approximately forty thousand acres of reserved land. He directed the commissioner to set aside the remaining twenty thousand acres and survey it in plots of twenty acres each. He further instructed them to sell these lots to selected heads of Afro-American families. The persons thus selected could procure these lots at not less than $1.25 per acre. Lincoln explained that this action was to be taken "for the charitable purpose of providing homes for such heads of families and their families respectively, so as to give them an interest in the soil."[20]

Since the lands thus set apart by Lincoln provided for only one thousand families, missionary Mansfield French and General Rufus Saxton attempted to circumvent these orders and procure land for as many as could afford to buy land at $1.25 per acre. On November 3, 1863, in the *Free South*, Saxton published his instructions to the freedmen. He assumed that the tax lands were now public lands and therefore subject to the preemption law which allowed a settler to file claim to land before it was offered at public auction. He encouraged the freedmen to exercise their right to preemption by building houses on

19. Willie Lee Rose, *Rehearsal for Reconstruction: The Port Royal Experiment* (New York: The Bobbs Merrill Company, 1964), 214; James M. McPherson, *The Struggle for Equality: Abolitionists and the Negro in the Civil War and Reconstruction* (Princeton: Princeton University Press, 1964), 251.

20. Basler (ed.), *The Collected Works of Abraham Lincoln*, VI, 453–59.

the land they wanted to buy and preempt the adjoining twenty acres. In this way he hoped that bidders would respect squatters' rights and permit the freedmen to purchase forty acres. On December 31, 1863, French secured approval of Saxton's plan from Salmon P. Chase, secretary of the treasury. Chase then issued new instructions, permitting preemption of twenty or forty acres at the rate of $1.25 per acre of all government lands on the island not reserved for military or educational purposes.[21]

Two of the direct tax commissioners decided to resist preemption passively by simply refusing to accept any money and by ignoring all preemption claims. They realized that the new instructions were poorly rooted in law and therefore the freedmen's legal claim to the land would be shaky once the war ended.[22] The commissioners convinced Chase that the best interest of both the freedmen and the government required that the freedmen not be permitted to preempt land. By early February, 1864, Chase withdrew the December instructions, thus thwarting Saxton's program.

When the sale occurred, all the reserved land was offered at open bidding. The land sold at an average price of more than eleven dollars per acre. Freedmen purchased only 2,276 acres at the low price of $1.25 per acre. Some Negroes on Wassa Island and on the Marion Chaplin plantation pooled their resources and bought their own land, intending to work it in common. They bought 470 acres, paying an average price of over $7.00 per acre in competitive bidding.[23]

The tax commissioners envisioned a mixed settlement of

21. Rose, *Rehearsal for Reconstruction*, 274, 284–85; McPherson, *Struggle for Equality*, 253.

22. Rose, *Rehearsal for Reconstruction*, 287–88.

23. *Ibid.*, 294–95; McPherson, *Struggle for Equality*, 255. It seems ironic that Saxton, in his efforts to assist as many blacks as possible in acquiring land, caused the initial instructions, reserving 20,000 acres, to be changed. This resulted in the loss of over 17,000 acres which the freedmen could have purchased at the low price of $1.25 per acre.

blacks and whites covering the islands with farms of widely varying sizes. They foresaw the Negroes with five to twenty acres
and northern white owners with larger farms. In this fashion the
owners of the larger farms could assure themselves of an
adequate labor supply while the Negro could assure himself of
sufficient work to supplement his earnings from his own small
farm. Though paternalistic in nature, this plan represented a
minor commitment to the idea that the government had some
responsibility for helping the freedmen gain economic security.[24]

Although General Saxton was one of the first of the military
commanders to become concerned with the problem of Negro
land ownership, he was by no means the only one. Wherever
Union troops gained control of southern territory, thousands of
escaped slaves made their way to the military camps in search of
freedom. Military commanders, faced with the problem of feeding the blacks, devised different methods of forcing them to help
support themselves.

In the Department of the Gulf confiscation and seizure of
abandoned plantations began under General Benjamin Butler in
1862. Prior to his departure from Louisiana Butler established a
system for leasing plantations and paying wages to former slaves.
Under Butler's wage scale men were to be paid $10 per month,
$3 of which could be paid in clothing. Women received $7 and
children between the ages of ten and sixteen received $5 per
month.[25] Butler's wage scale remained in effect until February,
1864, when it was replaced by one established by General
Banks. Under the new system first-class hands received $8 per
month, second-class hands $6 per month, third-class hands $5
per month, and fourth-class hands $4 per month. In addition to
these wages the laborers were permitted to cultivate land for
their own benefit: first- and second-class workers with families

24. Rose, *Rehearsal for Reconstruction*, 279, 296.
25. New York *Times*, January 16, 1863.

received one acre of land; first- and second-class workers without families received only a half acre of land; third- and fourth-class workers with families received one half acre of land, and those without families were allowed a quarter acre of land.[26] Although the motive behind both wage systems was a desire to protect the workers from exploitation by unscrupulous lessees, abolitionists and free blacks pointed out that under the wage system the condition of the laborer was worse than under slavery. One of the most devastating attacks on the entire system of confiscation and free labor was levied by the New Orleans *Tribune*. In an editorial on September 10, 1864, the *Tribune* condemned the confiscation program of the government as "one of the most striking evidences of hasty, imperfect and unwise legislation which our country presents." The editor stated emphatically that "The moment they [the planters] had departed, the government should have taken possession of the lands, divided them out into five acre lots, and distributed them among those persons who had, by dint of daily and long continued toil, created all the wealth of the South." The *Tribune* further charged that the plantations were leased to "avaricious adventurers from the North whose sole desire was to *exploit* the services of the freedmen, and make out of their labor as much money as possible. The slaves were made serfs and chained to the soil."[27]

By the end of October, 1864, it appeared that the *Tribune*'s objections may have had some effect. Control of the freedmen was transferred from the Freedmen's Bureau under Thomas Conway to the Treasury Department represented by Benjamin

26. *Ibid.*, February 15, 1864.
27. New Orleans *Tribune*, September 10, 1864. Emphasis in original. For an analysis of the conflict which developed between the military and the Treasury Department in Louisiana, as well as an analysis of the role of the *Tribune*, see C. Peter Ripley, *Slaves and Freedmen in Civil War Louisiana* (Baton Rouge: Louisiana State University Press, 1976).

F. Flanders. Prior to leasing plantations for 1865 Flanders helped organize several associations of freedmen to lease and work entire plantations together. One group of 130 leased the plantation of Confederate General Richard Taylor.[28]

Flanders joined with the *Tribune* and other interested free blacks to organize a bank and provide the capital needed by the freedmen to purchase mules, seed, plows, and other tools, and provisions. In order to ensure sufficient capital, the association called upon all black soldiers to invest twenty dollars from their back pay. This money would be lent to the various associations of freedmen who would repay the interest-free loans at the conclusion of the agricultural year. Since the freedmen could not offer any security, the Freedmen's Aid Association requested assistance from anyone who wanted to see the experiment in free labor succeed.[29]

The Third African Church of New Orleans even drew up a prospectus for a farming association. They recommended that groups of from five to ten families gather together, pool their resources, and lease land cooperatively. They even established a ratio for distribution of profits.[30]

As Flanders proceeded with his plan to assist the freedmen in leasing land on their own account, the military reassumed responsibility for the freedmen. Since the main function of the Freedmen's Bureau was to provide work for the freedmen, the name of the agency was changed to the Bureau of Free Labor. Military officials issued two orders which caused an uproar in the black community of New Orleans. The first of these orders created additional home farms or colonies for the care of the

28. *Ibid.*, November 1, 1864, February 22, 1865. In the Department of the Gulf the military agency assigned to provide for the freedmen was initially called the Freedmen's Bureau (not to be confused with the Bureau of Refugees, Freedmen, and Abandoned Lands, which was not created until March, 1865).

29. *Ibid.*, March 7, 1865, April 17, 1865.

30. *Ibid.*, February 3, 1865.

helpless freedmen. However, the order also commanded all able-bodied freedmen who were supported by the government to seek immediate employment.[31]

The second order instructed able-bodied freedmen to contract for labor and established a new pay schedule which provided wages of ten dollars per month for a first-class hand, "in addition to just treatment, wholesome rations, comfortable clothing, quarters, fuel and medical attendance, and the opportunity for instruction of children." Blacks objected to the new wage scale because they had anticipated one similar to the twenty-five dollar per month scale which the Treasury Department had established in Mississippi. However, their greatest opposition to the order was reserved for section twelve, which stated:

> For the purpose of reimbursing to the United States, some portion of the expenses of this system, and of supporting the aged, infirm, and helpless, the following tax will be collected in lieu of all other claims under these regulations:
> From each planter, for every hand employed by him between the ages of 18 and 50, two dollars per annum.
> From each hand between the same ages, one dollar per annum....
> Measures will be taken to collect the same Poll tax from all colored persons not on plantations, so that the active labor of this race may contribute to the support of their own helpless and disabled.[32]

Reaction to the order was immediate. Blacks held a meeting at Economy Hall on March 17, 1865. Thomas Conway, general superintendent of freedmen for the Department of the Gulf, attended the meeting. Captain James H. Ingraham, a free person of color, informed the gathering that Conway told him and all blacks that "we have been slaves until General Banks came here."[33]

31. General Order No. 7, Hq. Dept. of the Gulf, New Orleans, February 8, 1865, reprinted in New Orleans *Tribune*, February 14, 1865.

32. General Order No. 23, Hq. Dept. of the Gulf, New Orleans, March 11, 1865, reprinted in New Orleans *Tribune*, March 18, 1865: John Eaton, *Grant, Lincoln, and the Freedmen* (New York: Longman, Green and Company, 1907), 143.

33. New Orleans *Tribune*, March 18, 1865.

The assembly issued a resolution condemning Conway and stated that the existence of the Bureau of Free Labor was inconsistent with freedom. In an article entitled "Serfdom in Louisiana," the Cincinatti *Colored Citizen* pointed out that the order substituted a code of serfdom for one of slavery. The order rested on the concept that from the treason of the master the right to the labor of the slave was vested in the government.[34] Black opposition to the order had little effect on .the wages paid freedmen in the Department of the Gulf. However, the black population of New Orleans did succeed in having the city exempted from collection of the poll tax.[35]

By April, 1865, the Freedmen's Aid Association of the city of New Orleans reported that division of the large plantations had already begun and that some of the land had been rented to freedmen, who were cultivating the soil in squads of men, women, and children varying in number from fifteen to over one hundred. The association issued an open letter appealing to the friends of the freedmen for funds to provide seed, tools, draught animals, and rations. The association pointed out that this assistance was necessary since the freedmen had derived "little or no reward from their previous labors under the system of leases for the past year." The association pledged itself to supervise the expenditure of the funds provided to ensure that the freedmen derived maximum benefits.[36]

During the next few months the Freedmen's Aid Association of New Orleans assisted approximately seven hundred men, women, and children in the expense of cultivating fourteen plantations. In addition to the plantations leased to freedmen by the Treasury Department, the home colonies for helpless freedmen provided the opportunity for gainful employment to many others. Initially Conway established three home colonies, the Rost

34. Cincinnati *Colored Citizen* cited in New Orleans *Tribune*, April 13, 1865.
35. New Orleans *Tribune*, June 23, 1865.
36. *Ibid.*, May 2, 1865.

Home Colony in St. Charles Parish, which belonged to Pierre Rost, the Confederate envoy to Spain; the McHatten Home Colony, which included both the McHatten and Conrad plantations in East Baton Rouge Parish, and the Bragg Home Colony in Lafourche Parish, which had belonged to General Braxton Bragg.[37]

Since these were not able to handle the excess black population of New Orleans, General Canby seized the Sparks plantation near New Orleans and converted it to a home farm also. By July of 1865 over 1,300 freedmen were supported on Sparks, Rost, McHatten, and Bragg home colonies. The majority of their support came from the laborers who worked the home colonies for the government. Freedmen working these plantations cultivated for the government 640 acres of cotton, 975 acres of ratoon cane, 12 acres of garden vegetables, and 10 acres of potatoes. In addition these freedmen worked 60 acres of cotton, 100 acres of corn, and 310 acres of miscellaneous crops on their own account. Additional support for the home colonies came from the collection of the poll tax from planters and laborers outside the city of New Orleans.[38]

In the Mississippi Valley, General U. S. Grant, following a policy similar to that of Banks, appointed Chaplain John Eaton, Jr., as superintendent of contrabands in charge of the Freedmen's Department with responsibility for supervising the freedmen and the lands which had been taken over by the military.[39] There was considerable conflict between the military and the Treasury Department concerning the disposition of the land and the care of the Negroes. Originally the Freedmen's De-

37. *Ibid.*, July 11, 1865; Registers and Letters Received (BRFAL), in RG 105, NA, Microcopy 752, Roll 14, pp. 644–45.

38. White, *Freedmen's Bureau in Louisiana*, 67; New Orleans *Tribune*, June 23, 1865; Land Division (BRFAL), in RG 105, NA, Land Reports, Box 8.

39. Eaton, *Grant, Lincoln, and the Freedmen*, 5, 21, 26. Eaton was appointed on November 11, 1862.

partment had control over both land and blacks, with the understanding that the blacks would be provided for out of the proceeds from their labor on the land. In October, 1863, Treasury agents assumed control of all abandoned lands. By February, 1864, the Freedmen's Department complained that the Treasury Department was only interested in the proceeds from the land. Without the land the Freedmen's Department could not generate the funds necessary to care for the blacks.[40]

Of the many projects carried on by the Freedmen's Department, possibly the most noteworthy was in Mississippi. Davis Bend, seized under General Order No. 287, contained six plantations, two of which belonged to Jefferson Davis and his brother Joseph. Despite conflicting jurisdiction over the land, General Grant maintained partial military control over the area, hoping to convert Davis Bend into a Negro paradise. The Freedmen's Department moved more than ten thousand Negroes to the area, built hundreds of huts as housing, and then put the freedmen to work on the various plantations.[41] The Treasury Department subdivided and leased the plantations to both blacks and whites with the understanding that the lessee would supervise his laborers' work, provide them with sufficient quarters, and allow each family of four or more one acre of ground.[42]

In late November and December of 1864, the Freedmen's Department expelled all whites from the area and began organizing the blacks into a laboring community. Each head of a family was assigned a plot of ground with a house and allowed to

40. *Ibid.*, 143; Vernon Lane Wharton, *The Negro in Mississippi, 1865–1890* (New York: Harper Torchbooks, 1965), 39. These two sources should be consulted for a more thorough coverage of the conflict of authority.

41. S. Thomas to O. O. Howard, December 22, 1865, Registers and Letters Received (BRFAL), in RG 105, NA, Microcopy 752, Roll 20, pp. 8–13. This letter gives a general history of the Davis Bend experiment.

42. "Rules for leasing abandoned plantations and employing freedmen," Western Sanitary Commission and Treasury Department, in Record Group 105, National Archives, Microcopy 752, Roll 18, p. 837.

regulate his own affairs. At the beginning of the new year families received rent-free leases for the land they occupied in addition to permits to hold the necessary stock that was provided by the military. Many worked with nothing but hoes and their bare hands, while others borrowed money from northerners looking for lucrative investments.[43] Such were the conditions existing at Davis Bend when the Freedmen's Department turned the area over to the Freedmen's Bureau. Although the department made no provision to secure land for the Negroes, those who worked diligently and saved money could purchase land later when they became officially free.

While Eaton and his assistant superintendent concerned themselves with the problem of caring for the Negroes who flocked to the military encampments in the Mississippi Valley, the war continued. In November, 1864, General William T. Sherman began his famous march across Georgia. As the Army of Tennessee approached the coast, thousands of freedmen joined the march. They came with little but the clothes they wore and consequently had to be cared for or else they would have starved. Following the occupation of Savannah, Secretary of War Stanton and General Sherman met with a group of twenty Negro ministers in an effort to determine what could be done with the vast multitude following in the train of Sherman's army. The Negro leaders requested a temporary separation of the races as a means of reducing the existing antagonistic racial feelings.

The direct result of this meeting was the issuance, on January 16, 1865, of Special Field Order No. 15, which stated: "The islands of Charleston south, the abandoned ricefields along the rivers for thirty miles back from the sea, and the country bordering the St. Johns River, Florida, are reserved and set apart for

43. Eaton, *Grant, Lincoln, and the Freedmen*, 165–66; Wharton, *The Negro in Mississippi*, 39; S. Thomas to O. O. Howard, October 12, 1865, Registers and Letters Received (BRFAL), in RG 105, NA, Microcopy 752, Roll 22, p. 190.

the settlement of the negroes now made free by the acts of war and the proclamation of the President of the United States."[44] Under the terms of the order General Rufus Saxton was appointed as inspector of settlements and plantations. His major responsibility was to assign each head of family forty acres of land and "furnish... subject to the approval of the President of the United States, a possessory title."[45]

Saxton's concern for the welfare of the Negroes during the prior tax sale indicates the appropriateness of his selection. Some weeks earlier he complained to Stanton that the government had reneged on its promise of land for the freedmen.[46] Upon receipt of his orders, Saxton pleaded that he not be forced to assign land if the government did not intend to live up to its promise. With Stanton's assurance that the freedmen would be protected in their rights to the land, Saxton set to work settling them on the Sherman lands. By June, 1865, Saxton reported that approximately forty thousand Negroes had settled on about 400,000 acres of land reserved by Sherman's special field order.[47] In addition, Sherman instructed Saxton to lend the Negroes animals to work the land. These animals were too broken down for active military duty but under normal farm work they could recuperate sufficiently to be returned to active service. By that time, the Negroes supposedly would have earned enough to

44. William T. Sherman, *Memoirs of General William T. Sherman* (Bloomington: Indiana University Press, 1957), 248–52; *The War of the Rebellion: A Compilation of the Official Records of the Union and Confederate Armies* (Washington: Government Printing Office, 1880–1901), Ser. I, Vol. XLVII, Pt. 2, p. 37; hereinafter cited as *Official Records*. Unless otherwise indicated, all citations are to Series I.

45. *Official Records*, Vol. XLVII, Pt. 2, p. 37.

46. *Ibid.*, Series III, Vol. IV, 1022–31.

47. McPherson, *Struggle for Equality*, 258–59; R. Saxton to O. O. Howard, June 4, 1865, Registers and Letters Received (BRFAL), in RG 105, NA, Microcopy 752, Roll 17, p. 25; George R. Bentley, *A History of the Freedmen's Bureau* (Philadelphia: University of Pennsylvania Press, 1955), 98. Since the Sherman order specified forty acres for each head of family, one can assume from these figures that 10,000 families containing approximately 40,000 persons had settled on the reserved lands.

buy their own animals.[48] Had the terms of Sherman's special field order been sustained by the president and Congress, the history of Negro land ownership would have been quite different.

Although Civil War and Reconstruction historians have largely ignored the importance of land for the freedmen, one can hardly fail to note that every new act which brought emancipation brought with it some measure to bind the freedmen to the land. Almost immediately after the promulgation of the Emancipation Proclamation, Congress received a petition to create a bureau of emancipation. Over the next two years Congress debated and finally passed, on March 3, 1865, a bill creating within the War Department a Bureau of Refugees, Freedmen, and Abandoned Lands, with responsibility for helping the freedmen make the transition from slavery to freedom. The questions of authority and land were responsible for the two-year debate. As Congress debated, reports filtered in from the military and the Treasury Department, each claiming authority over the land. When Congress finally assigned the bureau to the War Department, congressional leaders thereby indicated their belief that only the military could protect the former slaves in their new freedom. Many of these same congressional leaders realized that the freedmen must have land if they were to be truly free. Otherwise, they would remain a landless mass of agricultural workers subject to the whims and fancies of the land owners. Section thirteen of the proposed bureau bill would have repealed the explanatory resolution appended to the second confiscation act. This would have given the government permanent tenure to confiscated land. However, section thirteen was amended out of the act creating the Freedmen's Bureau. Al-

48. *Official Records*, Vol. XLVII, Pt. 2, p. 115. Although most historians agree with Vernon Lane Wharton that the origin of the expression "forty acres and a mule" cannot be established, one must admit that Sherman's special field order and his letter to Saxton instructing that mules be lent to the freedmen gave substance to the expression.

though the friends of the freedmen failed to provide permanent tenure of land, they did provide for the distribution of land.[49] Section four of the act creating the bureau specified:

That the Commissioner, under the direction of the President, shall have authority to set apart, for the use of loyal refugees and freedmen, such tracts of land within the insurrectionary States as shall have been abandoned, or to which the United States shall have acquired title by confiscation or sale, or otherwise; and to every male citizen, whether refugee or freedmen as aforesaid, there shall be assigned not more than forty acres of such land, and the person to whom it was so assigned shall be protected in the use and enjoyment of the land for the term of three years at an annual rate not exceeding six per centum upon the value of such land as it was appraised by the State Authorities in the year of eighteen hundred and sixty for the purpose of taxation. . . . At the end of said term, or at any time during said term, the occupants of any parcels so assigned may purchase the land and receive such titles thereto as the United States can convey, upon paying therefore the value of the land as ascertained and fixed for the purpose of determining the annual rent aforesaid.[50]

The Freedmen's Bureau bill, therefore, although it did not offer free land, promised that by working diligently the freedmen would be able to purchase land.

49. New York *Times*, February 14, 1865.
50. U.S., *Statutes at Large*, XII, 508. While debating whether to create a freedmen's bureau, Congress appointed, under the War Department, the American Freedmen's Inquiry Commission. The commission issued a preliminary report on June 30, 1863, in which it recommended that the freedmen ultimately be given title to the farms and gardens they occupied. In its final report, issued May 15, 1864, the commission recommended that a freedmen's bureau be created with control of both freedmen and the land, thus avoiding conflict. *Official Records*, Ser. III, Vol. III, p. 443; *ibid.*, Ser. III, Vol. IV, p. 381. In order to provide that there would be adequate land to assign to the freedmen, Senator Lyman Trumbull proposed on June 27, 1864, that Congress revoke the explanatory resolution which had become a part of the second confiscation act. This would have eliminated the words "nor shall any punishment or proceedings under said act be so construed as to form a forfeiture of the real estate of the offender beyond his natural life." Although the Senate agreed to this amendment, the House refused to grant its approval and thus effectively nullified later efforts to assign land to the freedmen.

II

Confiscation and Restoration

THE EMANCIPATION OF four million slaves further complicated the social, economic, and political problems of a nation disrupted by war. Foremost among these problems—and urgently needing attention—was the alleviation of destitution among large numbers of freedmen. Hardly less important was the formulation of long-range plans for the economic welfare of the former slaves. Despite myriad proposals, programs, and alternatives, the freedmen's future was too often subject to the capricious expediency of those persons wielding power. Congress, nevertheless, by creating the Freedmen's Bureau, proposed to solve the problem of land and temporary rations. Unfortunately, the failure to provide appropriations forced all bureau activities to be self-supporting. Freedmen were to become self-sufficient by renting or purchasing land from the bureau. Out of the proceeds of their first crop they were to reimburse the government for any rations which they received.

Immediately following the cessation of hostilities, the War Department provided freedmen with surplus shovels, axes, and other tools of the disbanding armies. Based on recommendations of the Western Sanitary Commission and several assistant quartermasters, some military commanders turned over to the use of the bureau the horses and mules in excess of military needs. When the assistant commissioner for North Carolina requested the use of some of the five thousand mules and horses in that state not needed by the military, Howard had no difficulty securing the animals from the military commander of the district.[1] Furthermore, General Grant instructed his military commanders to dismount their cavalry and sell most of the horses at public auction. Freedmen who had accumulated money during the war attended these auctions and "bid freely and bought largely." [2] One such auction in Georgia was attended by over ten thousand persons of whom at least two thirds were freedmen. They purchased mules and horses at prices ranging from $150 to $300.

Thomas Conway, the assistant commissioner for Louisiana, began his bureau activities by purchasing mules, cotton seed, and farm implements, which he used to work some of the plantations under his control. In this manner he provided wages for the able-bodied, and out of the proceeds he was able to care for the destitute.[3] Land distribution, however, because of jurisdictional disputes and divided authority, proved to be the most perplexing of the economic problems.

At the close of the war the Treasury Department and the military controlled the land available for distribution to the freedmen. President Johnson, in July, 1865, ordered Treasury officials and military commanders to transfer to the Freedmen's Bureau control of all abandoned and confiscated property as well

1. New York *Times*, June 6, 1865; "Report of Inspection of the Western Sanitary Commission," Registers and Letters Received, Bureau of Refugees, Freedmen and Abandoned Lands (BRFAL), in Record Group 105, National Archives, Microcopy 752, Roll 18, pp. 827–28; C. H. Tompkins to O. O. Howard, May 21, 1865, Roll 1, Register 1, p. 459; E. Whittlesey to O. O. Howard, June 26, 1865, Roll 18, p. 735; O. O. Howard to E. Whittlesey, June 27, 1865, Selected Series of Records (BRFAL), in RG 105, NA, Microcopy 742, Roll 1, p. 83.

2. *Nation*, I (September 21, 1865), 354; U. S. Grant to G. Meade, July 17, 1865, to L. Thomas, July 17, 1865, to P. Sheridan, July 18, 1865, in Ulysses S. Grant Papers, Library of Congress, Ser. 5, Vol. 109, pp. 50–51; Alrutheus A. Taylor, *The Negro in South Carolina During the Reconstruction* (Washington: Association for the Study of Negro Life and History, 1924), 30.

3. T. Conway to O. O. Howard, July 3, 1865, Registers and Letters Received (BRFAL), in RG 105, NA, Microcopy 752, Roll 14, pp. 534–35.

as all funds derived from the rental of these lands. Despite these orders, bureau officials were thwarted on many occasions in retrieving the land and the money. In Tennessee, General Clinton B. Fisk experienced difficulty convincing Treasury agents to turn over the property under their control.

When the Treasury Department finally transferred the property on August 14, 1865, most of the land had not been surveyed. Fisk reported that he had received 42,168 acres of land. However, he did not include the acreage of six plantations. Furthermore, the above figures are deceptive since only 9,881 acres were tillable. In Florida, although there was relatively little farm property confiscated, the Treasury Department held 162 pieces of town property in Pensacola and one tract of one hundred acres in Escambia County. The rental from this property was urgently needed if the bureau was to help the freedmen in Florida. However, the Treasury agent, J. W. Rick, did not transfer the property until April 5, 1866.[4] In Alabama there was no abandoned or confiscated land. However, the military had captured considerable property belonging to the Confederate government. The military commander transferred the property to the bureau but the Treasury agent repossessed the land. Since the land was captured Confederate property and was neither abandoned nor confiscated, the property belonged to the Treasury Department, not the Freedmen's Bureau. After some delay Howard succeeded in regaining possession of the property, which provided over $62,000 in rent during the next year.[5]

General Rufus Saxton, in South Carolina and Georgia, complained that the military commanders restored nearly all abandoned property to the former owners. Colonel Orlando Brown

4. C. B. Fisk to O. O. Howard, July 5, 1865, *ibid.*, Microcopy 752, Roll 14, p. 995; June 30, 1865, p. 1265; Land Division (BRFAL), in RG 105, NA, Land Records, Boxes 7 and 10.

5. W. Swayne to O. O. Howard, September 16, 1865, Registers and Letters Received (BRFAL), in RG 105, NA, Microcopy 752, Roll 17, p. 700; Elizabeth Bethel, "The Freedmen's Bureau in Alabama," *Journal of Southern History*, XIV (1948), 62.

claimed that most of the rebels in Virginia reclaimed their abandoned lands before he could organize the bureau.[6] However, the Treasury agents and direct tax commissioners for Fairfax, Prince William, and St. Elizabeth counties transferred to Brown over 15,000 acres which had been confiscated but not sold. In addition, General Benjamin Butler transferred approximately 65,000 acres which he had seized. By the end of July, 1865, Brown reported that he had received control of 81,541 acres. Freedmen occupied 33,516 of the acreage, while whites occupied only 5,562 acres.[7]

Shortly afterwards, Brown and several other military commanders recommended that all property in Virginia which had been condemned for confiscation be retained for the use of the bureau. Brown reported that the planters resisted bureau efforts by offering subsistence wages, refusing to rent land to freedmen, and adopting non-employment agreements for any former slave who voluntarily left his former master. Since he believed this reduced the freedmen to a condition worse than slavery, Brown literally pleaded for permission to expropriate all lands liable for confiscation under the law. He recommended that if his request for confiscation were denied, the government should make provisions for those freedmen wanting to go west to take advantage of the homestead law of 1862. In addition, he proposed that the bureau furnish transportation for those who could secure positions as domestic servants in the North.[8] Upon receipt of

6. R. Saxton to O. O. Howard, September 18, 1865, Registers and Letters Received (BRFAL), in RG 105, NA, Microcopy 752, Roll 17, p. 215; D. Tillson to O. O. Howard, September 22, 1865, Roll 18, p. 111; O. Brown to O. O. Howard, May 19, 1865, Roll 13, pp. 798–99.

7. "Memoranda Relating to Abandoned and Confiscated lands, 1865–1868," Land Division (BRFAL), in RG 105, NA, Box 12, Land Reports, Box 11.

8. R. Cutts to H. W. Halleck, May 18, 1865, Registers and Letters Received, in RG 105, NA, Microcopy 752, Roll 13, p. 798; H. W. Halleck to E. M. Stanton, May 25, 1865, Roll 15, pp. 776–77; O. Brown to O. O. Howard, June 6, 1865, Roll 13, p. 893, June 15, 1865, p. 837, July 6, 1865, p. 915, July 28, 1865, pp. 865–66, and August 26, 1865, pp. 820–21; Land Division (BRFAL) in RG 105, NA, Land Reports, Box 11.

Brown's communication, Howard and Edwin Stanton, the secretary of war, took immediate action to declare a portion of the land in Amherst County, Virginia, vacant. In this manner the bureau gained control of an additional 5,300 acres. By assigning this land to the bureau, Stanton issued a warning to "those men who propose to nullify the Proclamation of the President and the laws of Congress."[9]

In Mississippi, Colonel Samuel Thomas revealed the resistance of whites to any land program benefiting the freedmen: "The whites know that if the negro is not allowed to acquire property or become a landholder he must return to plantation labor and work for wages that will barely support himself and family; and they feel this kind of slavery is better than none at all."[10] Consequently, since Thomas had an insufficient military force to protect the Negroes, he refrained from assigning them any land.

Thomas reported however that the Freedmen's Department relinquished control of the settlement at Davis Bend, where his officers converted one of the plantations into a home farm for the care of indigents. Transients performed the work on this farm. In September, the bureau land agent in Mississippi reported that the freedmen were cultivating all available land on Palmyra, Hurricane, and Banks, three of the plantations on Davis Bend which made up the freedmen's colony called Camp Hawley. Although the freedmen at Camp Hawley were growing a top grade crop, such was not the case on all plantations at Davis Bend. Brierfield, one of the plantations belonging to Jefferson Davis' brother Joseph, experienced considerable flooding. Con-

---

9. O. O. Howard to O. Brown, June 19, 1865, Selected Series of Records (BRFAL), in RG 105, NA, Microcopy 742, Roll 1, p. 69.

10. S. Thomas to O. O. Howard, Registers and Letters Received (BRFAL), in RG 105, NA, Microcopy 752, Roll 18, p. 46; July 31, 1865, p. 245, September 21, 1865, Roll 22, p. 52.

sequently, the freedmen's colony which the bureau attempted to establish there had to be abandoned.[11]

In order to assure that the bureau had sufficient funds to pay the expenses of the various colonies at Davis Bend, Colonel Thomas placed the gin and all its machinery under the command of a bureau agent who informed the freedmen that they would be allowed to gin their cotton "on as good terms as any other party across the river or elsewhere will gin for you."

The freedmen were willing to pay the cost of ginning their cotton but they resented the implications of the government actions. Fifty-six freedmen filed a formal petition with Colonel Thomas requesting that they be allowed to repair and operate the gin. They thanked the military for the protection it had afforded them and the right to till the soil they had been given. However they summarized their experiences that year in the following manner:

> At the commencement of the present year, this plantation was, in compliance with an order of our Post Commander, deprived of horses, mules, oxen and farming utensils of every description, very much of which had been captured and brought into Union lines by many of the undersigned; in consequence of which deprivations, we were, of course, reduced to the necessity of buying everything necessary for farming, and having thus far succeeded in performing by far the most expensive and laborious part of our work, we are prepared to accomplish the ginning, pressing, weighing, marking, consigning, etc., in business-like order if allowed to do so.[12]

When Colonel Thomas refused their request the freedmen wrote a letter to the New Orleans *Tribune* explaining their position. They pointed out that they did not intend that their petition offend anyone.

11. J. Weber, "Report of property in hands of Bureau," September 6, 1865, Records of the Assistant Commissioner for the State of Mississippi (BRFAL), in RG 105, NA, Microcopy 826, Roll 34, pp. 35–36.
12. New Orleans *Tribune*, July 29, 1865.

We are merely asking them to trust us in the management of our own affairs, as far as many of us have been intrusted with similar affairs of our late masters. . . . We wish every planter so engaged on this and other places to obtain the largest possible share of the produce of their labor, so that they may be encouraged to continue and others induced to commence. And further, we wish it distinctly understood that we do not claim the use of the above named machinery as a right, but desire it as a privilege to prevent the imposition of superfluous and unnecessary charges.[13]

Although the freedmen did not receive the right to operate the gin, the report on Davis Bend at the end of 1865 was extremely encouraging. The home farm, after paying all expenses, including wages and the cost of shelter, clothing, and rations for the old and infirm, showed a profit of over $25,000. The freedmen who worked rent-free land on their own account for that year made a profit of over $159,000. Although this was one of the most successful ventures by free Negro labor in 1865,[14] it did indicate that the freedmen, with minimal supervision and adequate protection, could provide for themselves.

Despite the success of the Davis Bend experiment, most freedmen found the lack of funds and the opposition of whites detrimental to their acquisition of land. In Louisiana, Chaplain Thomas Conway noted that Negro soldiers were saving money to buy land when they mustered out of service. Twenty such regiments in Louisiana had already saved sufficient money to

13. *Ibid.* The letter was dated July 11, 1865.
14. *Senate Executive Documents*, 39th Cong., 1st Sess., No. 2, p. 82; Vernon Lane Wharton Collection, Box 9, University of Southwestern Louisiana Archives; *House Executive Documents*, 39th Cong., 1st Sess., No. 70, p. 257; "Certificate of Negro Planters on Davis Bend," in RG 105, NA, Microcopy 752, Roll 20, p. 35; *Senate Executive Documents*, 39th Cong., 1st Sess., No. 27, pp. 30, 38. General Thomas reported that 181 companies or partnerships comprising 300 adults and 450 children received about five thousand acres of land, which they worked without interference, even from the bureau. They produced 12,000 bushels of corn worth $12,000, vegetables, potatoes, and melons which they sold for $38,000, and 1,736 bales of cotton which they sold for $347,000. They paid out $160,000 in expenses, paid their white partners $60,000, and the expenditures were $238,000, leaving a balance of $159,000.

buy all the confiscated and abandoned lands in the state. One of these regiments had saved fifty thousand dollars to buy four or five of the largest plantations on the Mississippi. Because of the attitude of the whites, Conway feared for the safety of the freedmen in the interior of the state where there was little military protection. He therefore decided to assign land on both banks of the Mississippi, where the Negroes would be near transportation and commerce, and the military could better protect them.[15]

Colonel Charles Bentzoni and Major Phillip Weinmann proposed the creation of military colonies in the West. The colonies would be settled one company to a county. Each soldier would receive about fifty acres of land with the government retaining title to the land until his military term of seven years expired. The Negroes would work the land as independent farmers, and then after the harvest, they would drill and serve as soldiers. They would thus protect the western frontier and in the meantime become self-sufficient.[16]

Sergeant S. H. Smothers, a black soldier from Indiana serving with the 25th Army Corps in Texas, also proposed the creation of a military colony. However, unlike Bentzoni and Weinmann, who envisioned the government giving the land to the colonists in return for military service rendered, Smothers proposed that

15. T. Conway to E. R. S. Canby, "Final Report of the Bureau of Free Labor, Department of the Gulf," in RG 105, NA, Microcopy 752, Roll 20, pp. 358; T. Conway to O. O. Howard, August 22, 1865, Roll 14, p. 608; Oliver O. Howard, *Autobiography of Oliver Otis Howard* (New York: The Baker and Taylor Company, 1907), 188–89.

16. C. Bentzoni to O. O. Howard, July 7, 1865, Registers and Letters Received (BRFAL), in RG 105, NA, Microcopy 752, Roll 13, p. 1024; Phillip Weinmann to O. O. Howard, June 13, 1865, Roll 18, pp. 599–601. Unlike Bentzoni and Weinmann, who proposed establishing the soldier colonies in the West, Chaplain H. H. Moore proposed to establish such military colonies in the South. He suggested that 50,000 to 100,000 acres of either public or confiscated land be appropriated to plant some eight hundred colonies of black soldiers. He pointed out that confiscated or abandoned improved land would be preferable for the experiment since a crop could be made the first year. H. H. Moore to Senator H. Wilson, March 29, 1865, Registers and Letters Received (BRFAL), in RG 105, NA, Microcopy 752, Roll 16, pp. 854–55.

the colonists settle in the lower Rio Grande valley where they could purchase land at from twenty-five cents to one dollar per acre. He pointed out that "the high prices of land in the old states, the competition of labor, and the strong prejudice in the minds of the whites against us, make it very difficult for us to rise to wealth and respectability in those states. By settling in new portions of the country we will not have these difficulties to contend with." Smothers proposed also that blacks form a society called the First United States Colored Pioneer Association. The association would select the location for the colony and assist the colonists in purchasing the land. The association would also include a military organization to which all male members would belong. The sole purpose of the military organization would be the protection of the lives and property of the colonists.[17]

The inability or refusal of landowners to pay wages to their black laborers deprived many of the opportunity to purchase land. In response to the complaint that the planters had no money, the New Orleans *Tribune* suggested that they either find some or sell some of their land, since they had no right to withhold wages from the laborers for an entire season. The *Tribune* also pointed out that there was no country in the world where the owners made the laborers wait more than fifteen days for their money. If the workers had the means to provide for their families for a year in advance they could easily become independent farmers. The planters claimed that they had no money. Therefore if they could not afford to pay, they should cease to be planters and become workers.[18]

Colonel Bentzoni reported procrastination in accepting the Emancipation Proclamation by Arkansas slaveholders. He found it necessary as late as July, 1865, to issue orders stating that all

17. New Orleans *Tribune*, October 11, 1865, reprinted Smothers' letter dated September 23, 1865.
18. *Ibid.*, December 31, 1865.

slaves were freed as of January 1, 1863. He also proclaimed that anyone who retained his chattels after that time owed them back wages for two and one-half years. Unfortunately, the rapid demobilization of the military deprived the bureau in Arkansas of the necessary personnel to enforce Bentzoni's order. Brown in Virginia requested permission to use the power of the bureau to collect back wages for some 300,000 Negroes retained illegally in bondage and forced to work.[19] Had either of these two men succeeded, thousands of Negroes would have had sufficient funds to purchase the land they needed to support their families.

While General O. O. Howard was organizing the Freedmen's Bureau, President Johnson, on May 29, 1865, issued an amnesty proclamation pardoning most southerners and restoring their property rights. Concerned about the effect of this proclamation on the freedmen's land needs, Howard requested an opinion from the attorney general concerning his authority under the act creating the bureau. The attorney general replied that Howard "has *authority*, under the direction of the President, to set apart *for the use* of loyal refugees and freedmen the land in question; and he is *required* to assign to each male of that class of persons not more than forty acres of such land."[20] Thus, Howard could maintain control of all confiscated and abandoned lands actually needed for refugees and freedmen, subject, however, to presidential approval. The Freedmen's Bureau never controlled more than two-tenths of one percent of the land in the South and President Johnson's amnesty proclamation forced restoration of most of that land.[21]

19. "General Order No. 30," Helena, Arkansas, July 7, 1865, reprinted in New York *Times*, July 21, 1865; J. W. Sprague to O. O. Howard, September 21, 1865, Registers and Letters Received (BRFAL), in RG 105, NA, Microcopy 752, Roll 17, pp. 240–41; O. Brown to O. O. Howard, July 27, 1865, Roll 13, pp. 878–79.

20. James Speed to E. M. Stanton, for transmittal to O. O. Howard, Registers and Letters Received (BRFAL), in RG 105, NA, Microcopy 752, Roll 13, p. 57 (Emphasis in original); O. O. Howard to J. Speed, July 1, 1865, Microcopy 742, Roll 1, p. 89.

21. Paul Skeels Peirce, *The Freedmen's Bureau: A Chapter in the History of Reconstruction* (Iowa City: University of Iowa, 1904), 129.

Basing his actions on the attorney general's opinion, Howard decided to resist the efforts of southerners to reclaim any of three types of land which the bureau actually controlled: confiscated, abandoned, and captured Confederate property. Most of the captured Confederate property was not suitable for agricultural purposes. In those areas that had come under federal military control by 1863 the federal district courts had been reestablished and the direct tax commissioners had been appointed. Much of the land that was confiscated for non-payment of the direct tax had been condemned and sold by the courts to northern investors, except for such lands in Virginia that Stanton, at Brown's request, had reserved from sale. In the Sea Islands of South Carolina and Georgia the direct tax commissioners also held some confiscated lands. By far the largest class of lands was abandoned property. Much of this was either soon reclaimed by the former owners or restored by military commanders. Nevertheless, the bureau did acquire considerable aggregates of abandoned property. Brown reported from Virginia on June 7, 1865, that he had taken control of fifty-eight plantations totaling 16,675 acres, on which he built 669 huts as housing for 2,955 freedmen.[22]

In Louisiana and Mississippi, Treasury officials did not transfer land to the bureau until the end of July, 1865. By then they had already leased fifty-eight plantations in Mississippi and twenty-three in Louisiana to freedmen. Within a month after the land was turned over to the bureau in Louisiana, Conway, settled freedmen on nine additional plantations.[23]

22. *House Reports*, 40th Cong., 2nd Sess., No. 30, pp. 11–12; O. Brown to O. O. Howard, June 7, 1865, Registers and Letters Received (BRFAL), in RG 105, NA, Microcopy 752, Roll 13, pp. 377–84; S. Thomas to O. O. Howard, June 28, 1865, Roll 1, Register 1, p. 460.

23. T. Conway to O. O. Howard, July 7, 1865, Registers and Letters Received (BRFAL), in RG 105, NA, Microcopy 752, Roll 14, p. 576; August 13, 1865, p. 468; New York *Times*, September 26, 1865; *Nation*, I (October 5, 1865), 42; New Orleans *Tribune*, November 14, 1865. The editor of the *Tribune* praised the New Orleans Freedmen's Aid Association for aiding freedmen in leasing fourteen plantations; New Orleans *Daily Picayune*, August 19, 1865.

On August 4, 1865, Conway reported that he had sixty-four plantations totaling 62,528 acres under his control. Only the 1,400-acre plantation of Richard Taylor in St. Charles Parish had actually been confiscated and title conveyed to the government by the district court. Treasury agent Benjamin Flanders had leased this plantation to an association of freedmen for one hundred dollars and one-eighth the proceeds of the crop. It appears that freedmen were farming on their own account approximately 10,000 acres of the 62,528 acres controlled by Conway.[24]

The Louisiana parishes of Tensas, Madison, and Carroll were controlled by the Treasury agent in Mississippi. Consequently, during 1865, the twenty-nine plantations confiscated in these parishes were carried on the Mississippi records. This has led to considerable confusion among historians concerning the actual amount of land held by the government in Louisiana. The twenty-nine plantations in these three parishes contained approximately 15,700 acres. During 1865 freedmen worked 3,372 acres of this land on their own account. Six associations planted 1,825 acres and fifty-one individual families worked 1,547 acres. Individual family holdings ranged from four to one hundred acres, whereas the association holdings ranged from eighty to eight hundred acres. One association, Eli Woodra and Company, leased eighty acres of land on which they produced a crop of thirty-five bales of cotton.[25]

In Warren County, Mississippi, fifteen families became self-supporting on small tracts which they leased from the government. John Smith leased forty acres on which he grew 10 bales of cotton and 250 bushels of corn. Ned Bohamon worked forty acres on which he grew a crop estimated at between 8 and 10

24. Land Division (BRFAL), in RG 105, NA, Land Reports, Box 8.
25. Land Report, September 6, 1865, Records of the Assistant Commissioner, Mississippi (BRFAL), in RG 105, NA, Microcopy 826, Roll 34, pp. 26–36; S. Thomas to A. Baird, Transfer of property, pp. 175–82; Land Division (BRFAL), in RG 105, NA, Land Reports, Box 8.

bales of cotton. Joseph Young and his family produced 10 bales on only thirty acres of land. A few, like John Winbush, apparently over-extended themselves and attempted to plant more land than their limited resources could bear. Winbush produced only 5 bales of cotton on fifty acres. Others, like one black who called himself King Herod, succeeded on a minimum amount of land. Herod planted only ten acres yet produced 3 bales of cotton.[26]

Although the time for planting staple crops was over when most bureau agents gained control of the land, Howard instructed them to make arrangements to divide the land and lease it to freedmen as rapidly as possible. In this manner freedmen would be able to start their vegetable gardens and thereby provide for themselves.

Conway, in Louisiana, seems to have developed a carefully thought-out plan for leasing land to the freedmen. On August 28, 1865, Conway issued Circular No. 10, instructing any freedman or refugee who wished to procure land for his own use to send an application to bureau headquarters prior to January 1, 1866. The applications were to contain the number in each family or association; the number of acres desired; and the amount of means commanded either by the individual or association in order to carry out the terms of the lease. Between September 5, 1865, and October 24, 1865, a total of 267 applications were made in Louisiana. Despite Conway's explicit instructions, of this total, 106 indicated that they had no rations to support themselves or tools to work the land. There were 1,054 men, 845 women, and 1,434 children involved in the 267 applications. Together they requested 23,919 acres of land.

Representative of the 161 applicants who could provide for themselves while preparing their first crop was Abraham Gordon, a freedman who had a wife and three children. He applied

26. Land Report, September 6, 1865, Records of the Assistant Commissioner, Mississippi (BRFAL), in RG 105, NA, Microcopy 826, Roll 34, pp. 26–36.

for twenty-five acres in Jefferson Parish and indicated that he had two horses, one plow, one cart, and $450.

One association, led by Miles Summerville and consisting of twenty-four other freedmen, twenty-five freedwomen, and thirty children, applied to rent 250 acres of government land in Terrebonne Parish. In order to assure success of the venture they had acquired thirteen horses with harness, five hundred barrels of corn, fifty hogs, six head of cattle, and six hundred dollars.[27]

While freedmen hopefully applied for land in Louisiana they received the support of the Negro press. The New Orleans *Tribune* praised General Howard's policy of dividing the land and pointed out that "the division of the lands is the only means by which a new, industrious, and loyal population may be made to settle in the South. . . . There is a large population of freedmen that has to settle on the divided lands." However, the *Tribune* also questioned the value of the title the settlers were to receive. "Shall they work under the threat of being expelled, from year to year, by returned rebels, taking what they call the 'mock oath' of amnesty?"[28] The fears of the *Tribune*'s editor were well founded.

As southern agitation for property restoration increased, Howard devised a plan to retain most of the land under his control. He refused to restore any abandoned property unless the owner could prove non-abandonment. Howard considered the president's pardon as insufficient to force restoration of the land which Congress, by law, had reserved for the use of the bureau. However, through a series of executive orders beginning early in July, the president gradually forced restoration of much of the property. Howard apparently believed that the

27. "Register of Applications of Freedmen for Land" (BRFAL), in RG 105, NA, Louisiana Records; *House Executive Documents*, 39th Cong., 1st Sess., No. 70, pp. 19, 25.

28. New Orleans *Tribune*, August 31, 1865.

immediate assignment of land to the freedmen would hinder presidential restoration. With this in mind he issued Circular No. 13 in July, 1865, instructing his agents not to restore any abandoned property but instead to assign this type of land to the freedmen as soon as possible.[29]

Some bureau agents acted in conformity with Howard's orders. Clinton B. Fisk in Tennessee set apart all abandoned plantations under his control and began making arrangements to sell the land to the former slaves in small lots of ten, twenty, thirty, or forty acres. Agents in Mississippi seized the property of former rebels worth more than $20,000, while General Saxton in South Carolina and Georgia seized 312,014 acres as abandoned until ordered to cease by the military commander of the district. Saxton reported that the order suspending the seizure of abandoned lands came just as he had completed arrangements for taking possession of all the remaining abandoned lands which had not yet been seized by the Treasury Department. He protested: "The stopping of our operation in this direction coming at the same time with the decision that a former abandonment does not forfeit the land if the owner returns before such lands are seized by U.S. authorities, will effectually prevent this bureau from gaining possession of any more lands until this confiscation act shall be enforced." Failure to continue his operation would effectively nullify section four of the act creating the bureau.[30]

In Arkansas, Assistant Commissioner John W. Sprague indi-

29. *House Reports*, 40th Cong., 2nd Sess., No. 30, pp. 11–12; *House Executive Documents*, 39th Cong., 1st Sess., No. 70, pp. 16–18. Immediately upon receipt of Circular No. 13, Conway, in Louisiana, issued his Circular No. 10, informing the freedmen to apply for land. The editor of the *Tribune* on September 5, 1865, stated that hundreds of freedmen were taking advantage of Circular No. 10. He praised the Negroes who in so short a time had accumulated sufficient capital to settle land.

30. *Senate Executive Documents*, 39th Cong., 1st Sess., No. 27, p. 139; C. B. Fisk to O. O. Howard, August 27, 1865, Registers and Letters Received (BRFAL), in RG 105, NA, Microcopy 752, Roll 14, p. 1288; Andrew Johnson to O. O. Howard, August 24, 1865, Roll 16, p. 596; G. G. Meade to R. Saxton, September 30, 1865, Roll 17, p. 530; R. Saxton to O. O. Howard, September 9, 1865, p. 522.

Table 1
COMPILATION OF LANDS HELD BY THE
FREEDMEN'S BUREAU 1865–1868*

	A	B	C
Virginia	75,600	49,800	9,336
North Carolina	36,500	10,800	2,540
South Carolina	435,000	181,600	74,669
Georgia		31,900	650
Alabama	3,400	3,200	None
Mississippi	43,500	22,600	None
Louisiana	78,200	47,900	3,040
Tennessee	65,600	40,900	21,582
Kentucky			None
Arkansas	106,100	66,100	27,717
Missouri		None	None
D.C. and Maryland	13,800	11,000	None
Florida	300	100	None
Texas	None	None	None
TOTALS	858,000	464,000	139,543

*The figures in column A reflect the greatest approximate number of acres held by the Freedmen's Bureau in 1865; the figures in column B reflect the approximate number of acres held on January 31, 1866; and the figures in column C reflect the approximate number of acres held in August, 1868. (Note the combined report for South Carolina and Georgia in 1865, for Tennessee and Kentucky in 1865 and 1866, and for Arkansas and Missouri in 1865.)

This table was constructed from information found in the Land Division Records, RG 105, BRFAL, Box 12.

cated, at the end of August, 1865, that he held 18,736 acres of land in addition to town lots and buildings. Most of the smaller tracts of land he rented on one-eighth shares until January 1, 1866. One plantation of 6,184 acres, known as the Pillow place, was subdivided into tracts and leased to the freedmen for one-eighth of the proceeds of the crop. In order to provide for helpless freedmen he established a home farm on one plantation of 1,018 acres. He indicated that the home farm contained 134 houses, 1 saw mill, and 1 school house. Upon receipt of Circular No. 13, Sprague seized confiscable and abandoned property in Arkansas and increased his holdings to 106,140 acres. Apparently Sprague's sentiments concerning land for the freedmen mirrored General Howard's concern.[31]

Since Howard's policy was in direct contravention to President Johnson's program, he ordered Howard to draw up a new circular restoring the lands. In compliance, Howard ordered restoration of abandoned lands to those southerners who secured a presidential pardon. However, because the order also contained provisions for retaining all confiscated lands, the president ordered it recalled. Johnson rewrote the restoration order to read: "Land will not be regarded as confiscated until it has been condemned and sold by decree of the United States Court for the district in which the property may be found, and the title thereto thus vested in the United States."[32] This new circular made the possession of land so uncertain that many bureau agents discontinued their policy of assigning land to the freedmen. Fortunately, the order instructed bureau agents to protect the rights of the freedmen to the crop which they had planted.[33]

31. Land Division (BRFAL), in RG 105, NA, Land Reports, Box 7.
32. George R. Bentley, *A History of the Freedmen's Bureau* (Philadelphia: University of Pennsylvania Press, 1955), 92; New York *Times*, September 6, 1865, September 14, 1865, December 20, 1865; Howard, *Autobiography*, 232, 235; New Orleans *Times*, September 23, 1865; New Orleans *Tribune*, September 26, 1865.
33. *House Executive Documents*, 39th Cong., 1st Sess., No. 70, pp. 21–22; *House Reports*, 40th Cong., 2nd Sess., No. 30, p. 13.

Assistant Commissioner Sprague in Arkansas reported at the end of October that he had restored a total of 6,434 acres of land, including the Pillow place, which had been divided previously among the freedmen. In addition to restoring the property, Sprague allowed the owner to collect the one-eighth lease which the freedmen had contracted to pay for the use of the land. By the end of December, 1865, Sprague reported that he had restored 39,400 acres but that he had also seized an additional 1,900 acres. He therefore held 68,641 acres as of January 1, 1866.[34]

Assistant Commissioner Eliphalet Whittlesey in North Carolina reported that although he had restored 38,735.5 acres of land under Circular No. 15 he still retained 61,663.5 acres as of October 31, 1865. He also indicated that much of the land that had been technically restored was still in the possession of the bureau since it was leased to the freedmen. Most of the owners preferred not to be responsible for the bureau's share of the crop and therefore only assumed informal possession of the dwellings on their land. By December 31, 1865, when most of the leases expired, the bureau in North Carolina controlled only 11,397 acres. [35] However, the bureau continued to lease to freedmen what land it actually controlled. One freedman, George Brown, on January 13, 1866, leased 750 acres, of which only 70 acres were cleared. Under the terms of the lease Brown was to pay , on or before January 1, 1867, a rent of one-fourth the production of any crop, turpentine, or tar from the plantation. All large leases in North Carolina during 1866 were for one-fourth of any products derived from the tract leased. Isaac Burnett leased 800 acres of turpentine land; Josiah Collins leased 125 acres of turpentine land; John Ventes leased 10 acres of farm land. Since the

34. J. W. Sprague, Land Report for Arkansas and Missouri, November, 1865, Land Division (BRFAL), in RG 105, NA, Land Reports, Box 7.

35. E. Whittlesey, Land Report for North Carolina, October 31, 1865, January 31. 1866, ibid.

bureau controlled little cleared land the farm leases were small. On one plantation there was only 61 acres of tillable land. Therefore, bureau agents leased the land in one-acre tracts to sixty-one families. The bureau agent in the Beaufort district of North Carolina reported that in March, 1866, he restored the Washington Thomas place of 10 acres. "However, Freedmen living on the place have leases to January 1, 1867, rent free with permission to remove their houses." He also indicated that 105 freedmen living in 22 shanties on the ten-acre Josiah Bell place were supporting themselves. On Roanoke Island the bureau controlled 1,114 acres, of which 890 were cultivated. However, Captain Frank A. Seely, the bureau agent for the island, reported in April, 1866, that 3,000 refugees and freedmen were scattered about on different tracts of land having about one acre each. Evidently, although the bureau only controlled a small portion of the island, the freedmen acted on the assumption that the entire island was under bureau control.

By the end of April, 1866, Whittlesey in North Carolina indicated that there were only 3,696 acres in the possession of the bureau, with 1,356 of that under cultivation. Fortunately, the freedmen who held rent-free leases on the land restored between January 30, 1866, and April 30, 1866, were protected in their right to use the land until January 1, 1867.[36]

Assistant commissioners in other states also grappled with the problem of how to obey Circular No. 15 as ordered by President Johnson and still provide justice to the freedmen who believed the land had been promised to them. Saxton in South Carolina, Brown in Virginia, Thomas in Mississippi, and Conway in Louisiana all reported that if they were forced to restore land

36. F. A. Seely to E. Whittlesey, October 31, 1865, Records of the Assistant Commissioner for the State of North Carolina (BRFAL), in RG 105, NA, Microcopy 843, Roll 36, pp. 29–39; April 5, 1866, pp. 89–93; F. A. Seely to G. Brown, Lease, January 13, 1866, p. 299; F. A. Seely to J. Smith, Lease, January 5, 1866, p. 293; F. A. Seely to J. Ventes, Lease, January 10, 1866, p. 295; E. Whittlesey to O. O. Howard, Report for month ending April 30, 1866, pp. 102–103.

according to the terms of the new restoration order, the freed-men would be forced either to leave the South or to become wage slaves on the land they had always worked. Brown esti-mated that at least twenty thousand freedmen in southeastern Virginia would be displaced.[37] Much of the condemned land in Virginia which Stanton had reserved for the use of the bureau was now subject to restoration.[38] Since some of the owners had not yet received their pardons, Brown, Judge John C. Under-wood, and the tax commissioner for Virginia recommended that the order suspending sale of condemned land be revoked. In this manner, at least some of the freedmen could secure a small homestead before the owners could be pardoned. Ironically, if instead of suspending the sale of these properties in June, Stan-ton had ordered the title transferred to the Freedmen's Bureau, there could have been no restoration. It is quite possible that Johnson would have approved such action at that time since he had not yet undergone the metamorphosis from enemy of the planter aristocracy to defender of their property rights.[39]

As restoration proceeded, Howard and certain of his agents continued their resistance. Howard established the policy that all restorations must be made by him in order to avoid a conflict of authority. Colonel Fullerton, who favored restoration and was a confidant of the president, attempted to circumvent Howard

37. Bentley, *Freedmen's Bureau*, 97; G. Whipple to O. O. Howard, November 15, 1865, Registers and Letters Received (BRFAL), in RG 105, NA, Microcopy 752, Roll 19, p. 243.

38. J. C. Underwood to O. O. Howard, October 12, 1865, Registers and Letters Received (BRFAL), in RG 105, NA, Microcopy 752, Roll 24, p. 924. Judge Underwood stated that at the September term of the U.S. District Court of Virginia, $2 million of condemned property was returned to former rebels.

39. *Ibid.*, J. C. Underwood to O. O. Howard, October 7, 1865, Roll 24, p. 926; October 12, 1865, p. 924; J. Havighurst to O. O. Howard, October 7, 1865, p. 930; *Senate Executive Documents*, 39th Cong., 1st Sess., No. 27, p. 165. During the war Judge Underwood, in *U.S.* vs. *the Rights Title and Interest of Hugh Latham*, ruled that the Constitution permitted the government to take the life of a traitor. Therefore it could take his property with full title. New York *Times*, November 22, 1863.

by ordering sub-agents of the bureau to restore land directly without first seeking Howard's approval. Howard countermanded Fullerton's orders and informed the assistant commissioners that under no circumstances were they to break a lease with the freedmen.[40] One sub-agent in Virginia interpreted Howard's instructions literally and as soon as he learned that certain plantations were to be restored he immediately leased them to freedmen for a long period. In this manner he succeeded in delaying restoration legally since the owner could not be given possession of land which was under lease.[41]

Apparently President Johnson anticipated Howard's delaying tactic. On September 7, 1865, he issued an executive order suspending his previous instructions to the Treasury to turn over funds collected from abandoned and confiscated lands to the bureau. In this manner he could weaken the efforts of the bureau, and its chief, by simply depriving them of financial support. Some Treasury agents who agreed with the president interpreted the new executive order as giving them authority to collect the rents from the lands in question.[42]

Secretary of the Treasury Hugh McCulloch impounded fifty thousand dollars derived from the sale of cotton raised by freedmen under General Saxton's direction. Saxton argued that the cotton was raised by old men, women, and children and sent to New York to be sold for their benefit. Therefore, the money "belongs to the freedmen, and should be restored to me, to be expended for their benefit." Secretary McCulloch cited Johnson's executive order of September 7 forbidding further transfer of such funds to the Freedmen's Bureau. Saxton ap-

40. N. M. Stinson to C. Woodhull, October 10, 1865, Registers and Letters Received (BRFAL), in RG 105, NA, Microcopy 752, Roll 17, p. 903; O. O. Howard to S. Thomas, Selected Series of Records (BRFAL), in RG 105, NA, Microcopy 742, Roll 1, p. 236.

41. O. O. Howard to O. Brown, October 25, 1865, Registers and Letters Received (BRFAL), in RG 105, NA, Microcopy 752, Roll 24, p. 59.

42. "Executive Order of September 7, 1865," ibid., Roll 21, p. 415; C. B. Fisk to O. O. Howard, p. 418.

pealed the decision but McCulloch was adamant. He pointed out that the entire proceeds could not belong to the laborers unless they also owned the soil. Since the lands were abandoned the government took possession of it as "the property of public enemies." Therefore, the products belonged to the government, not the freedmen. It appears that the Treasury finally allowed ten thousand dollars for the value of the labor and retained forty thousand as profit.[43]

Howard realized that his control of confiscated and abandoned land was entirely dependent on the president. Consequently he instructed Saxton to discontinue renting and selling land in the South Carolina parishes of St. Helena and St. Luke. He preferred to permit the tax commissioners to sell the land since they could actually convey title whereas the bureau could not. By November, 1865, approximately nine hundred freedmen had purchased small homesteads from the tax commissioners; many others deposited their money in the Freedmen's Savings Bank to pay for the parcels they were cultivating while waiting for their lands to be surveyed and offered at auction. The commissioner of the Internal Revenue, who favored the president's restoration policy, issued instructions halting the sale of lots in Beaufort, South Carolina. Tax Commissioner William Brisbane enlisted the support of Senator James Doolittle in an effort to continue the sale of lots of not more than twenty acres to freedmen. Brisbane proposed that the government sell the land which it had appropriated and recompense the original proprietors.[44]

When Congress finally convened in December, 1865, friends of the freedmen requested congressional action to halt property

43. R. Saxton to O. O. Howard, November 23, 1865, *ibid.*, Roll 24, p. 24; H. McCulloch to O. O. Howard, December 16, 1865, pp. 792–93; January 6, 1866, pp. 835–38.

44. O. O. Howard to R. Saxton, September 6, 1865, Selected Series of Records (BRFAL) in RG 105, NA, Microcopy 742, Roll 1, p. 167; W. Brisbane to J. R. Doolittle, November 28, 1865, in James R. Doolittle Papers, Library of Congress.

restoration. Congress was apparently more concerned with the disposition of abandoned lands than with confiscated land. Unlike the confiscation act of 1862 which limited the term of confiscation to the life of the offender, the act of July, 1864, provided for the sale of abandoned lands for the benefit of freedmen. The act defined abandoned lands as any land from which the owner was voluntarily absent while aiding the Confederacy in any manner.[45] Congress had intended that the seizure of abandoned lands be permanent and therefore issued a resolution in December, 1865, requesting information concerning lands restored under President Johnson's restoration policy. Howard reported that the bureau held a number of pieces of property which had been seized and condemned under the act of July 17, 1864, and allotted to freedmen. No property of this type had been restored. However, many abandoned plantations occupied by freedmen, but not allotted to them, had been restored to former owners. Howard also reported that many plantations included in General Sherman's Special Field Order No. 15 were occupied by freedmen as homesteads. None of these had been restored to former owners.[46]

Although Howard and some bureau agents continued to resist restoration, the bureau restored approximately 393,000 acres by January 31, 1866. However, bureau agents still retained approximately 464,000 acres. In response to a House resolution of March 5, 1866, concerning lands restored, Howard indicated on April 21, 1866, that the bureau had restored 15,452 acres confiscated under the act of July, 1862. Concerning lands seized as abandoned under the act of July, 1864, he indicated that the bureau restored 14,652 acres which had been allotted to freedmen. Therefore, by April 21, 1866, the bureau had restored approximately 430,104 acres of land to former owners or their

45. U.S. *Statutes at Large*, XII, 375–78.
46. New York *Times*, January 9, 1866.

agents. Nevertheless, the bureau still retained possession of well over 427,000 acres of confiscated and abandoned land. As late as August, 1868, the bureau retained possession of approximately 140,000 acres of confiscated or abandoned land.[47] Unfortunately, these figures are quite deceptive in that they represent all land held, rather than just tillable land. For instance, of the 42,168 acres which Treasury agents in Tennessee turned over to the bureau in August, 1865, only 9,881 acres had been cleared and were considered tillable. The remaining 32,287 acres were of no value as farmland since no freedman would lease or purchase the land for farming without assurance that the land, once cleared and made productive, would be his. These same conditions existed in the other southern states.[48] Therefore, without the power to convey title to the land, and in the face of the president's restoration order, the prospects of securing land for the freedmen were not bright. The only area where the bureau appeared to have some chance of acquiring title to abandoned land was in South Carolina, Georgia, and northern Florida where General Sherman had reserved for the exclusive use of the freedmen a thirty-mile-wide belt of land along the coast from Charleston, South Carolina, to the St. Johns River in Florida.

47. "Memoranda relating to abandoned and confiscated land, 1865–1868," Land Division (BRFAL), in RG 105, NA, Box 12.

48. Land Division (BRFAL), in RG 105, NA, Land Reports, Box 10, Tennessee; Box 7, Florida and Alabama; Box 8, Louisiana; Box 12, Virginia.

III

The Sherman
Reservation

GENERAL SHERMAN'S SPECIAL Field Order No. 15, issued after consultation with black leaders and with the approval of the secretary of war, created a reservation for the exclusive use of the freedmen. General Saxton, after being assured by Secretary of War Stanton that the government fully intended to keep its promise to the freedmen, began dividing the reservation into forty-acre tracts. General Sherman also turned over to Saxton all the horses and mules seized by his soldiers as they captured enemy territory. Since Sherman retained only those animals needed for his supply wagons and his cavalry units, the amount turned over to Saxton was considerable. Saxton assigned these animals to the freedmen as they settled on the land.[1] These actions by high-ranking government officials convinced many blacks that the government would indeed seize and distribute the land of their former masters.

Saxton and his subordinates worked tirelessly in providing the basic necessities for the freedmen who flocked to the Sherman reservation. When Stanton expressed concern that the freedmen on the reservation were a burden on the government, Saxton pointed out that all who had arrived during the planting season had received nothing from the government and were

1. *Official Records*, XLVII, 2, p. 15.

completely self-supporting and prosperous. By April 6, 1865, he had located approximately twenty thousand freedmen on 100,000 acres of land. He estimated that these would soon be self-sustaining. Although he admitted that about 70 percent of the freedmen under his charge were destitute, he explained that they had been fortunate to reach the safety of Union lines alive since "refugees are daily murdered, almost in sight of our advanced pickets, by guerillas, and are daily fleeing to us for protection in an utterly destitute condition."[2]

During the closing months of the war Saxton continued settling freedmen on the Sherman reservation. Unfortunately, the number of freedmen seeking land continued to increase while Saxton's staff remained unchanged. It was impossible to survey and mark every tract of land prior to settling the freedmen on the land. Consequently, Saxton issued land certificates which simply identified the settler, the plantation on which he settled, and the number of acres assigned to him. When the war ended Saxton reported to Howard that by June 4, 1865, he had settled an estimated forty thousand freedmen on the Sherman lands.[3]

Reports from bureau sub-agents working under Saxton during the summer of 1865 are incomplete and not uniform. However, a general picture of the condition of the freedmen can be drawn from the reports. It appears that Saxton continued to prohibit white civilians from entering the reservation. The freedmen, however, who had formerly lived there but had been brought to the interior by their former owners, returned now to their old homes. By the summer of 1865, word of Sherman's Special Field Order No. 15 had spread throughout the states covered by the order as well as to neighboring states. So great was the desire for land that blacks poured into the reservation in search of their forty-acre plots. The agent for St. Luke and St. Bartholemew's

2. New Orleans *Tribune*, May 19, 1865, reprinted Saxton's letter of April 6, 1865.
3. Register and Letters Received by the Bureau of Refugees, Freedmen, and Abandoned Lands (BRFAL), in Record Group 105, National Archives, Microcopy 752, Roll 24, p. 449; R. Saxton to O. O. Howard, June 5, 1865, Roll 17, p. 25.

parishes, South Carolina, indicated that between August 1 and August 28, 1865, the population under his charge grew from one thousand to two thousand and was being augmented daily. He pointed out that although most of the freedmen were self-supporting the rapid increase of population had caused considerable crowding, which had resulted in an epidemic. Although he controlled 57,825 acres, only one thousand were under cultivation and the epidemic made it improbable that additional acreage would be planted.[4]

Conditions of the freedmen in the Georgia sea islands appear to be worse than in other areas of the Sherman reservation. William F. Eaton reported that he controlled thirty-seven plantations containing approximately 29,350 acres of land. However, although 22,200 acres were cleared, only 445 acres had been planted by 911 freedmen. One plantation had 120 freedmen who had arrived too late to plant anything but two acres of beans. Fortunately, conditions were not this bad on all plantations in the Georgia sea islands. In some cases the former masters had abandoned not only the land but also the slaves. These ex-slaves remained on the land and grew the provisions they needed to survive. The 130 freedmen who remained on the Thomas Spaulding plantation on Sapelo Island were completely self-sustaining, although they had only planted sixty acres.[5]

Apparently Eaton attempted to settle freedmen on the Sherman lands without sufficient assistance. Between April and September of 1865, he helped 458 families consisting of 1,825 persons settle on small tracts of land. However, he only issued 84 certificates for a total of 1,839 acres of land.[6]

4. H. J. Judd to R. Saxton, August 1, 1865, Records of the Assistant Commissioner for the State of South Carolina (BRFAL), in RG 105, NA, Microcopy 869, Roll 33, pp. 6, 13–16.

5. "Report of Abandoned and Confiscated Lands in the Georgia Sea Islands for the Month of August 1865," Records of the Assistant Commissioner, South Carolina (BRFAL), in RG 105, NA, Microcopy 869, Roll 33, pp. 1–2.

6. "Registers of Lands assigned under General Sherman's Order," Records of the Assistant Commissioner for the State of Georgia (BRFAL), in RG 105, NA, Microcopy 798, Roll 36, pp. 1–30.

By August, 1865, Howard concluded that the three states included in the Sherman reservation were too great a responsibility for one assistant commissioner, regardless of how dedicated Saxton was. He therefore reassigned Saxton to control of South Carolina and appointed T. W. Osborne assistant commissioner of Florida and Davis Tillson assistant commissioner of Georgia. Saxton reported that prior to relinquishing Florida to Osborne he had settled approximately 1,900 families on 79,000 acres under the terms of Sherman's field order.[7]

By September, 1865, the former owners of land within the Sherman reservation demanded that they be provided the same rights as returning rebels in other states. Although exempted from the general amnesty, they had secured special pardons from President Johnson. They therefore demanded that their lands be restored to them. Saxton refused their demands and on September 5, 1865, wrote to Howard: "I consider that the faith of the Government is solemnly pledged to these people who have been faithful to it, and that we have no right now to dispossess them of their lands."[8] Four days later Saxton reiterated his position:

"The lands which have been taken possession of by this bureau have been solemnly pledged to the freedmen. The law of Congress has been published to them, and all agents of this bureau acting under your order have provided lands to these freedmen. Thousands of them are already located on tracts of forty acres each. Their love of the soil and desire to own farms amounts to a passion—it appears to be the dearest hope of their lives. I sincerely trust the government

7. R. Saxton to O. O. Howard, August 26, 1865, Registers and Letters Received (BRFAL), in RG 105, NA, Microcopy 752, Roll 17, pp. 612–16. Although Saxton reported that he relinquished 79,000 acres to the new assistant commissioner of Florida, Osborne reported on October 31, 1865, concerning abandoned agricultural lands that "there is very little of this class of property in Florida and what there is will be turned over to the legal claimants as rapidly as the proper applications are submitted."

8. R. Saxton to O. O. Howard, September 5, 1865, Registers and Letters Received (BRFAL), in RG 105, NA, Microcopy 752, Roll 17, p. 200; Registers of Letters Received (BRFAL), in RG 105, NA, Register 1, p. 423.

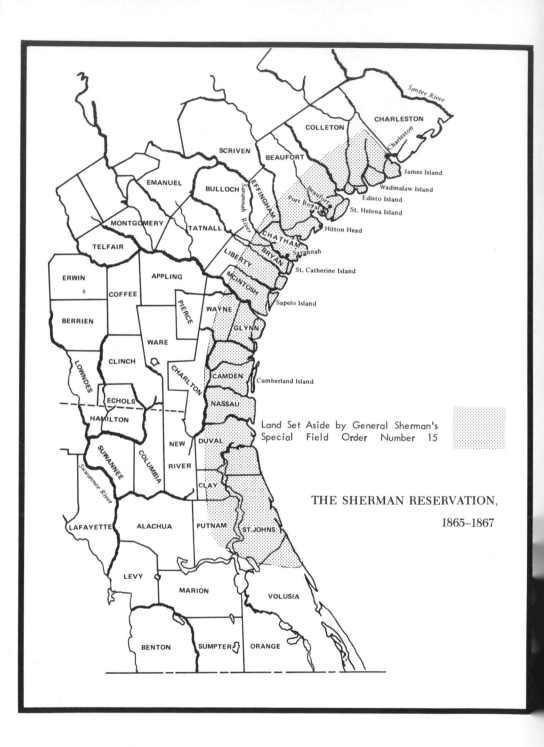

Land Set Aside by General Sherman's Special Field Order Number 15

THE SHERMAN RESERVATION, 1865–1867

will never break its faith with a single one of these colonists by driving him from the home which he has been promised. It is of vital importance that our promises made to freedmen should be faithfully kept.[9]

Yet, only three days later President Johnson forced Howard to rewrite and issue Circular No. 15. Armed with this new circular and their presidential pardons, the former owners demanded that Saxton restore their land. He forwarded each request for restoration to Howard with this endorsement:

The freedmen were promised the protection of the Government in their possession. This order was issued under a great military necessity with the approval of the War Department. I was appointed the executive officer to carry it out. More than forty thousand destitute freedmen have been provided with homes under its promises. I cannot break faith with them now by recommending the restoration of any of these lands. In my opinion this order of General Sherman is as binding as a statute.[10]

Saxton did, however, endorse the restoration of lands outside the Sherman reservation and on which no freedmen were residing. At the end of September he informed Howard that he was carrying out the restoration provisions of Circular No. 15.[11]

Former owners of the Sherman lands again appealed to President Johnson, who ordered Howard to inform Saxton that Circular No. 15 applied to the Sherman reservation also. In addition, Johnson ordered Howard to proceed to the Sherman reservation and arbitrate a mutually satisfactory agreement between the freedmen and the former owners.[12] Howard's first stop was at

9. R. Saxton to O. O. Howard, September 9, 1865, Registers and Letters Received (BRFAL), in RG 105, NA, Microcopy 752, Roll 17, p. 523.

10. *Nation*, I (October 26, 1865), p. 5; R. Saxton, Endorsement on application of Wm. Whaley, Records of the Assistant Commissioner, South Carolina (BRFAL), in RG 105, NA, Microcopy 869, Roll 32, p. 194; R. Saxton Endorsement on application of M. Whaley, pp. 219–20.

11. Registers of Letters Received (BRFAL), in RG 105, NA, Register 1, p. 446.

12. O. O. Howard to R. Saxton, October 6, 1865, Selected Series of Records, (BRFAL), in RG 105, NA, Microcopy 742, Roll 1, p. 199; Letters Received (BRFAL), in

Edisto Island, South Carolina, where he met with the freedmen and informed them that President Johnson had ordered him to restore the land. He assured them that although he could not retain the land for them he would not restore the land unless the owners provided work for all who were on the land. The freedmen objected to working for their former owners and pleaded for the privilege of renting or buying lands on the islands. After his meeting with the freedmen on Edisto Island, Howard wired Stanton that he had attempted to reconcile the freedmen to the surrender of the land to the former owners. He was evidently disturbed by his orders, for he concluded: "My task is a hard one, and I am convinced that something must be done to give these people and others the prospects of homesteads."[13] Stanton, who was completely opposed to the restoration of the Sherman reservation to the former owners, was more adept at interpreting executive orders so as to benefit the freedmen. He telegraphed Howard at Charleston that the president's order only called for him to see if the freedmen and the former owners could arrive at a mutually satisfactory agreement. If they could not, Howard should not have disturbed the freedmen in their possession.[14]

The freedmen on Edisto Island were unwilling to relinquish the land and contract to work for their former masters. They elected a committee of three freedmen, Henry Brown, Ishmael Moultrie, and Yates Sampson, to plead their case both with Howard and with President Johnson. They informed Howard:

RG 105, NA, Letter Book, p. 318; New York *Times*, December 20, 1865; *House Executive Documents*, 39th Cong., 1st Sess., No. 11, pp. 7, 42–43; George R. Bentley, *A History of the Freedmen's Bureau* (Philadelphia: University of Pennsylvania Press, 1955), 98–99; Oliver O. Howard, *Autobiography of Oliver Otis Howard* (New York: The Baker and Taylor Company, 1907), 240; Willie Lee Rose, *Rehearsal for Reconstruction: The Port Royal Experiment* (New York: The Bobbs Merrill Company, 1964), 352–54.

13. *House Executive Documents*, 39th Cong., 1st Sess., No. 11, p. 8.

14. William S. McFeely, *Yankee Stepfather: General O. O. Howard and the Freedmen* (New Haven: Yale University Press, 1968), 148; Bentley, *Freedmen's Bureau*, 99; Howard, *Autobiography*, 240.

General, we want [h]omesteads. We were promised [h]omesteads by the government. If it does not carry out the promises [i]ts agents made to us . . . we are left in a more unpleasant condition than our former. We are at the mercy of those who are combined to prevent us from getting land enough to lay our [f]athers['] bones upon. We have property in [h]omes, cattle, carriages, & articles of furniture; but we are landless and [h]omeless . . . . We cannot resist . . . [w]ithout being driven out [h]omeless upon the road.

You will see this is not the condition of really free men. You ask us to forgive the landowners of our [i]sland. *You* only lost your right arm [i]n the war and might forgive them. The man who tied me to a tree and gave me 39 lashes[;] who stripped and flogged my mother & sister & who will not let me stay in his empty hut except [unless] I will do [h]is planting & be satisfied with [h]is price & who combines with others to keep away land from me, well knowing I would not [h]ave anything to do with [h]im [i]f I had land of my own—that man, I cannot well forgive. Does it look as if he has forgiven me . . . [since] he tries to keep me in a condition of [h]elplessness.

General, we cannot remain [h]ere . . . [under] such condition[s] and if the government permits them to come back we ask it to help us to reach land where we shall not be slaves nor compelled to work for those who would treat us as such."[15]

Their petition to President Johnson is even more touching in that it states simply the beliefs and attitudes held by so many freedmen:

This is our home. We have made [t]hese lands what they are. [W]e were the only true and [l]oyal people that were found in possession of [l]ands. [W]e have been always ready to strike for [l]iberty and humanity, yea to fight if need be [t]o preserve this glorious Union. Shall not we who [a]re freedman [*sic*] and have been always true to this Union have the same rights as are enjoyed by [o]thers? Have we broken any laws of these United States? Have we forfeited our rights of property [i]n land—If not[,] then, are not our rights as [a] free people and good citizens of these United States [t]o be considered before the rights of those who were [f]ound in rebellion against this

15. Registers and Letters Received (BRFAL), in RG 105, NA, Microcopy 752, Roll 19, pp. 839–41. The writer capitalized the first word of every line rather than the first word of every sentence.

good and just government[?].... If [the] [g]overnment does not make some provision by which we as [f]reedmen can obtain [a] [h]omestead, we have [n]ot bettered our condition.

We have been encouraged by [the] [g]overnment to take [u]p these lands in small tracts, receiving [c]ertificates for the same. We have thus far [t]aken sixteen thousand (16000) acres of land here on [t]his [i]sland. We are ready to pay for this land [w]hen [the] [g]overnment calls for it. [A]nd now after [w]hat has been done will the good and just government take from us as this right and make us [s]ubject to the will of those who cheated and [o]ppressed us for many years[?] God forbid! We the freedmen of this [i]sland and of the State of South Carolina—

Do therefore petition to you as the President of these United States, that some provisions be made by which [e]very colored man can purchase and [h]old it as his own. We wish to have [a] home, if it be but a few acres.... [W]e therefore look to you ... for protection and [e]qual [r]ights, with the privilege of [p]urchasing [a] [h]omestead right here in the [h]eart of South Carolina.[16]

This petition contains three items which are central to understanding the position of the freedmen on the Sherman reservation. First, they wanted land because without it they were not truly free. Second, they did not expect the land to be given to them but were ready to pay whatever the government asked. Third, they wanted the land which their toil had made productive. Howard soon learned that these same sentiments were held by freedmen settled on the Sherman reservation in Georgia and Florida.

Prior to returning to Washington, Howard instructed his aide, Captain A. P. Ketchum, to remain on the reservation to handle the details of restoration. He ordered Ketchum to establish a committee to adjudicate between the former owners and the freedmen. The committee was to consist of Captain Ketchum, a representative of the owners, and a representative of the freedmen. The landowners complained that Ketchum, in defiance of

16. *Ibid.*, Microcopy 752, Roll 23, pp. 437–38.

Howard's positive instruction, had appointed a Negro to the committee. It appears that the landowners may have misunderstood Howard's instructions. He ordered Ketchum to ask Edward Whaley, the representative for the landowners, if he refused to serve on the board of supervisors because one member was black. Ketchum explained that the freedmen would not accept any decision of the board unless a black was a member of the board. They did not trust any of the former owners because most of the settlers on Edisto were refugees from the mainland who had been driven away from their former homes, without money or produce, by the planters who had solemnly promised them a share of the crop. Therefore, if the owners wished to reach an agreement with the freedmen they would have to accept a committee on which a black served.[17]

William Eaton, the bureau agent in the Georgia sea islands, also reported that many freedmen were moving to the islands from the mainland. He pointed out that as soon as the crops were harvested the planters on the mainland drove away their former slaves empty handed. He reported that the former owners, armed with their presidential pardons, had become defiant of bureau authority and threatened his life daily since he was the only obstacle to their regaining the sea islands. Eaton doubted whether he could continue to protect the freedmen on the islands without resorting to force. He therefore requested a guard of ten or fifteen men.[18]

17. McFeely, *Yankee Stepfather*, 148; New York *Times*, December 20, 1865; *House Executive Documents*, 39th Cong., 1st Sess., No. 11, p. 7; A. P. Ketchum to O. O. Howard, November 30, 1865, December 12, 1865, Registers and Letters Received (BRFAL), in RG 105, NA, Microcopy 752, Roll 21, p. 490; W. H. Trescott to O. O. Howard, December 1, 1865, Roll 24, p. 763; *Nation*, I (December 21, 1865), 772, A. P. Ketchum endorsement on letter of Edward Whaley, December 1, 1865, Records of the Assistant Commissioner, South Carolina (BRFAL), in RG 105, NA, Microcopy 869, Roll 32, p. 55; E. Whaley to A. P. Ketchum, December 2, 1865, p. 89.

18. W. F. Eaton, Land Report for October, November 16, 1865, Records of the Assistant Commissioner, South Carolina (BRFAL), in RG 105, NA, Microcopy 869, Roll 33, pp. 58–59.

During October, 1865, Saxton and Ketchum restored eighty plantations to former owners. However, they seized an additional thirty-six plantations in the sea islands as abandoned. Both Saxton and Ketchum apparently realized that if President Johnson was really determined to restore Sherman reservation lands to the former owners, only Congress could stop him. They therefore made certain recommendations to Howard concerning possible courses of action. Saxton pointed out that since the war had ended Congress must enact legislation extending the bureau. He proposed that this new legislation include a section adopting General Sherman's Special Field Order No. 15 as a law of Congress, and that the land be assigned to the bureau for distribution to the freedmen. "The complete right of possession [should] be given to the land assigned them or which they occupy in pursuance of the said order, and... they [should] be assured in their titles to the same, and receive from Congress, a deed for the property." Should Congress not be willing to go that far, Saxton suggested as an alternative that Congress could appropriate money to purchase the entire reservation at a fair price. The former owners would be offered either the land or the money. Should they choose the land, the money would be paid to the freedmen who occupied the land. Should they choose the money, the freedmen would retain the land and eventually receive titles after refunding to the government the cost of the land. Ketchum agreed with the recommendation and assured Howard: "I believe the freedmen will relieve the U.S. of all expenses by purchasing the land from the government at the prices it may agree to pay the owners."[19] Howard forwarded both suggestions to Congress with the recommendation that

19. R. Saxton, Land Report for October, 1865, *ibid.*, Roll 33, pp. 61–72; A. P. Ketchum, Land Report, November 20, 1865, pp. 75–87. R. Saxton to O. O. Howard, November 20, 1865, Registers and Letters Received (BRFAL), in RG 105, NA, Microcopy 752, Roll 24, p. 177; December 6, 1865, p. 253; A. P. Ketchum to O. O. Howard, Roll 21, p. 516; *Senate Executive Documents*, 39th Cong., 1st Sess., No. 27, p. 141.

some action be taken as soon as possible since the season for planting was at hand.

Senator Charles Sumner accepted Saxton's initial proprosal and sponsored a bill to confirm all land titles issued under Sherman's field order. The New Orleans *Tribune* applauded Sumner's bill as a movement in the right direction, and the first of a series of statutes which contemplates the confiscation of the estates of those guilty of treason and their division among those who are, by viture of their past labor and present rights, entitled to the same—the freedmen." Since Congress was not prepared for such a drastic attack on property rights, Sumner's bill was pigeonholed and finally postponed indefinitely.[20]

As Congress debated the fate of land, bureau, and freedmen, the former owners, through President Johnson, continued pressing for restoration of their property. During December of 1865, the bureau restored at least twenty-three plantations within the Sherman reservation. Ketchum restored only those plantations on which no freedmen held possessory titles. However, he did give some owners informal possession of plantations on which freedmen held possessory certificates. He explained that the former owners were only permitted to reside on the premises pending any decision by Congress. As a condition of restoration, owners obligated themselves to secure to the freedmen the crops grown in 1865 and to claim no portion of the proceeds for themselves. In the case of former slaves who were old or infirm, the landowners usually obligated themselves to provide for them in some way. For instance, William Whaley, who had badgered President Johnson constantly concerning Saxton's unwillingness to restore his land, finally had one plantation restored by Ketchum on December 28, 1865. He agreed to allow the three aged and infirm former slaves who remained on his plantation each a house and two acres of land rent free. He also agreed to

20. *Congressional Globe*, 39th Cong., 1st Sess., pp. 16–17; New Orleans *Tribune*, December 30, 1865.

feed them in return for whatever small services they could perform.

Ketchum attempted to win as liberal terms as possible for the freedmen. Some planters provided each person on the plantation as much as five acres rent free for 1866. Most former owners, however, provided one-half acre rent free to the freedmen who chose to stay on the plantation and contracted to work for 1866. In the event that the freedmen chose not to contract, the owners could not evict them until the supervisory board could find homes and employment for them elsewhere.[21]

Reports from agents sent to inspect the plantation prior to restoration indicate that on most of the plantations which were restored the freedmen who had planted crops the previous year had already left the plantations to return to their former homes on the mainland. By January, 1866, many of the freedmen who had formerly lived on the plantations within the reservation had also returned to their homes. Some plantations were completely abandoned; others had only two or three freedmen residing on them. In most cases the inspecting agent reported that very little land had been cultivated in 1865, usually less than one acre per person on the plantation. Some plantations were abandoned and uncultivated until freedmen flocked to them in November and December of 1865. Even on these plantations Ketchum secured the right to one-half acre rent free for those freedmen who chose to remain on the plantations and work for the former owners.[22]

21. A. P. Ketchum, Land Report, December 8, 1865, Records of the Assistant Commissioner, South Carolina (BRFAL), in RG 105, NA, Microcopy 869, Roll 33, pp. 89–91, January 5, 1866, p. 106; J. A. Alden, Land Report, December 31, 1865, pp. 87–99; A. P. Ketchum to Joseph Whaley, Restoration Order, December 28, 1865, Roll 32, pp. 200–201; A. P. Ketchum to Henry Seabrook, Restoration Order, December 28, 1865, p. 226; A. P. Ketchum to John Stoddard, Restoration Order, January 10, 1866, pp. 268–73, 279. Stoddard was trustee for several plantations.

22. A. P. Ketchum to O. O. Howard, January 22, 1866, Records of the Assistant Commissioner, South Carolina (BRFAL), in RG 105, NA, Microcopy 869, Roll 32, pp. 293, 333, 341, 345, 376, 659.

Although well over a hundred estates were restored in
November and December, 1865, Governor James L. Orr of
South Carolina complained to President Johnson that the bureau
was imposing unnecessary delays in restoration by requiring
the completion of a variety of forms. He also charged that the
bureau interpreted the phrase "mutually satisfactory" so loosely
that if the freedmen refused any terms, no matter how just, the
agents of the bureau refused to restore the land. Saxton refused
to restore any land which he had assigned to freedmen and for
which he or his agents had issued possessory titles. He was
finally removed from his position by order of President Johnson
on January 15, 1866.[23]

With Saxton's removal Ketchum realized that he was power-
less. On January 19, 1866, he restored Ephraim Clark's plantation on James Island. Although only three of the twenty-two
adults on the plantation had arrived there prior to November
and only two of these held certificates, this was the first planta-

---

23. J. L. Orr to O. O. Howard, January 17, 1866, Registers and Letters Received
(BRFAL), in RG 105, NA, Microcopy 752, Roll 24, p. 556; January 19, 1866, p. 553;
James M. McPherson, *The Struggle for Equality: Abolitionists and the Negro in the Civil
War and Reconstruction* (Princeton: Princeton University Press, 1964), 409; McFeely, in
Yankee Stepfather, 71–72, stated that: "Rufus Saxton, offered a head-office inspector-
ship, said he 'would not touch [it] with a thousand foot pole.' He flatly refused to deprive
the freedmen of the last service he could render them—the publicity attendant on his
being removed for taking their part in the struggle for land in the South." This may
portray Saxton as more self-sacrificing than he actually was, for in a private and confiden-
tial letter to Howard he pleaded: "Pray do not insist upon my performing inspection duty
in states where I have once been Commissioner. It will be distasteful and humiliating to
me in the last degree. I would not write this note could I afford to resign but I cannot. In
the name of that friendship *you once* professed for me I now ask you to grant the official
request I have made you and leave me to go back to my legitimate quartermaster
duty."(Emphasis in original.) In a second letter, written the same day, Saxton explained
that any assignment with the bureau, other than that of assistant commissioner, would
result in a reduction of pay. Unless he was reassigned to the quartermaster corps he
would be reduced to his permanent rank of captain. He pointed out that he could not
support his family on captain's pay and therefore repeated his request to be allowed to
return to his quartermaster duties. R. Saxton to O. O. Howard, January 17, 1866,
Registers and Letters Received (BRFAL) in RG 105, NA, Microcopy 752, Roll 24, pp.
476–77; January 17, 1866, pp. 462–63.

tion restored by Ketchum on which any of the residents actually
held possessory titles. During the next month Ketchum restored
some estates on which a small number of freedmen held possessory titles. He still refused, however, to restore those on
which large numbers had been settled under General Saxton's
direction in 1865. For instance, on February 3, 1866, he refused
to restore the estate of Mitchell Whaley since he felt that the
freedmen had acquired a "possessory title to the land they occupy under the order of General Sherman and... unless they
will voluntarily give up their possessory rights this plantation
cannot be restored." After January 26, 1866, all restoration orders contained a statement that restoration in no way affected
the possessory titles given to the freedmen.[24]

One planter had the audacity to request that the bureau assist
him in securing a portion of the crop raised on his plantation the
previous year. General Robert K. Scott, the new assistant commissioner, forwarded his request to Ketchum, who replied:
"Mr. Rose by a solemn obligation on file in this office bound
himself in the following words: 'The undersigned James Rose
does hereby solemnly promise and engage that he will secure to
the refugees and freedmen now resident on his within mentioned estates *the crops of the past season* harvested or unhar-
vested.'... Without this condition and express stipulation his
estate could not have been restored to him."[25]

While Saxton and Ketchum delayed the restoration of the
Sherman lands, Congress continued debating the bureau extension bill. The most that Congress would do at the time was to
confirm and protect the occupancy of the freedmen on the

24. A. P. Ketchum to E. M. Clark, Restoration Order, January 19, 1866, Records of
the Assistant Commissioner, South Carolina (BRFAL), in RG 105, NA, Microcopy 869,
Roll 32, p. 366, A. P. Ketchum to Joseph Whaley, Restoration Order, January 26, 1866,
p. 505; A. P. Ketchum endorsement to application of Mitchell Whaley, February 3,
1866, p. 64; A. P. Ketchum endorsement to application of B. L. Walpole, February 5,
1866, p. 64.

25. A. P. Ketchum endorsement to letter of J. Rose to R. K. Scott, February 6, 1866,
ibid., Roll 32, p. 64. Rose signed the agreement with Ketchum January 22, 1866.

Sherman lands for three years from the date of the order. When President Johnson vetoed the measure as unconstitutional because it deprived former owners of land by legislation rather than by due process of law, the friends of the freedmen failed to muster enough votes, even from the enemies of the South, to override the veto.[26]

The former owners claimed that the language used by Johnson in his veto message was sufficiently clear to require immediate restoration of their land. Howard, on the other hand, felt that neither Congress nor the president had taken decisive action. Reluctant to make sweeping restorations unless he received more definite instructions from either the president or the War Department, Howard wrote Johnson in February, 1866, asking for such instructions. Since President Johnson did not reply, Howard decided to locate those who held valid titles to land and protect them in their possession until "some definite action is had by the government." All other lands would be restored as soon as possible. Howard recalled Ketchum to Washington and assigned the responsibility for validating possessory titles to the assistant commissioners of South Carolina and Georgia, Robert K. Scott and Davis Tillson respectively. He informed them that they were to caution all holders of certificates to preserve their certificates carefully. In the South Carolina sea islands Scott validated 906 warrants by May, 1866.[27] There was considerable conflict between the bureau and the military at this point.

General James C. Beecher, the military commander, took it

26. New York *Times*, February 22, 1866; J. D. Richardson (comp.), *A Compilation of the Messages and Papers of the Presidents* (18 vols.; Washington: Government Printing Office, 1896–1907), VI, 398–405.

27. O. O. Howard to Andrew Johnson, February 22, 1866, in Andrew Johnson Papers, Library of Congress, Series 1, Roll 20, pp. 9306–07; O. O. Howard to R. K. Scott, March 8, 1866, Registers and Letters Received (BRFAL), in RG 105, NA, Microcopy 752, Roll 29, p. 853; R. K. Scott to O. O. Howard, May 29, 1866, Roll 35, p. 323. Special Order No. 27, February 24, 1866, ordered Ketchum to return to Washington for reassignment. He remained on Howard's staff as his aide and by 1867 rose to the rank of brevet lieutenant colonel. Records of the Assistant Commissioner, Georgia (BRFAL), in RG 105, NA, Microcopy 798, Roll 34, p. 365.

upon himself to determine the validity of the warrants and proceeded to evict all whom he judged to possess invalid warrants.
In February, 1866, he issued the following instructions: "In case
freed persons have so called land titles or warrants you will
inspect these and ignore any which do not state a special number
of acres. If the specified number of acres is included in the
document you will demand to be shown the lot claimed, which
lot must be measured and staked out. If such lot cannot be
shown, you will ignore the claims and proceed as though it did
not exist." [28] Scott immediately issued rules for determining the
validity of the warrants—an action which, in effect, countermanded Beecher's orders. Scott informed Beecher that he was not
to eject freedmen from plantations on which they held possessory
titles. He pointed out that General Sherman's order had never
been revoked and was therefore still in full force. Beecher, his
orders thus thwarted, claimed: "I am informed by a party claiming to have been present, that on or about 14 inst. [the 14th of
this month] complaint having been made that I presumed to
judge the validity of land warrants, the Assistant Comm'r. ordered a staff officer to proceed to James Island and 'confirm
every title which Gen. Beecher has disapproved.'"[29] If this actually occurred the freedmen may have benefited from this particular conflict of authority.

In Georgia, General Davis Tillson seems to have been opposed to permitting the Negroes to remain on the Sherman
lands. In December, 1865, he proposed that the freedmen on
the Sherman reservation sign labor contracts with the former
owners. Saxton told him that he had no authority for such action.
Nevertheless, Tillson held meetings between the owners and

28. Beecher's Circular No. 7, February 11, 1866, Registers and Letters Received
(BRFAL), in RG 105, NA, Microcopy 752, Roll 19, pp. 860–61.

29. W. H. Smith to J. C. Beecher, February 26, 1866, *ibid.*, Roll 27, p. 856; R. K.
Scott to General Denvers, p. 824; W. H. Smith to Lt. Everson, March 17, 1866, p. 804;
R. K. Scott to O. O. Howard, March 26, 1866, p. 837; J. Beecher to W. L. M. Berger,
March 20, 1866, p. 837.

the freedmen, trying to convince the freedmen to contract to work the land for which they held warrants. A month later, he proposed an order temporarily restoring the lands to the owners with the understanding that this restoration would in no way affect the rights of either group to the land. Congress would still have the final word on whether to ratify the possessory titles or not. Tillson claimed to be interested only in the well-being of all parties concerned since the former owners had the capital which the freedmen needed to operate the farms.[30]

In February, 1866, Tillson accompanied two northerners who had leased St. Catherine's Island from the former owners and wanted to take possession and hire the freedmen living there. Of the six hundred people on the island some two hundred had just arrived and were destitute. The entire island had already been divided under Special Field Order No. 15 by a civilian agent, a Negro preacher named T. G. Campbell from New York, who claimed "verbal" authority from General Saxton to issue land warrants. Campbell was the official bureau agent for the island and reported earlier that as of December 15, 1865, there were 369 freedmen on the island. Between November 15 and December 15, 1865, a total of fifteen persons arrived and settled on land for which Campbell issued fifteen certificates. Either he ignored or was unaware of Howard's order that no certificates be issued to anyone who arrived after October 19, 1865. Campbell also reported that on December 14, 1865, seven persons left St. Catherine's to settle on land of their own near Savannah.

When Tillson visited the island he found that the freedmen were armed and did not want to allow any whites on the island. After Tillson convinced them that he was the assistant commissioner for Georgia, they requested that he provide them with partial rations during the coming year. They insisted that they

30. D. Tillson to O. O. Howard, December 13, 1865, Roll 20, p. 815; January 15, 1866, pp. 1014, 1018; *House Executive Documents*, 39th Cong., 1st Sess., No. 70, p. 352.

had all the animals, implements, seed, and nearly all the food required to enable them to plant on their own.

Tillson reported to Howard that he refused their request for partial rations because they had been fed the previous year and had failed to grow even enough to feed themselves. Campbell's report of rations received and distributed in 1865 indicates that most of the freedmen on St. Catherine's must have been self-sufficient, otherwise they might have gone hungry had they depended on government rations. He received and issued one-eighth barrel of salt, two barrels of meal, one-eighth barrel of sugar, one-eighth barrel of soap, five boxes of bread, two barrels of meat, three-fourths barrel of hominy, one-half cask bacon, and one-fourth keg of vinegar. Obviously, these rations were not sufficient to maintain 369 persons. Therefore, Tillson's statement that the freedmen on St. Catherine's had been fed by the government in 1865 was an exaggeration.[31]

In spite of this inaccuracy, Tillson was indeed faced with a serious problem, since over two hundred newly arrived freedmen were without land or provisions. As assistant commissioner for Georgia, Tillson had an obligation to all the freedmen under his jurisdiction. He explained that Scuyler and Winchester represented the owners and were willing to furnish money, supplies, and machinery in exchange for labor. The freedmen chose a committee to meet with Scuyler and Winchester. Since the majority of the freedmen on the island held grants, the majority of the members of the committee represented their interests and therefore refused to accept any offer made by the northerners. Those who had arrived recently, however, had no land and were therefore willing and anxious to contract.

Tillson called the freedmen together and informed them that

31. T. G. Campbell, Monthly report, Records of the Assistant Commissioner, South Carolina (BRFAL), in RG 105, NA, Microcopy 869, Roll 33, pp. 95–96; D. Tillson to O. O. Howard, February 12, 1866, Registers and Letters Received (BRFAL), in RG 105, NA, Microcopy 752, Roll 26, p. 1073.

in order to be fair to all he had decided that he would recognize the validity of all titles given by General Saxton and his adjutant general. He would also "recognize the titles given by Mr. Campbell, as to give a man holding one, not forty acres, but as much land as he could work *well*, say from ten to fifteen acres— and that the balance of the land should be turned over to Messrs. Scuyler and Winchester, who should be allowed to hire the remaining freed people who wish to work for them . . . and then, in case Congress did not give the freed people titles to their lands, they were to pay their proportional part of the $5,000 rent paid to the owners of the island by Messrs. Scuyler and Winchester, which would amount to some $2 or less per acre."[32]

In order to justify this action reducing the size of the grants, Tillson accused Campbell of having made grants to himself, his sons, and others who were born free and who were on the island "simply to speculate and take advantage of the poverty of others."[33]

William F. Eaton, the bureau agent for several of the Georgia sea islands, including St. Simon's, informed General Tillson that all of the Sherman lands in Georgia had finally been surveyed, but as late as February, 1866, the titles had not been issued to the freedmen. Only those having titles were to be permitted to keep the land upon which they had settled. On February 17, 1866, Tillson issued an order permitting restoration of much of the land on St. Simon's Island. He ordered Eaton to consolidate all grants held by freedmen on one portion of each plantation; the remainder of the plantation was to be restored to the former owner who agreed to hire those freedmen holding invalid war-

32. D. Tillson to O. O. Howard, February 12, 1866, Registers and Letters Received (BRFAL), in RG 105, NA, Microcopy 752, Roll 20, pp. 1074–78; Report of Operations, September 1865 to November 1866, Records of the Assistant Commissioner, Georgia (BRFAL), in RG 105, NA, Microcopy 798, Roll 32, pp. 17–22.

33. D. Tillson endorsement to letter of T. G. Campbell, Registers and Letters Received (BRFAL), in RG 105, NA, Microcopy 752, Roll 27, p. 561.

rants. Unlike Scott, who provided that whenever the grants were consolidated the owners would have to pay the freedmen for whatever improvements had been made on the land vacated, Tillson made no provision to indemnify the freedmen who were dislocated by his orders.[34]

Tillson reported in November, 1866, that on St. Catherine's Island 147 freedmen contracted with Schuyler and Winchester while 420 planted on tracts of their own on the southern and most fertile portion of the cleared land on the island. He noted that notwithstanding the difference in the number of laborers, Scuyler and Winchester's crop would be at least three times as large as that raised by the freedmen. He concluded that this clearly demonstrated that "the freedmen[,] if left to work for themselves, and control their own labor, will not attain any considerable success."[35] Of course, he ignored the differences in resources that existed between the freedmen and the planters. His comparison assumed that the freedmen commanded the same capital resources as did the two northern entrepreneurs. He also assumed that the freedmen were interested in planting cotton as a cash crop. The vast majority of the freedmen at this time were much more concerned with growing the provisions which they would need for the following year. Furthermore, each freedman worked his small plot individually, whereas the northern entrepreneurs worked one large tract using the gang system which had been prevalent in the antebellum South, and which was undoubtedly more efficient, though repungnant to the former slaves, who wanted to be on their own. Tillson therefore presented a non sequitur argument. Fol-

34. D. Tillson to O. O. Howard, February 12, 1866, Roll 20, p. 1078; Special Field Order No. 1, February 14, 1866, Records of the Assistant Commissioner, Georgia (BRFAL), in RG 105, NA, Microcopy 798, Roll 34, p. 221; Special Field Order No. 3, p. 222; W. H. Smith, Instructions to Lt. Everson, March 17, 1866, p. 804.

35. D. Tillson to O. O. Howard, November 1866, Records of the Assistant Commissioner, Georgia (BRFAL), in RG 105, NA, Microcopy 798, Roll 32, p. 21.

lowing the same line of false reasoning, he believed that there were no more than ten families in all of the sea islands of Georgia who would benefit from their land grants. He felt that they would be better off if, at the end of the year, they went to work for wages, rather than try to work the land with insufficient means.[36]

Yet, in spite of his apparently negative attitude, Tillson did everything possible to protect those who appeared to have a valid claim to land under Sherman's order. He even issued new certificates for land to some freedmen who had lost their warrants. His main concern was that the freedmen become self-sufficient as quickly as possible. He firmly believed that this could best be accomplished by working for wages under the protection of the bureau.

One can see the diversity of bureau efforts to solve the freedmen's economic problem. Some bureau officers helped the freedmen in every way possible to secure land immediately, while others, who were equally concerned about the welfare of the freedmen, preferred to establish them as workers until they had sufficient financial resources to become successful landowners.

Congress was surely cognizant of these efforts when it finally took action by passing the second Freedmen's Bureau bill over the president's veto. The bill included provisions for those freedmen holding land under valid warrants to purchase, at not more than $1.50 an acre, up to twenty acres of land held by the direct tax commissioners in South Carolina. In order to protect the freedmen the bill further stipulated that the purchasers could not alienate the land for six years. Since those who held valid warrants had worked their land and improved it, this action by Congress, although guaranteeing them the right to purchase

36. D. Tillson to O. O. Howard, March 5, 1866, Registers and Letters Received (BRFAL), in RG 105, NA, Microcopy 752, Roll 27, p. 522.

land, deprived them of the improvements they had made. However, they apparently had profited from the year during which they held the land rent free. In December, 1866, the direct tax commissioner for South Carolina reported that he had collected twenty thousand dollars in the months of November and December from the sale of tax lands on St. Helena Island under the act of July 16, 1866. In April, 1867, the Freedmen's Savings and Trust Company representative at Beaufort reported that the freedmen had paid the direct tax commissioner $31,000 for land.[37]

Now that Congress had finally taken decisive action, Scott in South Carolina and Tillson in Georgia were able to assist the freedmen who held Sherman grants in securing permanent title to land of their own. The act identified two classes of freedmen: first, those who held valid warrants and were still in possession of land; and second, those who had received valid warrants but had been dispossessed by the restoration of the land to former owners.

Tillson informed Howard that in order to avoid any difficulty he would furnish the direct tax commissioners with a list of all warrants granted and would notify them when he issued the last warrant. In this manner the direct tax commissioners would be able to judge if there was sufficient land for sale to both first and second class applicants. Saxton's records indicate that his agents had settled 458 families, consisting of 1,825 persons, between April and September of 1865. However, Saxton or his adjutant general had only issued 84 warrants for 1,839 acres of land. Tillson issued vouchers to all freedmen who had lost their certificates. He also issued vouchers to all who had not received

37. U.S., *Statutes at Large*, XIV, 175–76; New York *Times*, July 19, 1866; W. E. Wording to O. O. Howard, December 19, 1866, Registers and Letters Received (BRFAL) in RG 105, NA, Microcopy 752, Roll 45, p. 251; S. L. Harris to J. W. Alvord, April 29, 1867, Roll 46, p. 896.

certificates but had been settled on the land by Saxton's agents prior to October 19, 1865. Between November 14, 1866, and January 19, 1867, Tillson issued a total of 160 first-class warrants and 16 second-class warrants for land in Georgia. The lots claimed ranged in size from ten to forty acres.[38]

In South Carolina Scott reported on November 1, 1866, that he had validated 1,565 warrants for 62,600 acres of land. He also indicated that although the bureau had restored 146,650 acres on the mainland and 64,545 acres in the sea islands of South Carolina, he still retained under his control 29,093 acres on the mainland and 72,600 acres on the sea islands. Since the freedmen holding valid warrants had two years to select their land from the direct tax commissioner, the bureau retained control of much of this land until it was dropped from the rolls on January 1, 1869.[39]

Section seven of the second bureau bill specified that the freedmen's warrants were to be exchanged for lands in Beaufort County, South Carolina, to which the government had acquired title through the tax sales of 1863 and 1864. This would, in effect, create a predominantly black area in the state. It is interesting that the bureau agent for the district was Martin R. Delaney, a black abolitionist who had coedited the *North Star* with Frederick Douglass. Delaney was also a black nationalist

38. D. Tillson to O. O. Howard, September 24, 1866, Registers and Letters Received (BRFAL), in RG 105, NA, Microcopy 752, Roll 37, pp. 1067–68; "Registers of Land Titles Issued to Freedmen, April to September, 1865," Records of the Assistant Commissioner, Georgia (BRFAL), in RG 105, NA, Microcopy 798, Roll 36, pp. 233–352; Sample land warrant issued by Tillson, Roll 13, p. 732; List of warrants issued, November 14, 1866, to January 19, 1867, Roll 36, pp. 353–62.

39. R. K. Scott, Land Report, November 1, 1866, Records of the Assistant Commissioner, South Carolina (BRFAL), in RG 105, NA, Microcopy 869, Roll 33, pp. 308–312. The figures alone are misleading. Although Scott reported 146,650 acres restored, the figures actually total 145,042. Furthermore, on forty plantations, acreage had been estimated at 500 acres. These were changed to 700 acres. "Memoranda Relating to Abandoned and Confiscated Lands, 1865–1868," Land Division (BRFAL), in RG 105, NA. Consolidated schedule of operations from October, 1867, to August, 1868, indicates that as of August, 1868, the bureau still controlled 74,669 acres of land in South Carolina.

who had attempted in the late 1850s to secure a grant of land in the Niger River valley of Africa.[40] It seems fitting that he should serve as bureau agent for Beaufort County.

At the end of February, 1867, Delaney reported that a great number of people who did not have grants had left the district for the mainland. He controlled twenty-one plantations containing 21,150 acres, of which 6,900 acres were under cultivation. He indicated that the freedmen were cultivating 5,400 acres which they leased from the government at one dollar per acre. Although the freedmen were self-supporting, he pointed out that some had taken too little land and consequently would not be able to support themselves throughout the planting year. He advised that in the future the minimum quantity of land leased to a working family of four should be ten acres.[41]

By February, 1868, the entire county of Beaufort, with the exception of the plantations bought by northerners at tax sales during the war, had been divided into ten and twenty acre plots and sold to freedmen holding validated warrants for land. William Henry Brisbane, the chairman of the direct tax commissioners for South Carolina, reported that over two thousand families had acquired homesteads.[42]

In 1869, after the bureau had been disbanded for all practical purposes, Brisbane requested that the attorney general of the United States protect the freedmen in their possession of the land they bought. He pointed out that in the absence of the bureau the former owners and owners of lands adjoining freedmen were

40. Jane H. and William H. Pease, *Bound with Them in Chains: A Biographical History of the Antislavery Movement* (Westport, Conn.: Greenwood Press, Inc., 1972), 185.

41. M. R. Delany, Monthly Report for November 1865, December 21, 1865, Records of the Assistant Commissioner, South Carolina (BRFAL), in RG 105, NA, Microcopy 869, Roll 33, pp. 87–88; Report for February, 1867, p. 350; Report for March, 1867, p. 360; Report for June, 1867, p. 408; Report for July, 1867, p. 437.

42. H. M. Stuart to O. O. Howard, February, 1868, Registers and Letters Received (BRFAL), in RG 105, NA, Microcopy 752, Roll 55, p. 226; W. H. Brisbane to E. R. Hoar, October 22, 1869, Roll 66, p. 733.

seeking action in state court to have the freedmen ejected from their homes. He reported one case in which a northerner claimed that the plantation he had purchased at the tax sale included the land on which three black families had settled. Since the freedmen had no one to appear for them, they were evicted by the sheriff. Brisbane pointed out that had he been called upon he could have testified that the claimant had never purchased the land. However, when he learned of the case it had already been decided. He urged the attorney general's office to provide some means whereby the freedmen would be protected in their investment. Fortunately for the freedmen, the lands involved had been sold to them in fee simple and they had paid taxes on the land after purchasing it.[43]

When Congress assigned tax lands to the freedmen holding valid land warrants, it settled the question of what to do with the Sherman titles. However, the legislation was inadequate to meet the needs of the vast majority of the former slaves who were being evicted throughout the South as restoration continued. Friends of the freedmen, undaunted by the loss of the abandoned and confiscated lands, sought alternative means of making land available.

43. W. H. Brisbane to E. R. Hoar, October 22, 1869, *ibid.*, Roll 66, p. 733; Howard *Autobiography*, 193; Rose, *Rehearsal for Reconstruction*, 397. Rose pointed out that as late as 1890, 75 percent of the land in Beaufort County, South Carolina, was owned by blacks.

IV

Alternative Proposals and the Southern Homestead Act

NOT UNAWARE OF the potential consequences of restoration under the president's pardoning policy, bureau agents, in particular, and others sought alternative answers to the freedmen's plight of landlessness. Many agents offered proposals to Howard, who acted on some while rejecting others; some such proposals eventually were forwarded to Congress, where they were influential in passage of the Southern Homestead Act and in the act extending the life of the bureau.

Quartermaster M. C. Meigs devised a plan whereby many of the freedmen could secure land in the South. He proposed, as a condition for receiving pardons, that those southerners with a net worth of at least twenty thousand dollars (who were excluded from automatic pardon in Johnson's amnesty proclamation) give to each head of family of their former slaves from five to ten acres of land. The freedmen would receive full title to the land with the stipulation that the land could not be alienated during the lifetime of the grantee. This would prevent sharpers from depriving the freedmen of their land. The planter would only sacrifice a small portion of his plantation in order to secure his pardon, while assuring himself of a small settlement of freedmen to serve as an adequate labor supply. Meigs pointed out that unless landowners were willing to adopt such measures the freedmen would be forced to seek homes in the western homestead lands. This type of emigration would impoverish the South, whose fields, without labor, would be worthless. Howard forwarded the recommendation to Stanton, who sent it on to President Johnson.[1] Johnson chose not to adopt the recommendation, but it might have been the basis of Thaddeus Stevens' later confiscation plan.[2]

Carl Schurz and John W. Sprague proposed that the government assign freedmen land along the route of the Union Pacific Railroad and furnish them with transportation. In this manner, the land would be settled and the freedmen would protect the railroad from Indian attack. This plan would remove some of the surplus Negro population from the South and would make the labor of those remaining more valuable. Howard received several recommendations that freedmen on the lands be colonized along southern railroads. By colonizing freedmen on the lands belonging to the railroad companies these roads, which had suffered extensive damage during the war, could be restored to full service and in many cases could be extended.[3]

The Memphis and Little Rock Railroad Company offered to hire from five hundred to one thousand Negro ex-soldiers and other freedmen to construct a railroad from Duvall's Bluff,

1. M. C. Meigs to O. O. Howard, August 22, 1865, Registers and Letters Received (BRFAL), in RG 105, NA, Microcopy 752, Roll 16, pp. 818–19; O. O. Howard to E. M. Stanton, September 4, 1865, in Andrew Johnson Papers, Library of Congress, Roll 17, Ser. 1, p. 6537; New York Times, December 20, 1865.

2. Ralph Korngold, Thaddeus Stevens: A Being Darkly Wise and Rudely Great (New York: Harcourt Brace and World, 1955), 286. In 1867 Stevens proposed that the government confiscate the property of all former slaveholders who owned more than two hundred acres of land. The property thus seized was to be assigned to the freedmen in lots of forty acres. The remaining land was to be sold and the proceeds used to reimburse loyalists whose property had been seized, destroyed, or damaged. Any remaining funds were to be used to increase the pensions of Union soldiers and to pay the national debt.

3. J. W. Sprague to O. O. Howard, November 1865, Registers and Letters Received (BRFAL), in RG 105, NA, Microcopy 752, Roll 22, p. 572; H. Pinner to O. O. Howard, Roll 16, p. 602; Senate Executive Documents, 39th Cong., 1st Sess., No. 2, p. 45.

Arkansas, to Memphis, Tennessee. The contractor, Nathan Bedford Forrest, proposed to pay the blacks one dollar per day, plus
rations and land from the railroad grant. Since Arkansas, under
its "temporary" black codes, forbade Negro ownership of land,
Forrest and his associates agreed to "bind themselves to secure
the [f]reedmen in the possession of the land they earn."[4] Upon
the request of bureau agents in Tennessee, Howard provided
transportation to Arkansas for several hundred destitute freedmen in Alabama. He instructed General E. O. C. Ord to detail a
capable, discreet officer, interested in the work of the bureau,
as superintendent in the district embraced by the proposed railroad. His primary function was to protect the freedmen in all
their rights and interests. Howard also informed Ord: "N. B.
Forrest is the contractor and from a personal interview with him
I am of [the] opinion that he is disposed to do everything that is
fair and right for the negroes which may be employed."[5] From
this one might assume that Howard did not know Forrest's reputation. General Nathan Bedford Forrest had commanded the
Confederate troops who attacked Fort Pillow. Union forces
claimed that after black troops at Fort Pillow surrendered under
a flag of truce they were butchered by the Confederate soldiers.
The Confederates claimed that after they saw the truce flag they
ceased fire and relaxed their guard, whereupon the Union forces
recommenced firing. Angered by this duplicity, they attacked
again and resolved to show no mercy. Union officers charged
that, as commanding officer of the Confederate forces involved
in the slaughter, Forrest was responsible for the action of his
soldiers.[6] Howard was fully aware of the charges, for in a letter

4. J. W. Sprague to O. O. Howard, November, 1865, Registers and Letters Received (BRFAL) in RG 105, NA, Microcopy 752, Roll 22, p. 572.
5. O. O. Howard to E. O. C. Ord, December 29, 1866, Selected Series of Records
(BRFAL), in RG 105, NA, Microcopy 742, Roll 2, p. 294.
6. M. J. Seanning to B. Wade, July 22, 1865, in Benjamin Wade Papers, Library of
Congress.

to Forrest on December 15, 1866, he stated: "My great objection would be your own agency. You are a stranger to me personally, therefore I depend upon your reputation for my opinions. Yet I do not wish to act with a view to your personal injury, and would suggest that your Directors send with their letter some agent to General Ord with your practical proposition."[7] Obviously, Howard was willing to experiment with any type of labor which would help the freedmen become self-sufficient.

Colonel S. M. Preston in Mississippi proposed that the pay due the soldiers of his black regiment be used to purchase sixteen thousand acres of land in Mississippi, thus providing some eight hundred families with twenty acres each. The families could work the land while the men completed their active service. With the money from their first crop and their final settlement from the military, the men could pay for the lands purchased and have enough to provide for their needs for the next year. Howard approved the proposal and returned all communications to Colonel Thomas, the assistant commissioner for Mississippi, for further action. However, Thomas hesitated to violate Mississippi's black codes, which prohibited Negroes from renting or leasing land. He informed Howard that he would sustain all leases or contracts made before the passage of the codes. Unfortunately, this statement implied that he would not sustain any leases, contracts, or sale of land made after the passage of the codes.[8]

Howard informed Thomas that while the bureau remained in Mississippi it would protect the freedmen in their right to lease land. He pointed out that "the whole power of the gov-

7. O. O. Howard to N. B. Forrest, December 15, 1866, Selected Series of Records (BRFAL), in RG 105, NA, Microcopy 742, Roll 2, p. 287.
8. S. M. Preston to S. Thomas, October 9, 1865, Registers and Letters Received (BRFAL), in RG 105, NA, Microcopy 752, Roll 19, p. 199; S. M. Preston to J. W. Farnsworth, January 18, 1866, Roll 23, pp. 788–93; S. Thomas to O. O. Howard, December 13, 1865, Roll 22, p. 556.

ernment... [was] pledged to sustain the freedom of the negro."
He therefore instructed Thomas to secure from the department
commander whatever military forces were necessary to protect
the freedmen in their leases.[9]

The actions and statements of Colonel Thomas are enigmatic.
In August, 1865, he warned the planters not to expect too much
from the freedmen immediately because "slavery made them
what they are; if they are ignorant and stupid, do not expect
much of them, and give them at least time to get out of the ruts
of slavery, before judgeing [sic] them by the highest stan-
dards."[10] He also warned the planters, however, that slavery
had ended and that they must recognize and respect the freedmen's right to own property that they acquired legitimately.
Then, in September he adopted a position similar to that which
Fredrick Douglass had proposed in 1862 in an address to the
Emancipation League of Boston. Douglass, in response to the
question of what to do with four million slaves if they were
emancipated, advised: "Do nothing with them, but leave them
like you have left other men to do with and for themselves.... If
we cannot stand up, then let us fall down.—We ask nothing at
the hands of the American people but simple justice and an
equal chance to live."[11] Thomas echoed this same belief when
he advised Howard that the freedmen needed nothing but justice, a chance to own property, and "the free exercise of their
right to have schools and churches—and then, let them
alone."[12]

The following month, when the Mississippi legislature

9. O. O. Howard to S. Thomas, November 30, 1865, Records of the Assistant
Commissioner, Mississippi (BRFAL) in RG 105, NA, Microcopy 826, Roll 28, p. 405.

10. Circular No. 9, August 4, 1865, *ibid.*, Roll 28, p. 84.

11. Frederick Douglass, "The Future of the Negro People in the Slave States,"
Douglass' Monthly (March, 1862); Thomas R. Frazier (ed.), *Afro-American History:
Primary Sources* (New York: Harcourt Brace Jovanovich, Inc. 1970), 136.

12. Registers and Letters Received (BRFAL), in RG 105, NA, Microcopy 752, Roll
22, p. 51.

enacted black codes, Thomas vacillated between his obligation to aid the freedmen and his unwillingness to violate the laws of the state until ordered to ignore those laws by Howard. By December, 1865, Thomas reverted to his earlier position and informed Howard that the freedmen only wanted the "right to buy property, to be paid for their labor, to protection before the courts, to have schools and churches, and freedom from personal abuse."[13] He asked Howard if it would be consistent with his position as assistant commissioner if he were to act as an agent for the freedmen in the purchase of a large tract of land. The freedmen had the money, but no one would sell them land. Thomas felt, therefore, that if he or one of his officers acted as their agent the land could be purchased and the freedmen would be able to settle on their own land. Howard encouraged Thomas to proceed with the proposal but warned that only sub-agents who were scrupulously honest be appointed.[14]

General Davis Tillson submitted a plan to Howard for colonizing freedmen in southwestern Georgia. Some of the men had accumulated from one hundred to five hundred dollars and were anxious to purchase land for themselves. One society of freed people had already saved over seven thousand dollars and planned to raise that amount to ten thousand dollars. Tillson sent two members of the society to Thomas County to examine and make arrangements to purchase land. Since the whites in the area wanted assurances of white leadership of the colony, he appointed Major Hastings as commander. He also asked the American Union Commission to supply the seeds and implements needed by the colonists. The only expense to the government was the cost of transportation. In addition Tillson suggested, without success, that the American Union Commission purchase a large tract of well-selected land in southwestern

13. S. Thomas to O. O. Howard, December 13, 1865, *ibid.*, Roll 22, p. 557.

14. *Ibid.*; M. Woodhul to S. Thomas, December 27, 1865, Records of the Assistant Commissioner, Mississippi (BRFAL), in RG 105, NA, Microcopy 826, Roll 28, p. 405.

Georgia to be sold to the freedmen at cost. In this way speculators would not be able to take advantage of them.[15]

In North Carolina a former Union army officer suggested that northern men, including bureau agents, form a company to buy land which could be cultivated immediately. Freedmen would be employed as wage laborers to work the land under the supervision of an agent of the company. The company would select those who proved to be the most industrious and sell them from ten to twenty acres on reasonable terms to be paid over a long period of time. The freedmen would be given title to the land. Howard encouraged Assistant Commissioner Whittlesey to foster this plan and "any scheme which will ensure the freedmen homes and farms of their own."[16]

Blacks in Virginia proposed that the freedmen not depend on northerners to purchase land for resale but rather that they form local associations. Members would make regular payments of small installments, thereby creating a fund to purchase land for subscribing members. The association would hold a mortgage on the land until the sum advanced by the association and the interest were paid, at which time the purchaser would receive clear title to his land.[17]

Other blacks believed that only through government action could a sufficient amount of land be secured for the freedmen. Although the New Orleans *Tribune* had opposed the poll tax on black laborers in March, 1865, it apparently did not represent the sentiment of all blacks. Alex Spriggs, a black from West

15. D. Tillson to O. O. Howard, December 2, 1865, Registers and Letters Received (BRFAL), in RG 105, NA, Microcopy 752, Roll 20, pp. 766–69; O. O. Howard to D. Tillson, December 13, 1865, Selected Series of Records (BRFAL), in RG 105, NA, Microcopy 742, Roll 1, p. 237.

16. A. W. Tourgee to E. Whittlesey, July 29, 1865, Registers and Letters Received (BRFAL) in RG 105, NA, Microcopy 752, Roll 18, p. 192.

17. *Ibid.*, Roll 23, p. 543; Thomas Bayne and John Brown, *An Address from the Colored Citizens of Norfolk, Virginia, to the People of the United States* (New Bedford, Mass.: E. Anthony and Sons, Printers, 1865), 8.

Virginia, suggested that Congress levy a tax of five dollars on every black adult male and one dollar on every black female in the entire country. He believed that in this manner a sum of $2,244,000 could be raised to be applied to the purchase of land for the freedmen.[18]

Because of the depressed economic condition prevailing in the South at the conclusion of hostilities, some bureau agents concentrated on restoring the economy as a means of assisting the freedmen. One agent in Virginia proposed that the government settle the freedmen on forty-acre tracts and furnish each family a pair of mules or horses, a set of harness, a wagon or cart, a set of farming implements, seed, rations, and forage. He suggested that out of the proceeds of the first crop the government would collect the cost of rations, seed, and forage and then pay, out of the balance, one-third to the owner and two-thirds to the cultivator. The teams, implements, harness, and cart were to be sold to either the owners or cultivators as soon as they were able to purchase. In this manner the freedmen would receive a fair return on their labor and would be able to save money to purchase land. This plan, unfortunately, was predicated on continued control of abandoned lands by the bureau.[19]

The restoration of property rendered many freedmen homeless. Most of the plantation owners, impoverished by the war, were unable to utilize all their land; hence their need for the services of their former chattels diminished considerably. One owner in Virginia informed the freedmen that the government had returned the land to him. He offered to sell at three hundred dollars per acre, then drove off all who could not afford to buy or would not pay his price. The freedmen requested that the government take some action to provide them with homesteads. This situation prompted a refusal in December, 1865, by

18. A. Spriggs to O. O. Howard, December 7, 1865, Registers and Letters Received (BRFAL), in RG 105, NA, Microcopy 752, Roll 24, p. 288.
19. G. Armes to O. O. Howard, July 29, 1865, *ibid.*, Roll 13, p. 160.

bureau agents in Virginia, to restore any plantation unless the owner agreed to employ all his former slaves.[20] In spite of the precautions taken to protect the freedmen, many were evicted by their former owners. Brown estimated that in the district of southeastern Virginia alone some twenty thousand would be displaced as a result of the president's restoration policy. The American Missionary Association, on the other hand, estimated in their report to President Johnson in November, 1865, that in actuality some 105,000 freedmen in Virginia were rendered "houseless, homeless, and helpless."[21]

A delegation from the association requested that the president either retain all the land promised to the freedmen by Congress or furnish transportation to the western homestead lands and guarantee sufficient rations until a crop could be planted and harvested. The president replied that the blacks were as much entitled to the homestead lands as anyone else. However, his general attitude towards the freedmen's plight is indicated in his belief that they were "wards" of the government and those who were destitute would receive rations. He objected to any plan to establish separate colonies of freedmen on public lands. He considered it necessary for the Negroes to be interspersed with the white population. The delegation also visited Secretary of War Stanton to enlist his support. Stanton pointed out that "the abandoned as well as confiscated lands should have been given them [the Negroes] beyond recall, and that the Government, having freed the slaves, was bound to provide for the helpless and suffering among them, to the fullest extent to which the master was morally bound before emancipation."[22]

When George Whipple reported the outcome of the dele-

20. *House Reports*, 40th Cong., 2nd Sess., No. 30, p. 13; *House Executive Documents*, 39th Cong., 1st Sess., No. 70, pp. 141–42.

21. Registers and Letters Received (BRFAL), in RG 105, NA, Microcopy 752, Roll 25, p. 2; Roll 19, pp. 243–52; Roll 19, p. 249.

22. *Ibid.*, Roll 19, p. 252.

gation's visits to Johnson and Stanton, Howard promised that if the American Missionary Association, or any other organization, would indicate its good faith by guaranteeing to provide ten black families who were dependent on the government with tools, stock, huts, and adequate supervision, he would provide the transportation and rations necessary to establish them on homesteads under the Homestead Act of 1862.[23]

In early June, 1865, Brown, who was extremely concerned over Virginia's "excess" black population, recommended that the families of Negro soldiers stationed in Texas be permitted to join them. Howard approved the plan, ordered transportation and subsistence, and instructed the newly appointed assistant commissioner for Texas to provide for these families. Unfortunately, of the eight to ten thousand black Virginia soldiers sent to Texas, only forty-five families chose to follow. Brown protested that many would have emigrated but the reduction of family rations by one-half and failure to pay the soldiers for ten months caused considerable discontent. Virginia whites, aware that Brown's proposal would reduce the labor supply, also aided in thwarting the plan. They spread rumors that the blacks were to be "colonized in Texas." The freedmen, who remembered Ile a Vache, viewed the prospect of colonization with great horror.[24]

As unemployment and destitution increased, Brown continued to press for some form of colonization of the excess laboring population in Virginia. His fear, which appears justifiable, was that the return of ten thousand Negro soldiers from Texas would aggravate an already deteriorating situation. He therefore proposed that the government induce the Negro soldiers to

23. O. O. Howard to G. Whipple, November 27, 1865, Selected Series of Records (BRFAL) in RG 105, NA, Microcopy 742, Roll 19, p. 237.

24. H. M. Stinson to O. Brown, June 15, 1865, *ibid.*, Roll 1, p. 60; O. Brown to O. O. Howard, June 17, 1865, Registers and Letters Received (BRFAL) in RG 105, NA, Microcopy 752, Roll 13, p. 809; O. O. Howard to M. C. Meigs, June 28, 1865, Selected Series of Records (BRFAL) in RG 105, NA, Microcopy 742, Roll 1, p. 225.

select their bounty lands in Texas and compel their families to join them. This step would reduce the number of Virginia freedmen dependent on the government by at least five thousand. If this plan was not feasible, then the government should set aside from the public lands of Florida sufficient land to provide forty acres to each male freedman willing to emigrate. In this fashion all the surplus laborers in Virginia could become self-supporting immediately by cutting and selling the timber on their land.[25] Since the government owned no public land in Texas, Howard asked Brown to develop his Florida proposal for submission to the president and the Congress.

In formulating his proposal Brown recommended that the government set aside in Florida 500,000 acres of public land, subject to the 1862 homestead law, for exclusive settlement by fifty thousand Virginia freedmen, as well as by the soldiers stationed in Texas. The government would furnish the necessary farm stock, farming utensils, seed, and other essentials. For each ten thousand emigrants the government should appoint an assistant quartermaster to ensure that the freedmen repaid the government for their supplies. As soon as they reimbursed the government they should be issued titles to their land.[26]

Upon receipt of Brown's proposal, Howard informed Secretary of the Interior James Harlan of the Florida plan and requested information concerning the public lands in that state. Harlan replied that Howard lacked authority under the act creating the bureau to set aside any public land for the exclusive use of the freedmen. He reminded Howard that Congress limited the authority of the bureau to "such tracts within the insurrectionary states as have been confiscated, abandoned, or pur-

25. O. Brown to O. O. Howard, October 4, 1865, Registers and Letters Received (BRFAL) in RG 105, NA, Microcopy 752, Roll 25, p. 21; O. Brown to O. O. Howard, December 1865, Roll 25, p. 216; O. Brown to O. O. Howard, November 20, 1865, Roll 25, p. 166; M. Woodhull for Howard to O. Brown, November 21, 1865, Selected Series of Records (BRFAL) in RG 105, NA, Microcopy 742, Roll 1, p. 225.

26. O. Brown to O. O. Howard, December 1865, Registers and Letters Received (BRFAL) in RG 105, NA, Microcopy 752, Roll 25, pp. 217–18.

chased."[27] Brown countered with a suggestion that since Florida was under martial law the commanding officer of the department could issue an order stating that no lands set apart by the bureau could be preempted. This move would hold the lands long enough for the freedmen to reach Florida and establish their claims under the Homestead Act of 1862. Unfortunately, President Johnson did not authorize the reservation of public lands in Florida.[28]

Howard then submitted Brown's proposal to Congress. With a view to aiding Congress in its deliberations, he instructed Colonel T. W. Osborne, assistant commissioner for Florida, to inspect part of the public lands and determine which areas would be suitable for the type of settlement envisioned. Osborne recommended that the federal government purchase from Florida all territory south of latitude twenty-eight and organize it under a territorial form of government. He envisioned this new territory as a settlement exclusively for freedmen, with each family permitted to preempt or purchase eighty acres of land. He estimated that approximately nine million acres of land was suitable for the settlement of 115,000 families, or about 575,000 persons.

Should the government not wish to purchase this land from Florida, then some 1,376,000 acres of land still belonging to the national government could be set aside. Osborne recommended that if Brown's proposal was accepted, the government immediately provide for a resurvey of the area, cutting the land up into eighty-acre lots and allowing only one lot per family. He also suggested that each township be completely settled before another township was opened for settlement. This move would facilitate both settlement and government of the territory. In order to assure that freedmen would not be defrauded of their

27. J. Harlan to O. O. Howard, December 17, 1865, *ibid.*, Roll 21, pp. 233–35.

28. O. Brown to O. O. Howard, December 17, 1865, *ibid.*, Roll 25, p. 266; M. Woodhull for Howard to O. Brown, December 19, 1865, Selected Series of Records (BRFAL) in RG 105, NA, Roll 1, p. 226; O. O. Howard to O. Brown, December 21, 1865, p. 269.

lands, he recommended further that they should not be allowed
to sell the land thus settled in less than ten years. Except for the
eighty-acre provision and the restriction on sale, the freedmen
should be settled according to the terms of the Homestead Act of
1862.[29] Once the settlers were on the land the only thing they
would need would be military protection.

Based on the actions and recommendations of the various
agents of the bureau, Senator Lyman Trumbull introduced a bill
in December, 1865, extending the life of the Freedmen's
Bureau. The bill also contained provisions for setting aside the
unoccupied public lands in Florida, Mississippi, and Arkansas
for exclusive homesteading by blacks. Approximately three million acres of land in the above-named states would be available
for allotment to freedmen in parcels not exceeding forty acres.
Each settler would be furnished a house and the necessary provisions for farming, such as stock, seed, and tools. In the ensuing
debate on the bill, one senator estimated that these provisions
would cost the taxpayers forty-five million dollars; no similar bill
had ever been introduced in Congress to furnish homes and
houses for the white men of the country. One proposed amendment would have eliminated the names of the states and permitted the freedmen to locate on any public lands. Senator Thomas
A. Hendricks replied, "I am not willing to withdraw from settlement, from homesteading or pre-emption, lands in the latitude
where white settlers are most likely to go."[30] In other words,

29. T. W. Osborne to O. O. Howard, January 1, 1866, Registers and Letters Received (BRFAL) in RG 105, NA, Microcopy 752, Roll 20, pp. 499–505; January 2, 1866,
Roll 20, pp. 488–94; *Nation*, II (February 1, 1866).

30. *Congressional Globe*, 39th Cong., 1st Sess., 209, 363, 371–72. President
Johnson, in explaining his reason for vetoing the bill stated: "The President of the United
States stands toward the country in a somewhat different attitude from that of any
member of Congress. Each member of Congress is chosen from a single district or State;
the President is chosen by the people of all the States. As eleven States are not at this
time represented in either branch of Congress, it would seem to be his duty on all proper
occasions to present their just claims to Congress." Richardson (comp.), *Messages and
Papers of the Presidents*, VI, 404.

the freedmen could have public lands, but only so long as they restricted their activity to southern states. Congress enacted the bill essentially as Trumbull proposed but even this minor commitment to the freedmen met with defeat when Congress was unable to muster enough votes to override Johnson's veto.

Undaunted by this setback, Howard and his subordinates continued their efforts to secure legislation providing land. He instructed the assistant commissioners for Georgia, Alabama, Arkansas, Louisiana, and Mississippi to inspect the public lands in their respective states to determine the availability of tracts suitable for colonization of freedmen, preferably away from whites.[31] Bureau officials in two states filed reports. The assistant commissioner for Alabama recommended that public lands be set aside for the freedmen. He believed that since most whites refused to sell land to the freedmen, many blacks in the state would embrace the opportunity thus offered to obtain a home.[32] After an investigation of St. Landry and Calcasieu parishes in Louisiana a bureau agent concluded that there were no lands in those parishes "which the Government of the United States could control that would be suitable for the colonization of negroes, and where they could be granted homesteads and permanently located in homes of their own."[33] He based his conclusion on the fact that the land available was along the route of a proposed railroad to Texas and consisted primarily of swampy lands unsuited for immediate tillage. Only if the freedmen settled near the areas already cleared and owned by whites could

31. M. Woodhull for Howard to D. Tillson, copies sent to W. Swayne, A. Baird, S. Thomas, and J. Sprague, January 18, 1866, Selected Series of Records (BRFAL), in RG 105, NA, Microcopy 742, Roll 2, p. 61.

32. W. Swayne to O. O. Howard, January 20, 1866, Registers and Letters Received (BRFAL), in RG 105, NA, Microcopy 752, Roll 19, p. 538.

33. J. Cromie to A. Baird, March 7, 1866, *ibid.*, Roll 28, p. 362. The lands Cromie inspected were alternate sections fifteen miles in depth on either side of the right of way of the proposed New Orleans, Opelousas, and Great Western Railroad. It must be remembered that Howard's instructions were to search for lands on which the freedmen could be established in separate colonies away from the whites.

the public lands be of any benefit.[34] This, however, might not have been too wise, considering the hostile attitude of the whites in the interior portions of the state where the public lands were located. The whites had already purchased the best public lands and did not want blacks to settle near them.

Howard did not limit his efforts to inspection of the public lands in these five southern states. He proposed to use the power of the bureau to settle freedmen in Florida under the terms of the homestead law of 1862. He appointed an agent of the bureau to organize a colony of freedmen in Virginia for settlement in Florida. Initially hundreds of Virginia families demonstrated interest in the project, but fear of colonization (based on the Ile a Vache experience) and the continued belief that the government would give them land in Virginia soon reduced the number to fifty families, or about two hundred persons. By the time the colony was finally organized in late March, 1866, operating funds for the bureau were so low that Howard had to depend on the military for transportation. The request was regretfully denied because the War Department funds were low and the project was delayed until Congress provided a specific appropriation for the bureau.[35] Howard encouraged Thaddeus Stevens in the House and William Fessenden in the Senate to initiate legislation providing funds for transporting freedmen to public lands.[36]

Stevens and Fessenden, as well as other congressmen, were concerned over restoration, which dispossessed the freedmen of

34. A. Baird to M. Woodhull for Howard, March 17, 1866, *ibid.*, Roll 28, pp. 366–67.

35. W. H. Hunt to O. O. Howard, March 22, 1866, *ibid.*, Roll 27, p. 728; G. Chahoon to O. O. Howard, February 1866, Roll 27, p. 734; O. O. Howard to E. M. Stanton, April 26, 1866, Roll 27, p. 738. O. O. Howard to E. M. Stanton, April 26, 1866, Selected Series of Records (BRFAL), in RG 105, NA, Microcopy 742, Roll 2, p. 126; A. P. Ketchum for Howard to G. Chahoon, April 28, 1866, Roll 2, p. 129.

36. O. O. Howard to T. Stevens, April 27, 1866, Selected Series of Records (BRFAL), in RG 105, NA, Microcopy 742, Roll 2, p. 128; O. O. Howard to W. P. Fessenden, May 4, 1866, Roll 2, p. 134.

lands assigned them under the act creating the Freedmen's Bureau. A bill was introduced in the House providing for the disposal of public lands in the South. In Arkansas, Alabama, Florida, Louisiana, and Mississippi there remained 46,398,544.87 acres of unsold public lands. Proponents pointed out that Congress could not give freedom, protection, and justice without homesteads. "With free lands to occupy and cultivate and own, no combinations of capital, no monopolies, no vagrant laws, nor all these combined, can make slaves of the laboring masses in any country." Furthermore, the bill was necessary because Congress had failed to adopt any extensive system of confiscation.[37]

The bill provided for setting aside all public lands in the above-named states for the exclusive use of freedmen and loyal refugees until January 1, 1867. The measure was truly one of reform in that it limited all public lands in these five states to "homesteading for actual settlement." No cash sales or preemptions would be permitted. Freedmen would not have to expend their meager cash reserves for registration fees until they actually received their patents. This would allow them five years to improve their homesteads and save the $5.00 needed to complete registration of their land. For two years, no entry could be made for more than 80 acres of minimum land (previously valued at $1.25) or 40 acres of double minimum land (previously valued at $2.50 per acre). The Senate amended the bill to increase the amount of land to 160 acres, but the conference committee reduced the maximum to 80 acres. The bill, usually referred to as the Southern Homestead Act, became law on June 21, 1866, with President Johnson's signature.[38]

While debating the Southern Homestead bill, several congressmen introduced new legislation extending the life of the Freedmen's Bureau. Congress requested Howard's views on the

37. *Congressional Globe*, 39th Cong., 1st Sess., 715–17.
38. *Ibid.*, 3155; New York *Times*, May 23, 1866; U.S., *Statutes at Large*, XIII, 66–67.

necessity of legislation continuing the existence of the bureau. Howard pointed out that since the bureau had been obliged to restore the land under its control, more land was needed. He suggested that "an equivalent in public lands could be set apart, under the same or similar conditions to those of this [Freedmen's` Bureau Act of March 3, 1865] law."[39] Howard emphasized his belief that land must be made available for the freedmen to purchase. He apparently equated the fees required for homesteading with the purchase price of land.

Because the fate of the Southern Homestead bill under debate at this time was uncertain, the Committee on Reconstruction included a public lands section in the Freedmen's Bureau extension bill setting aside one million acres of public lands in the southern states. This land was not intended as a gift since freedmen would be permitted to lease in lots of forty acres each and purchase the land from the government at an agreed valuation.[40] With the passage of the Southern Homestead Act this section became superfluous and Congress deleted it.

Several sections of the new Freedmen's Bureau bill were concerned with the Sherman lands and the lands condemned under the tax laws. Congress confirmed the title of the lands bought in the tax sale in 1863 and provided that all leases made to "[h]eads of families of the African race" be changed to certificates of sale, thus redeeming the promise made by Lincoln in 1863.[41]

By this time President Johnson had completed his metamorphosis to defender of the planter class and their property rights. He vetoed the bill extending the life of the Freedmen's Bureau because it continued the bureau courts. He also opposed the Sherman land section as a bill of attainder and considered the

39. T. Elliott to O. O. Howard, April 2, 1866, in Andrew Johnson Papers, Library of Congress, Ser. 1, Roll 21, p. 10579; O. O. Howard to T. Elliott, April 8, 1866, Roll 22, pp. 10574–78.

40. *Congressional Globe*, 39th Cong., 1st Sess., 2773, 79.

41. U. S., *Statutes at Large*, XIV, 175–76. (See page 9 herein.)

entire bill class legislation. The House read the veto message and, without debate, voted to override. Some Senators opposed overriding the veto because the bill would place the labor of the South under the control of the bureau, and might enable unscrupulous agents to use their position to amass wealth. One senator protested that the Sherman land provision for sale of the tax lands at not more than $1.50 an acre was a gift for cotton land worth from fifty to one hundred dollars per acre. He pointed out that all sixty thousand acres could be sold at ten dollars an acre without even leaving the Senate. In spite of these objections the Senate voted to override by a vote of thirty-three to twelve.[42]

Congressmen were surely cognizant of the fact that without the bureau to help and protect the freedmen, few indeed would be able to avail themselves of the provisions of the Southern Homestead Act. Therefore, by extending the life of the bureau, Congress at least guaranteed that some freedmen would receive help in locating and settling on land of their own.

42. *Congressional Globe*, 39th Cong., 1st Sess., 3838, 3840, 3842, 3850.

V

Homesteading in Mississippi, Alabama, and Arkansas

THE PROMISE OF LAND contained in the Southern Homestead Act led friends of the freedmen to believe that now at last the blacks would be established on land of their own.[1] Unfortunately, this dream failed to materialize. Numerous factors worked against success in this endeavor; not the least was lack of commitment to the idea of Negro land ownership on the part of some agents of the bureau. During the two years following passage of the homestead law, many freedmen attempted to acquire the land promised to them. Some, who secured the aid of sympathetic bureau agents, met with success. Others succeeded in spite of the bureau, but most were destined to remain landless.

Homesteading activity was sporadic and did not seem to follow a specific pattern. In some states bureau agents reported much activity, whereas in others there was either less activity or there were fewer agents concerned with helping the freedmen. Since most bureau agents in Mississippi, Alabama, and Arkansas seemed little concerned with homesteading, these three states will be discussed in this chapter. Louisiana, which provides an example of the conditions of the land records, and Florida, in which most of the homesteading activity actually occurred, will be discussed in later chapters.

1. Richard Cadbury to O. O. Howard, June 15, 1866, Registers and Letters Received (BRFAL), in RG 105, NA, Microcopy 752, Roll 31, p. 563; D. Gosorne to O. O. Howard, August 11, 1866, Roll 32, p. 669.

Shortly after the passage of the Southern Homestead Act, Howard issued orders urging all assistant commissioners to aid the freedmen in securing homesteads. He recommended that, wherever possible, freedmen should be settled in colonies isolated from the whites.[2] He hoped in this way to reduce the possibility of friction between the races while at the same time he intended that the blacks should protect and assist each other.

After issuing these orders Howard wrote an explanatory letter to all assistant commissioners urging them to use every means at their disposal to inform the freedmen of the terms of the Southern Homestead Act, especially that section which restricted entry to freedmen and loyal whites until January 1, 1867. He apparently feared that six months was insufficient time to settle the freedmen before they would have to compete with former Confederates. He therefore urged all officers to take the necessary steps to make the bureau an efficient agency for homesteading the public lands.[3]

In order to assist the freedmen, Howard authorized his subordinates to furnish transportation and one month's rations to any freedmen attempting settlement on the public lands. He also instructed the assistant commissioners to hire civilians with special training as locating agents. The assistant commissioners should also assign agents whose primary responsibilities would be to communicate with the register of the local land office and to answer all questions from those seeking information concerning homesteading. In this way, freedmen would be assured of proper professional assistance in locating their claims.[4]

---

2. *House Executive Documents*, 39th Cong., 1st Sess., No. 1, p. 763; *Nation*, III (July 12, 1866), 23.

3. O. O. Howard to assistant commissioners for Alabama, Mississippi, Arkansas, Louisiana, and Florida, July 9, 1866, Selected Series of Records (BRFAL), in RG 105, NA, Microcopy 742, Roll 2, p. 170; July 19, 1866, p.176.

4. O. O. Howard to J. C. Robinson (in North Carolina) August 22, 1866, copies sent to assistant commissioners of South Carolina, Florida, Alabama, Mississippi, and Louisiana, Selected Series of Records (BRFAL) in RG 105, NA, Microcopy 742, Roll 2, p. 187; August 31, 1866, p. 199; O. O. Howard to assistant commissioners for Alabama,

Howard instructed the assistant commissioners of the five southern states containing public lands to report immediately on the location and quality of such lands in their states. This information could be given to all wishing to avail themselves of the benefits of the act.[5] During the congressional debate on the Southern Homestead Act, the assistant commissioners for Louisiana and Mississippi sent Howard some of this information.

In Louisiana relatively little of the public land was suitable for settlement by freedmen in separate colonies. The land was either heavily forested and therefore not suitable for immediate tillage, or open prairie devoid of trees. In either case the limited financial resources of the freedmen rendered settlement difficult.[6]

The assistant commissioner for Mississippi estimated that there were approximately three and one-half million acres of unsold public lands. The land was of undetermined quality. Nevertheless, as late as December, 1866, the new assistant commissioner could not locate the lands in Mississippi; bureau agents in South Carolina and Virginia waited for a report on the location of the public lands in Florida. It appears that only the assistant commissioner for Alabama made an early report on the public lands in the state under his charge. There, of the six and one-half million acres available, only four million acres were arable. Most of the public lands in the state could be reached easily by train or water.[7]

Mississippi, Arkansas, Louisiana, and Florida, July 9, 1866, p. 170; *House Executive Documents*, 39th Cong., 1st Sess., No. 1, p. 764.

5. O. O. Howard to assistant commissioners for Alabama, Mississippi, Arkansas, Louisiana, and Florida, July 19, 1866, Selected Series of Records (BRFAL), in RG 105, NA, Microcopy 742, Roll 2, p. 176; *House Executive Documents*, 39th Cong., 1st Sess., No. 1, p. 765.

6. A. Baird to M. Woodhull, March 12, 1866, Registers and Letters Received (BRFAL), in RG 105, NA, Microcopy 752, Roll 28, p. 367.

7. *Senate Executive Documents*, 39th Cong., 1st Sess., No. 27, p. 44; *Senate Executive Documents*, 39th Cong., 2nd Sess., No. 6, p. 19; S. Thomas to O. O. Howard, February 6, 1866, Registers and Letters Received (BRFAL), in RG 105, NA, Microcopy 752, Roll 22, p. 896; C. Cadle, Jr., to O. O. Howard, July 25, 1866, Roll 31, pp. 352–56.

The assistant commissioners for Virginia, Georgia, and North Carolina all attempted to send freedmen from their districts to the homestead land. In Virginia, the homesteaders desperately needed assistance. According to one report, if given information concerning the condition and location of the public lands and assurance of adequate provisions, most Virginia freedmen would avail themselves of the offer. The superintendent of schools in Georgia reported that several colonies were organized to emigrate to Arkansas. He indicated that the desire for land was so great that freedmen without sufficient financial resources had to be restrained. He had organized one colony of four hundred persons possessing fifteen thousand dollars to effect settlement. In North Carolina, a proposed colony prepared to go either to Florida or to Arkansas. The bureau arranged transportation for a representative of the colony, but he had not left by December, 1866.[8]

In South Carolina, the bureau's assistant commissioner took no action to encourage emigration to the homestead lands of other states. Bureau agents in that state completely ignored Howard's directive to supply rations and transportation to homesteaders. Although the assistant commissioner protested that he had not received the letter, it was subsequently found. He was familiar with the Southern Homestead Act and reported that approximately two or three hundred freedmen from South Carolina would file claims either in Arkansas or in Florida after January 1, 1867.[9]

In Texas, General J. B. Kiddoo published the information concerning the Homestead Act but did not give the matter any special attention. He believed that the Negroes in Texas could

8. *Senate Executive Documents*, 39th Cong., 2nd Sess., No. 6, pp. 57, 104, 162, 168; F. D. Sewall to O. O. Howard, December 15, 1866, Registers and Letters Received (BRFAL), in RG 105, NA, Microcopy 752, Roll 39, pp. 856, 871; O. Brown to O. O. Howard, Roll 40, p. 559.

9. F. D. Sewall to O. O. Howard, December 3, 1866, Registers and Letters Received (BRFAL), in RG 105, NA, Microcopy 752, Roll 39, p. 774; December 15, 1866, p. 861.

secure better land and at less cost if they bought from the state of Texas than if they attempted to travel to the areas open to homesteading. He tried to encourage immigration to Texas rather tham emigration from Texas.[10]

Howard agreed to supply transportation and rations for freedmen who chose to go to Texas if it were possible for them to secure permanent homes. He informed Kiddoo that one company of freedmen had already left Virginia for Texas and that representatives from Norfolk, Fortress Monroe, and Yorktown in Virginia, as well as from Newbern, North Carolina, were on their way to look over the country and report back to their companions. Howard was reluctant to encourage Negroes to go to Texas as long as there were reports of freedmen being abused and murdered.[11]

It seems somewhat ironic that freedmen could not homestead in Texas because all public lands belonged to the state of Texas and were not included in the Southern Homestead Act. In October, 1866, the Texas legislature voted to grant 640 acres of public land to every Confederate soldier who had been wounded, and 640 acres to the widows and orphans of Confederate soldiers. Angered by this action, one Union man proposed to a congressman that Congress confiscate the state lands of Texas and award them to Union soldiers and freedmen.[12]

The Southern Homestead Act opened the public lands of five southern states to exclusive settlement by freedmen and loyal whites until January 1, 1867. At the time the bill became law, most of the freedmen who could have benefited were unable to take advantage of the act. They were either under contract to

10. *Senate Executive Documents*, 39th Cong., 2nd Sess., No. 6, p. 147.
11. O. O. Howard to J. M. Schofield, August 22, 1866, Selected Series of Records (BRFAL), in RG 105, NA, Microcopy 742, Roll 2, p. 186; O. O. Howard to J. C. Robinson, August 22, 1866, p. 186; O. O. Howard to J. P. Kiddoo, September 11, 1866, p. 206; O. O. Howard to P. Sheridan, September 18, 1866, p. 210.
12. J. L. Brisbin to Z. Chandler, October 5, 1866, in Zachariah Chandler Papers, Library of Congress.

work until the end of the year, or had leased land and planted it. Many agents reported these facts to Howard and requested that Congress take some action to extend the time limit; otherwise, the purpose of the act would be defeated. Congressman George W. Julian pushed through the House of Representatives a bill requiring the continuance of an oath of past allegiance from those seeking eligibility under the Southern Homestead Act. Unfortunately, the Senate failed to act on the measure.[13]

The black codes of Mississippi made land ownership by freedmen difficult, if not impossible, until they were canceled in 1867; afterwards whites remained hostile to the Negroes and the Freedmen's Bureau. Agents in some counties found it impossible to travel without an armed escort. Many whites in Mississippi purchased public lands from the Confederate government during the Civil War, which sale they now found to be invalid. Consequently, they opposed any policy which might deprive them of this land.[14]

In October, 1866, about three hundred heads of families of freedmen in Vicksburg, deprived of information by officials in Mississippi, sent a petition to Howard concerning the homestead lands in Mississippi. They asked Howard to "hurry up these laggard land officers." These men all planted their own crops that year and paid rent as high as twelve dollars per acre. With the homestead lands they hoped to improve their lot.[15]

As early as July, 1866, the assistant commissioner for Mississippi requested that the land office at Jackson be opened for business since the register could not act until the president appointed a receiver. He informed Howard that he had no maps

13. Roy M. Robbins, *Our Landed Heritage: The Public Domain, 1776–1936* (Lincoln: University of Nebraska Press, 1962), 213.

14. *Nation*, III (October 4, 1866), 263; S. Thomas to O. O. Howard, February 6, 1866, Registers and Letters Received (BRFAL), in RG 105, NA, Microcopy 752, Roll 22, p. 896; A. C. Gillem to O. O. Howard, January 20, 1867, Roll 43, p. 55.

15. A. W. Ross to O. O. Howard, October 6, 1866, Regi ters and Letters Received (BRFAL), in RG 105, NA, Microcopy 752, Roll 39, p. 279.

MISSISSIPPI, 1866

of the public lands in Mississippi and was unable to procure them from the general land office. He requested that Howard endeavor to secure the maps. By December, 1866, a private citizen, John F. H. Claiborne, had assisted almost two hundred of his former slaves in settling on homesteads near Meridian. Bureau agents throughout the state indicated that there were numerous applications for entry under the Homestead Act but that they could not assist the freedmen unless the land office was opened. The time for exclusive entry by freedmen was fast coming to an end and there was an urgent need to secure the maps and land records which "must be in the land office at Washington," one assistant commissioner reasoned.[16]

In 1867, a new assistant commissioner for Mississippi was appointed. He reported that thousands of freedmen were being brought to Mississippi from Virginia, North Carolina, South Carolina, and Georgia. This immigration resulted from two factors: the desire for homesteads and the high wages being offered by Mississippi planters. That same month the sub-assistant commissioner for the Meridian district reported that many families had entered land and were preparing it for cultivation. The bureau agent for the Pass Christian district reported that seventy-five or eighty families had entered homesteads in the various counties of the district.[17]

For the next year there seems to have been relatively little homesteading activity, but in March, 1868, Howard encouraged increased efforts to settle freedmen on the public lands. He

16. J. T. Wood to O. O. Howard, December 10, 1866, *ibid.*, Roll 38, p. 865; *Senate Executive Documents*, 39th Cong., 2nd Sess., No. 6, p. 96; *House Executive Documents*, 39th Cong., 2nd Sess., No. 1, p. 747; Vernon Lane Wharton, *The Negro in Missi sippi 1865–1890* (New York: Harper Torchbooks, 1965), 60.

17. A. C. Gillem to O. O. Howard, February 15, 1867, Registers and Letters Received (BRFAL), in RG 105, NA, Microcopy 752, Roll 43, pp. 153–67, March 15, 1867, p. 211; March 15, 1867, p. 214.

suggested the creation of a dual position: locating agent for the state and bureau agent for Jackson district, where the land office was located.[18]

Spurred by Howard's request for action, the new assistant commissioner inspected the land office records and then made an inspection tour of the available land. He reported that most of the land was either sandy pine barrens or swamp totally unfit for agricultural purposes. The land was valuable for the timber growing on it, but the assistant commissioner apparently was not imaginative enough to realize that a homesteader could satisfy the terms of the homestead law by cutting and selling some of the lumber. In addition to clearing his land for farming, a homesteader could also produce turpentine from the pine trees. The assistant commissioner did point out, however, that many freedmen had settled near Lowell along the line of the railroad from Vicksburg to Meridian.[19]

Although a locating agent was appointed in March, he did not open his office in Jackson until August, 1868. All bureau agents were directed to inform freedmen that they would be assisted by locating agents. The locating agent prepared and distributed maps and charts showing what lands were open for entry. The assistant commissioner pointed out that all the homestead land had been available for sale prior to the war at the nominal price of twenty-five cents per acre and therefore was not of great value. Good land, ready for planting, could be purchased from planters at reasonable rates. Later events proved his assumption

18. O. O. Howard to A. C. Gillem, March 4, 1868, Selected Series of Records (BRFAL), in RG 105, NA, Microcopy 742, Roll 4, p. 215; A. C. Gillem to O. O. Howard, March 17, 1868, Registers and Letters Received (BRFAL), in RG 105, NA, Microcopy 752, Roll 54, pp. 377–79; E. Whittlesey for O. O. Howard to A. C. Gillem, March 28, 1868, Selected Series of Records (BRFAL), in RG 105, NA, Microcopy 742, Roll 4, p. 234.

19. A. C. Gillem to O. O. Howard, March 17, 1868, Registers and Letters Received (BRFAL), in RG 105, NA, Microcopy 752, Roll 54, pp. 377–79.

correct, for eight years later the state was still trying to sell the land at five cents per acre.[20]

During the period from 1866 to 1876, 8,797 homesteads were entered in Mississippi with 1,915, or 25 percent of these entries completed and final certificates issued. In addition, in the National Archives, there are seven packages of homestead applications which were not acted upon.[21] These attest to the initial interest by freedmen in homesteading in Mississippi prior to the opening of the land office. Although it is impossible to determine with any accuracy how many Negroes actually entered homesteads, from the extensive activity reported by bureau agents one can safely estimate that at least 5 percent, or 440 of the entries were made by blacks, and that of that number 20 percent, or approximately 88 freedmen, received final certificates.

In spite of the request from the assistant commissioner for Alabama that his state be included in the public lands bill, relatively little early activity occurred. After passage of the Southern Homestead Act, the inspecting agent reported that most of the lands were refuse lands and had long been open to unlimited purchase. Cleared land that could be planted immediately was abundant and inexpensive, so agents did not advise the freedmen to homestead.[22] When the freedmen learned that the whites would not sell land to them, they became more interested in securing homesteads on the public lands.

Some of the best land in the state was the railroad land, which

20. A. C. Gillem to O. O. Howard, October 1, 1868, *ibid.*, Roll 59, p. 873: *House Executive Documents*, 40th Cong., 3rd Sess., No. 1, p. 1048; Wharton, *The Negro in Mississippi*, 60.

21. *House Executive Documents*, 40th Cong., 3rd Sess., No. 1, p. 23; Harry P. Yoshpe and Philip P. Brower (comps.), *Preliminary Inventory of the Land Entry Papers of the General Land Office: Preliminary Inventory No. 22* (Washington: National Archives, 1948), 45–46; Paul W. Gates, *History of Public Land Law Development* (Washington: Government Printing Office, 1970), 414.

22. *Senate Executive Documents*, 39th Cong., 2nd Sess., No. 6, p. 19.

had been certified to the state by the federal government under grants of June 13, 1856, and May 17, 1857. Since the railroad companies had not fulfilled the requirements of the grants, these lands should have reverted to the central government. A recommendation to Congress advocated the appointment of a set of loyal "Commissioners of Railroad Lands" to facilitate opening the lands for homesteading. [23] George W. Julian attempted unsuccessfully to secure passage of a bill which would have restored these lands to the public domain.

The land office at Montgomery opened in 1866, but the one at Mobile, in the district where most of the best remaining lands were located, did not fully open until 1869. The register of the land office at Mobile accepted entries in 1868, but in the absence of a receiver charged a twelve-dollar fee to enter land. He defended his action by stating, "It is optional with me if a man can enter at all until the appointment of a Receiver, if he does it is because I allow him and not that I am duty bound." [24] Before permitting freedmen to enter land, the register insisted that they procure certificates of location. Surveyors charged freedmen from fifteen to twenty-five dollars for the certificates, although they were issued from maps in the land office without going out of the city. Thus, many freedmen paid as much as thirty-seven dollars for taking the "preliminary steps toward acquiring titles to land which Congress designed as a gift to actual settlers." [25] Many freedmen complained that they paid the twelve dollars demanded, lived upon and improved their land for a year, then received certificates for other than the desired tracts. This situation resulted from the practice of issuing surveyor certificates on locations made from office

23. W. H. Smith to O. O. Howard, December 20, 1866, Registers and Letters Received (BRFAL), in RG 105, NA, Microcopy 752, Roll 44, pp. 47–48.
24. J. Gillette to O. L. Shepherd, May 29, 1868, *ibid.*, Roll 52, p. 305.
25. *Ibid.*, 303.

maps rather than by actual survey. In the southern part of Mobile County a few freedmen lived on their land for over a year after paying their twelve dollars without receiving certificates. Since the land was being surveyed for a proposed railroad, they feared being evicted from their land. One man paid twenty-four dollars to the register, but received no certificate.[26]

The sub-assistant commissioner for the Mobile district indicated that hundreds of freedmen wished to enter land, but would exhaust their financial reserves by doing so. They would then be unable to maintain themselves on their homesteads until they could produce their gardens and first crop. Under these conditions he deemed it best to advise all who applied to him to defer making applications until the commissioner of the general land office declared the office at Mobile to be properly opened.[27]

Based on this and similar reports from other bureau agents, the assistant commissioner for Alabama suggested that Howard inform the general land office of conditions in Alabama and request immediate action. Otherwise, the bureau would be unable to assist the freedmen in settling on public lands.[28] Since Alabama whites in 1868 still opposed the sale or occupancy of land by freedmen, only through the Southern Homestead Act could blacks secure homes.

In spite of the difficulty that freedmen encountered in Alabama, the commissioner of the general land office reported that 1,646 homesteads were entered in that state during the fiscal year ending June 30, 1868. All of these entries were for eighty acres or less. During the period in which the Southern Homestead Act was in force, 1866–1876, a total of 16,288 entries

26. Ibid., 304; L. Moore to J. Gillette, April 32, 1868, pp. 321–22.
27. J. Gillette to O. L. Shepherd, May 29, 1868, ibid., Roll 52, p. 305.
28. O. L. Shepherd to O. O. Howard, Monthly Report for May 1868, ibid., Roll 52, p. 351.

ALABAMA, 1866

were filed, and 4,343, or 28 percent, were completed. Although the records do not separate the entries by race, one can safely assume that blacks filed at least 5 percent or 815 entries, of which they completed at least 20 percent, or 163 homesteads.[29]

Unlike Alabama, in which there was relatively little early homesteading activity, considerable interest existed among freedmen and bureau agents in Arkansas. The state selecting agent in Arkansas misconstrued the terms of the Swamp Land Act of September 28, 1850, and certified all bottom land as swamp land, thus invalidating the land as potential homesteads. Since most of this land still belonged to the state and adjoined the government lands, the state land register recommended that the bureau locate freedmen on eighty-acre tracts of government land and 160 acres of state land. The cost of the state land was seventy-five cents per acre if within six miles of a navigable stream and fifty cents per acre if farther away. The register pointed out that state law allowed preemption claims to hold the land for one year. The cost of any improvements made during that year would apply toward the cost of the land.[30]

The assistant commissioner for Arkansas, in October, 1866, reported that although little had been accomplished, he had appointed Dr. W. W. Granger as surveyor and locating agent for the bureau. Assistant Commissioner Sprague and Dr. Granger experienced difficulty in obtaining reliable information concerning available land because the land books had not been posted for twenty years. Although the land officers assisted the bureau as much as possible, only Arkansans knew which lands were

29. *House Executive Documents*, 40th Cong., 3rd Sess., No. 1, p. 21; Yoshpe and Brower (comps.), *Preliminary Inventory No. 22*, p. 14–15; Gates, *History of Public Land Law Development* 414. These estimates were determined by compiling the various reports from the sub-assistant commissioners concerning homesteading activities by blacks and opposition on the part of some southern whites.

30. G. W. Dennison, U.S. Land Register, to D. H. Williams, August 4, 1866, Registers and Letters Received (BRFAL) in RG 105, NA, Microcopy 752, Roll 38, p. 628; and M. S. Andrews, State Land Agent, to D. H. Williams, August 24, 1866, pp. 630–32.

valuable and subject to entry, and they were unwilling to provide any information which would aid the freedmen in any way. Nevertheless, by October 1, 1866, thirty black families, or approximately 125 persons, entered land in Arkansas and moved to their land. In November, 1866, twenty families around Pine Bluff were preparing to locate a colony on the public domain.[31]

As interest in homesteading intensified, Sprague reported an increased tempo in outrages against freedmen and Union men. The rapid demobilization of the army left the freedmen in Arkansas practically helpless. Sprague mustered out on September 1, 1866, and was immediately retained as a civilian agent until an officer could be assigned to replace him. In October, he asked to be relieved since he had no power to prevent the outrages being perpetrated against the freed people.[32]

One of the greatest problems facing the freedmen who wanted to homestead in Arkansas was the lack of provisions and tools. With barely enough to sustain their families, they could hardly attempt homesteading without guaranteed rations until they could complete their crops. Flooding in 1866 caused additional suffering. General E. O. C. Ord, the new assistant commissioner, requested authority to issue tools to the freedmen. He pointed out that since the army issued tools to the Indians the bureau should be able to do likewise for the freedmen. When Howard informed him that the tools were supplied to the Indians under a special appropriation, he recommended, without success, that Congress appropriate one hundred thousand dol-

31. *Senate Executive Documents*, 39th Cong., 2nd Sess., No. 6, pp. 2, 29–30; J. T. Sprague to O. O. Howard, October 5, 1866, Registers and Letters Received (BRFAL), in RG 105, NA, Microcopy 752, Roll 38, p. 624; October 12, 1866, Selected Series of Records (BRFAL), in RG 105, NA, Microcopy 742, Roll 2, p. 292; J. W. Dawes to J. Sprague, November 30, 1866, Registers and Letters Received (BRFAL), in RG 105, NA, Microcopy 752, Roll 38, p. 935.

32. J. Sprague to O. O. Howard, Monthly Report for August, 1866, Registers and Letters Received (BRFAL), in RG 105, NA, Microcopy 752, Roll 39, pp. 639–41; October 5, 1866, p. 619.

lars to buy tools to replace those washed away by the flood.[33]

At Fort Smith, Arkansas, a colony of about 150 families wanted to homestead despite their difficulty in sustaining themselves. Both the post chaplain and the superintendent of freedmen requested a temporary supply of agricultural and other implements needed to clear and cultivate farms. General Ord forwarded the request to Washington, asking for permission to issue the requested items. The chief quartermaster refused the request, claiming lack of authority because there had been no appropriation for such needs. He advised Howard to appeal to Congress for some provision for the issuance of the needed supplies.[34] In the meantime Howard received a gift of $1,072.83 from the American Freedmen's Union Commission to be used "for the benefit of the freedmen in settling them upon the lands of their own purchase under the Homestead Act."[35] Howard informed Ord of the gift and ordered him to send an honest and trustworthy officer to Fort Smith to secure seeds and implements for the destitute settlers. Ord carried out these instructions and the settlers received some of the supplies they needed.[36]

By the end of February, 1867, the bureau in Arkansas, under the leadership of Ord and Granger, succeeded in settling many of the former slaves on land of their own. Several hundred

33. E. O. C. Ord to O. O. Howard, January 22, 1867, with all endorsements, Selected Series of Records (BRFAL), in RG 105, NA, Microcopy 742, Roll 2, p. 473. Ord pointed out that since the freedmen were abused by the whites he favored colonization of the blacks under the Homestead Act and requested all supplies necessary to make such an endeavor successful. E. O. C. Ord to O. O. Howard, March 15, 1867, Registers and Letters Received (BRFAL), in RG 105, NA, Microcopy 752, Roll 41, pp. 388–89.

34. F. Springer to C. Banzhof, December 19, 1866, with all endorsements, Registers and Letters Received (BRFAL), in RG 105, NA, Microcopy 752, Roll 41, pp. 1–6.

35. J. M. McKim to O. O. Howard, November 27, 1866, *ibid.*, Roll 38, pp. 103–105. Note the use of the word *purchase*; apparently Howard was not alone in his belief that homesteading was equivalent to purchase.

36. O. O. Howard to E. O. C. Ord, *ibid.*, Roll 38, p. 106; O. O. Howard to E. O. C. Ord, February 4, 1867, with all endorsements, Roll 41, pp. 9–12. The final notation on the papers indicated that the supplies were distributed and paid for by August 12, 1867.

ARKANSAS, 1866

Route and Land Grant Area of the
Memphis and Little Rock Railroad

families settled near Fort Smith. There was, however, considerable delay. The land office at Clarksville failed to open; therefore, those who settled in the western section of the state around Fort Smith had to wait before they could enter their land. Although their papers were as nearly complete as possible, the only claim they had to their land was squatters rights. In addition, another group from Georgia proposed to settle near Fort Smith. This group, numbering some 150 families, sent agents to Arkansas to enter their claims for them.[37]

The agents waited until the Clarksville office opened, then experienced further delay. The commissioner of the general land office instructed the register not to accept any affidavits unless they were in complete accord with all of the homestead laws. Section 3 of the amendatory act of March 21, 1864, permitted an applicant to make the affidavit required by the homestead law before the clerk of court for the county in which he was an actual resident. However, this provision was only available "to those who reside, not only in the State, but in the particular *Land District*, as well, in which the entry is sought to be made."[38]

Because of this restriction, the agents sent by the colonists from Georgia were unable to file the required affidavits to secure the entries of land for their group. Congress was urged to amend the act to permit settlers from other states to make the affidavits before the clerk of the circuit court for the county or parish in which the applicants actually resided. Only in this manner would the homestead act help the freedmen who depended on their entry papers to secure one month's rations and transportation to their land.

37. E. O. C. Ord to O. O. Howard, February 22, 1867, *ibid.*, Roll 41, pp. 217–19; March 15, 1867, p. 387.

38. J. Wilson to W. W. Granger, June 1, 1867, *ibid.*, Roll 46, p. 144; W. W. Granger to C. H. Smith, June 29, 1867, pp. 140–41 (emphasis in original); J. Wilson to O. O. Howard, August 23, 1867, Roll 47, p. 11.

Granger pointed out another factor delaying homesteading that could easily be remedied. With proper authorization a survey party could take the field and remain there until it was able to "report, from personal examination, the character of every forty acres in a given area, and to tell applicants at once where, what kind, and what number of homesteads could be formed."[39] The survey party could accomplish in six months what would require six years under the system in use. Without an organized survey party, Granger had to wait until enough freedmen could gather to organize a party to take the field. Most of the freedmen could not afford to leave their work for more than a few days to examine the land.

By the end of February, 1867, Granger convinced Ord of the need for an organized survey expedition. He employed four men at twenty dollars per month plus rations and set out to survey the valleys along the tributaries of the Arkansas River. These valleys, though narrow, contained land second in fertility only to the river bottom lands. By June, 1867, he settled forty families on land surveyed by this expedition.[40]

In spite of all the efforts in Arkansas to aid the freedmen in securing land, bureau agents were only partially successful. When the land office at Clarksville finally opened in mid-1867, bureau agents discovered that much of the land entered by freedmen the previous autumn and cleared and cultivated by them may have been previously entered by other parties whose claims had not expired. The bureau tried to determine whether this land actually was open for settlement, in an effort to protect the rights of the freedmen.[41]

After Ord's replacement as assistant commissioner by General

39. Report of W. W. Granger, Surveyor, February 1, 1867, *ibid.*, Roll 41, p. 228; W. W. Granger to Dr. Kirkwood, February 24, 1867, Roll 42, pp. 365–71.
40. Report of W. W. Granger, Surveyor, March 5, 1867, *ibid.*, Roll 41, p. 394; S. N. Clark to O. O. Howard, June 5, 1867, Roll 46, pp. 565–66.
41. S. N. Clark to O. O. Howard, June 5, 1867, *ibid.*, Roll 46, pp. 566–67.

C. H. Smith, Granger remained one of the few agents in Arkansas still concerned about the freedmen and homesteading. Smith did not even mention the homestead act in any of his monthly reports until February, 1868, when he reported that one agent was discouraging freedmen from homesteading unless they had sufficient means to guarantee their success.[42] Under Sprague, then under Ord, there was considerable activity. Yet, under Smith, when more freedmen could afford to homestead, such efforts diminished. From this one might conclude that homesteading succeeded only when the assistant commissioner was himself very concerned about the welfare of the freedmen.

Under the Southern Homestead Act, 26,395 entries were made in Arkansas and 10,807, or 44 percent, were carried to completion.[43] Obviously, most of these entries were made by whites, but, based on the reports of bureau agents and Dr. Granger, a safe estimate would be that at least one thousand entries were made by freedmen. Because of opposition to Negro land ownership in Arkansas, probably only 250 or 25 percent completed their entries.

Although freedmen throughout the South demonstrated considerable interest in homesteading, their activity was relatively moderate and far from successful. Much of this lack of success stems from the disorganized condition of the land offices in the various states. Louisiana provided an excellent example of this lack of organization.

---

42. C. H. Smith to O. O. Howard, April 24, 1867, *ibid.*, Roll 41; February 27, 1868, Roll 52, p. 198.
43. Gates, *History of Public Land Law Development*, 414.

VI

Homesteading in Louisiana

WHEN CONGRESS, in passing the Southern Homestead Act, restricted entry to freedmen and loyal whites until January 1, 1867, congressmen evidently intended that these people have first choice of the available public land. After January 1, 1867, anyone who took an oath of allegiance to the United States could enter land for homestead. The special provisions for freedmen and loyal whites did not adequately take into account the ravages of war and nature, the depressed economic conditions of the freedmen, the quality of the public land, the condition of the land offices in the southern states, and the slow working of the government bureaucracy. Furthermore, any provisions intended for the exclusive benefit of blacks and loyal whites aggravated the existing racial and political tensions. Although these factors varied in different states, a study of their effect on homesteading in Louisiana can serve as an example of the awesome obstacles faced by freedmen in their struggle to acquire a stake in the land.

In Louisiana one of the major deterrents to homesteading was the actual physical condition of the land. Throughout the Civil War neglect of the levee system resulted in flooded fields, which prevented the state from recovering economically. Flooding in 1865 was so extensive that General E. R. S. Canby, the military commander of the district, provided seed corn for replanting to those whose lands were affected by the flooding. General Thomas Conway, bureau assistant commissioner, provided 4,028 rations to refugees and 225,735.5 rations to freedmen in Louisiana in 1865. While Congress debated the Southern Homestead Act in late winter and early spring of 1866, the raging Mississippi again overflowed its banks, broke through the levee at Morganza bend above Baton Rouge, and rushed toward the Gulf of Mexico, flooding an area fifty miles wide by one hundred miles long. Below New Orleans, the Chinn and Roberts levees also collapsed. As a result, everything east of Bayou Teche near Barre's Landing and west of the Mississippi was inundated. The Red River, swollen by winter and spring rains, also overflowed and flooded much of its valley. Approximately two-thirds of the state's alluvial land was under from ten to twelve feet of water and crops worth thirty million dollars were destroyed.[1]

Since the overflow of 1866 was more disastrous than that of 1865, Freedmen's Bureau Assistant Commissioner Absalom Baird and General Canby both recommended that measures similar to those of 1865 be taken. They estimated that such action would cost approximately $400,000 for Louisiana. Although Congress, which was debating the bill extending the bureau, provided no funds to replace seed and implements which had been destroyed by the flood, the bureau did provide emergency rations to those dislocated by the disaster. Between January 1, 1866, and October 31, 1866, the bureau in Louisiana issued 229,554.5 rations to freedmen and 153,463 rations to refugees at a cost of $71,760.57.[2] Obviously, because of the destitu-

---

1. Samuel H. Lockett, *Louisiana As It Is: A Geographical and Topographical Description of the State*, ed. Lauren Post (Baton Rouge: Louisiana State University Press, 1969), 20; O. O. Howard to E. M. Stanton, summary of rations issued in 1865, Registers and Letters Received (BRFAL) in RG 105, NA, Microcopy 752, Roll 49, p. 345; Howard Ashley White, *The Freedmen's Bureau in Louisiana* (Baton Rouge: Louisiana State University Press, 1970), 67–68.

2. White, *The Freedmen's Bureau in Louisiana*, 68–69.

tion caused by the flood, few settlers, either white or black, were able to take advantage of the homestead act in 1866.

The economic situation in Louisiana did not improve in 1867, as the state suffered still another flood. The new bureau assistant commissioner, General J. S. Mower, informed General Howard that whole parishes were submerged and that he would require rations for at least fifty thousand persons, most of whom were freedmen. Because there had been charges of graft and corruption against various bureau agents, General Mower issued stringent regulations which specifically forbade the issuance of rations to those living on land which was still under cultivation. In addition to this action by the bureau, Congress ordered the bureau to transfer fifty thousand dollars to the department of agriculture for the purchase and distribution of seed in the South. Although this action helped to replace some of the seed destroyed by flooding, little seed could be planted before mid-July, 1867, since much of the land was still inundated.[3] Most garden vegetables and cereals require from two to three months to mature. Hence, crops planted in July could not provide sustenance until late September or early October.

The New Orleans *Republican* reported, "There never was a time in the history of Louisiana when so many of the people were in peril of starvation." The *Republican* estimated in August, 1867, that not one plantation in one hundred had met expenses that year. Conditions deteriorated to the point that by the end of August the planters, who had provided subsistence for their workers as well as for 35,905 aged and helpless freedmen, were finally forced to call upon the bureau for assistance just at a time when the bureau received orders to discontinue issuing rations.[4]

3. *House Reports*, 40th Cong., 2nd Sess., No. 30, p. 3; New Orleans *Tribune*, April 17, 1867; White, *The Freedmen's Bureau in Louisiana*, 66–73.
4. New Orleans *Republican*, April 25, 1867, August 28, 1867; Lockett, *Louisiana As It Is*, 20.

While Congress and the bureau concentrated on the temporary solutions of seed and rations, Louisiana blacks joined with interested planters and politicians in urging that the levees be rebuilt. One black from St. John the Baptist Parish, Dennis Burrel, a former slave and delegate to the constitutional convention of 1867, reminded the editors of the New Orleans *Republican* that in 1865 the military had rebuilt the levees in his parish at the expense of the planters in the parish who had paid "without objection or complaint; and I do not see any reason why the same cannot be done now. I would therefore suggest that Major General Mower, commanding, be respectfully requested to order the work done, and a tax of one per cent, or more if required, be collected on the assessed value of the property in each parish . . . no person will object, as the amount to be paid by each taxpayer will be so small."[5]

The convention established a committee to study the situation. On December 6, 1867, the committee reported that the breaks in the levees through which the river had poured its vast flood the previous year had not been closed and it urged the convention to petition Congress to provide funds to rebuild the levees. One convention delegate proposed that the state not assist in the rebuilding of the levees unless the land owners established a system to "secure to the real tiller of the soil the just and legitimate fruits of his labor, by the equitable distribution of the right of ownership in homestead farms."[6]

By the end of December, 1867, the *Republican* assumed the position taken earlier by Burrell, and warned that unless the federal government assisted the state in rebuilding the levee system, the cost of feeding the destitute would place an undue

5. New Orleans *Republican*, November 10, 1867, the letter was dated November 2, 1867.

6. *Official Journal of the Proceedings of the Convention for Framing a Constitution for the State of Louisiana, 1867–1868* (New Orleans: N.p., 1868), December 5–6, 1867; New Orleans *Republican*, December 6, 25, 1867.

burden on the government. On the other hand, if the military would employ half of the estimated fifty thousand unemployed but able workers in Louisiana to rebuild the levees, the cost of rations for the unemployed would be greatly reduced and the government would be reimbursed from the proceeds of the next crop.[7] Unfortunately for Louisiana and other southern states, Congress failed to see the logic in the argument and continued to dole out rations through the bureau. Although Louisiana experienced more flooding than some of the other southern states in 1866 and 1867, economic conditions which prevailed in Louisiana also prevailed throughout most of the South.

Of the five southern states involved in the Southern Homestead Act, Louisiana provides probably the best example of the chaotic conditions prevailing in the land offices. Considerable confusion had resulted from the sale of federal lands by Louisiana officers during the Civil War; and to compound that confusion the New Orleans land office burned in 1864. Following the war, unionists in Louisiana complained that the land office in New Orleans, though rebuilt and reopened, had not been reorganized. They also complained that the register had resigned, and therefore, no business could be transacted since all official acts required the joint action of the register, who recorded the entry, and the receiver, who assessed and collected the fees. Finally, at the time Congress passed the Southern Homestead Act many of the records lost in the New Orleans fire had not yet been duplicated. Consequently, the register and receiver had relatively little information concerning which lands were available in the southeastern district of Louisiana.[8]

Shortly after the passage of the Southern Homestead Act, J. M. Edmunds, the commissioner of the general land office alerted the New Orleans register and receiver and explained the

7. New Orleans *Republican*, December 25, 1867.
8. New Orleans *Times*, May 23, 1866.

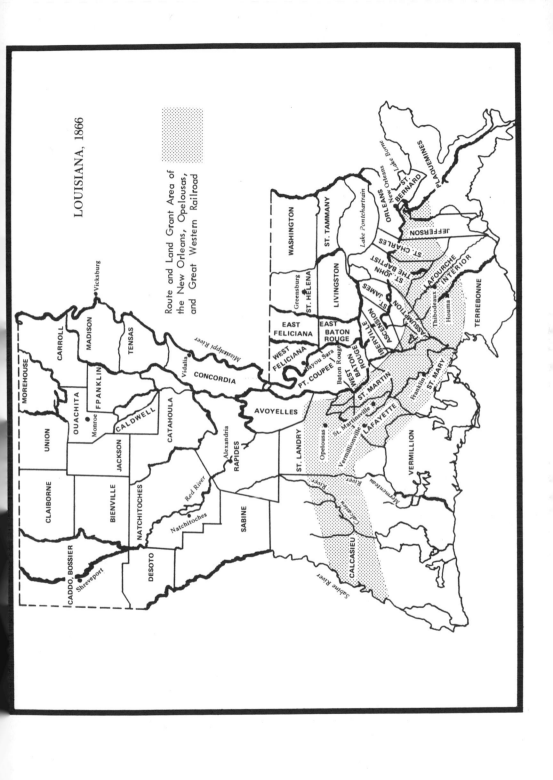

LOUISIANA, 1866

Route and Land Grant Area of
the New Orleans, Opelousas,
and Great Western Railroad

eighty-acre restriction. However, as late as August 23, 1866, the general land office in Washington was still waiting for detailed instructions of the obligations and responsibilities of the register and receiver under the act. In the meantime, Joseph Wilson became commissioner of the general land office in Washington and Simon Jones became the register of the land office in New Orleans. Since Wilson had served as assistant to Edmunds, he was familiar with the operation of his office. Jones, on the other hand, was completely unfamiliar with his responsibilities. The confusion in Louisiana continued when Jones resigned and was replaced by John Tully, in November, 1866.[9]

Even if the land office in New Orleans had been open for business, homesteaders would have had difficulty filing their entries since it was the only office open in the state. Prior to the war Louisiana had been served by five land offices: New Orleans, Greensburg, Opelousas, Monroe, and Natchitoches. All five offices would have been required to facilitate homesteading freedmen on the public lands. President Johnson began considering in August, 1866, whether to reopen all offices but did not make a final decision until October. In the meantime only the New Orleans office was open and the land officers could only dispose of public lands within the southeastern district.[10] President Johnson's decision to close the land offices at Opelousas and Greensburg made it impossible for homesteaders to file entry before January 1, 1867, the deadline for exclusive entry for blacks and loyal whites.

Against this background of chaos and confusion, the organized activities of the Freedmen's Bureau in Louisiana provides a con-

9. J. M. Edmunds to Register and Receiver, June 28, 1866, J. Wilson to S. Jones, August 23, 1866, Letters of the Commissioner of the General Land Office on file in the Louisiana State Land Office, Baton Rouge, Louisiana; New Orleans *Times*, November 17, 1866, Opelousas (La.) *Courier*, November 24, 1866.

10. J. Wilson to S. Jones, August 16, 1866 and August 23, 1866, Letters of the Commissioner, Louisiana State Land Office; J. Wilson to Register and Receiver, October 15, 1866.

trast. In order to assist Congress in its deliberations concerning the Southern Homestead Act, General Howard requested that the assistant commissioner examine the remaining public lands in their respective states to determine whether there was any land on which large groups of freedmen could be colonized in isolated settlements. Assistant Commissioner Absalom Baird sent Lieutenant James Cromie to examine the public lands of Louisiana. Cromie reported that although there were some excellent tracts of land along the proposed route of the New Orleans, Opelousas, and Great Western Railroad, there were few areas where the type of colonies envisioned by Howard could be established. Most of the best lands had been taken already by whites, who were not anxious to have freedmen as neighbors. Furthermore, the land was either swampy or heavily forested, or open prairie with few trees for building.[11]

When the Southern Homestead Act became law, Assistant Commissioner Baird appointed J. J. Saville as locating agent for the bureau. Baird encouraged freedmen to settle in companies of at least ten families to assist one another in cultivating their farms, establishing churches and schools, and protecting their investments. Since the Southern Homestead Act did not provide implements and seed, Baird and Saville discouraged freedmen from homesteading unless they had the equipment to cultivate the land and the means to support thenselves until they produced a harvest. Baird urged that each company of ten families have at least two wagons and teams. Each family in the company should have a horse or mule and the implements necessary to clear and cultivate the land.

11. M. Woodhull for Howard to D. Tillson, copies sent to W. Swayne, A. Baird, S. Thomas, and J. Sprague, January 18, 1866, Selected Series of Records (BRFAL), in RG 105, NA, Microcopy 742, Roll 2, p. 61; J. Cromie to A. Baird, March 7, 1866, Registers and Letters Received (BRFAL), in RG 105, NA, Microcopy 752, Roll 28, p. 362. The lands Cromie inspected were alternate sections fifteen miles in depth on either side of the right of way of the proposed railroad.

Since many blacks were under contract to work until the end of the harvest, they would not be able to select their land until after the period for exclusive entry. Baird urged those interested in homesteading to continue to work and save their money in order to have the necessary finances when they were free to homestead. He recommended that they forward their applications to Saville's office, indicating the number of acres desired, the approximate location in the state where they wished to settle, and the number of members in the family. While they continued to work, Saville would select for them suitable land in the locale they requested. He would prepare all documents and surveys in order to facilitate the move to the land should the prospective homesteader approve of the land selected for him.[12]

During the month of September, 1866, Saville assisted forty-nine black families consisting of 183 persons possessing cash totaling $6,260 in settling on land of their own. General Sheridan, the new bureau commissioner for Louisiana, doubted whether the blacks would be allowed to remain peaceably on the land selected for them. The Southern Homestead Act had only been in force one month when New Orleans erupted into a political riot with definite racial overtones. Throughout the remainder of 1866 there were numerous incidents of outrages against freed people and at least twenty-five authenticated cases of freedmen murdered by whites.

The assistant commissioner reported that many people were cutting and selling the best timber on the public lands. This action depreciated the value of the land and hindered freedmen from locating on those lands for fear of coming into contact with these lawless characters. The new settlers relied on the sale of the timber on their tracts until they had sufficient time to make a crop. Therefore, it was imperative that depredations on the public lands be halted. Without the assignment of a battalion of

12. New Orleans *Tribune*, September 15, 1866.

cavalry which could move rapidly to places distant from the military posts, it was impossible to protect the freedmen.[13]

The families whom Saville located on homesteads in September were unable to file their claims at the land office in 1866 because during that time either the register or the receiver was absent collecting the archives and effects of the closed land offices at Greensburg and Opelousas. The two officials were also occupied with transferring records to the land offices at Monroe and Natchitoches in order that those offices could be reopened as soon as possible. Since most of the land available for homesteading was located in the southern and western portion of the state, the New Orleans and Opelousas offices should have remained open. In fact, most of the best lands were located in the district formerly controlled by the Opelousas land office.[14]

By December 31, 1866, Saville located a total of eighty-seven families of freedmen on homestead lands. Yet, a month later only seven of these families had filed their applications at the land office. The New Orleans land office finally opened for business on January 17, 1867, but the register and receiver apparently did not understand the regulations established by the

13. *Senate Executive Documents*, 39th Cong., 2nd Sess., No. 6, pp. 2, 72; *Nation*, III (October 25, 1866), 232; P. Sheridan to O. O. Howard, October 1, 1866, Registers and Letters Received (BRFAL), in RG 105, NA, Microcopy 752, Roll 38, p. 371; October 17, 1866, p. 380; E. Whittlesey to O. O. Howard, January 24, 1867, Roll 45, p. 397; O. O. Howard to E. M. Stanton, November 1, 1866, Selected Series of Records (BRFAL), in RG 105, NA, Microcopy 742, Roll 2, p. 259.

14. White, *The Freedmen's Bureau in Louisiana*, p. 59. Absalom Baird reported in September, 1866, that the best available tracts were in St. Landry, Calcasieu, Rapides, Desoto, and Sabine parishes. He noted that it would be difficult to settle the public lands of those parishes because of bad roads and inaccessibility. He failed to note that most of the land controlled by the Natchitoches office that had not been sold had not yet been surveyed and therefore was not open to homesteading. The decision to reopen the Monroe office was also of questionable value since there was almost no homesteading activity in northeast Louisiana until 1872 when lumber companies began filing dummy entries on cypress and pine lands. From 1867 to 1878 only 1,200 entries were made and only 166 final certificates issued from the Monroe office. St. Landry and Calcasieu parishes, on the other hand, constituted the entire southwestern quarter of the state. Yoshpe and Brower (comps.), *Preliminary Inventory No. 22*, p. 40.

Southern Homestead Act. They charged the receiver fee of $2 as well as the registration fee of $5, an irregular action since the law directed that the registration fee not be collected until the issue of the patent for land. The Southern Homestead Act also required an applicant to file an affidavit stating that he was twenty-one years of age, or the head of a family, or that he had served in the army or navy of the United States during actual war, and that he had not borne arms against the United States. The register and receiver contended that the affidavits had to be sworn to in their presence. Therefore, those who settled in the western part of the state had to travel from one hundred to two hundred miles in order to file their affidavits, a trip costing from twenty to fifty dollars.

This presented a set of circumstances which were completely illogical to Saville. He pointed out that under the earlier public land laws, land once surveyed was offered for sale at a minimum price of $1.25 per acre if it was more than six miles from either a railroad or navigable stream. Lands within the six-mile limit— double minimum land—sold for $2.50 per acre. After the land had been offered for a number of years the price was reduced according to a scale established by the graduation law. By the time of the Civil War the price of most public lands in Louisiana had been reduced to twenty-five cents per acre. A purchaser could therefore secure eighty acres for twenty dollars plus a two-dollar registration fee and receive title to his land immediately. Saville therefore contended that if the freedmen were forced to travel to New Orleans to file their affidavits, the cost of the trip would be more than the value of the land under the graduation law. It would be better to allow the freedmen to purchase and receive title immediately rather than homestead with the hope of receiving title after five years.[15]

In addition, Saville pointed out that the land had been sur-

15. J. J. Saville to W. H. Sterling, January 28, 1867, Registers and Letters Received (BRFAL) in RG 105, NA, Microcopy 752, Roll 45, p. 609.

veyed in irregular half quarter sections, some of more than eighty acres and some of less than eighty acres. However, the applicants were required to pay $1.25 for each acre or part acre above eighty included in the tracts selected. Saville felt that it was unjust to compel anyone to purchase unwanted land. Instead, a freedman should be permitted to enter the land by surveyor subdivisions instead of on a straight eighty-acre basis.[16]

When the commissioner of the general land office learned of Saville's objections and recommendations, he notified the register and receiver that when a homestead claimant was prevented by reason of "distance, bodily infirmity, or other good cause" from personal attendance at the district land office, he could make the affidavits required before the clerk of court for the county in which he resided and "transmit the same with the fee and commissions to the Register and Receiver."[17] These instructions solved the problem of affidavits but it was not until May, 1867, that the fees established under the Southern Homestead Act were finally explained.[18]

Meanwhile, on March 29, 1867 (for some unexplained reason) the functions of register and receiver in the New Orleans office were suspended and the officials ordered to close the office and await instructions. In April, they were instructed to execute new bonds and then reopen the office. The receiver resigned and President Johnson did not replace him until fifteen months later. Although the land office was not open for business, the register was instructed to keep the office open in order to furnish information to persons interested in land. From January 17 to March 26, 1867, 259 entries were made, and an additional 238

16. *Ibid.*
17. J. Wilson to Register and Receiver, February 15, 1867, Letters of the Commissioner, Louisiana State Land Office. On July 16, 1868, Wilson returned 64 of the 106 entries made during the month of February, 1867. He instructed that new affidavits be prepared and forwarded to his office; otherwise the entries would be invalid. Obviously the general land office was as inefficient as the local offices.
18. J. Wilson to J. Tully, May 15, 1867, Letters of the Commissioner, Louisiana State Land Office.

entries from July 17 to December 30, 1868. It is apparent that homesteading activity was delayed by the absence of a receiver.[19] Since appointments of registers and receivers were made by the president, he could defeat the intention of the Southern Homestead Act by simply refusing to appoint either of these officers in a state, and, indeed, homesteading was delayed in most southern states because of the absence of either the register or receiver. Therefore, one can only question the president's intention.

Since the register was no longer burdened with registering homestead claims, he was finally able to effect the transfer of records from his office to Natchitoches and from Opelousas and Greensburg to New Orleans. In May, 1867, he completed an inventory of the records in his office and requested that the general land office supply him with sixty-five township plats for the Greensburg and Opelousas districts. A few months earlier he had requested the missing plats for the southeastern district. He was informed that the entire drafting division of the general land office had been engaged for two years in duplicating the lost plats for the five states covered by the Southern Homestead Act and that it would be several months before the maps for the Louisiana consolidated district could be prepared. In August, 1867, the general land office sent 126 plats for the southeastern district and informed the register that the remainder of the missing plats would be forwarded as soon as possible. Unfortunately, as late as November 3, 1869, the files of the New Orleans office were still incomplete.[20]

While the register reorganized his office, Saville continued his efforts to settle freedmen on the public lands of Louisiana. He noted the expiration, on June 3, 1866, of the grant of 621,266

19. J. Wilson to Register and Receiver, March 29, 1867, Letters of the Commissioner, Louisiana State Land Office; April 27, 1867, July 10, 1868; List of Homestead Entries in Louisiana found in Louisiana State Land Office.

20. J. Wilson to Register and Receiver, April 12, 1867, Letters of the Commissioner, Louisiana State Land Office; J. Wilson to J. Tully, May 7, 1867; May 13, 1867; May 17, 1867; August 14, 1867; J. Wilson to Register and Receiver, November 3, 1869.

acres of land to the New Orleans, Opelousas, and Great Western Railroad, and consulting a lawyer was informed that the land was subject to entry. On the basis of this legal opinion, he settled several families of Negro ex-soldiers on the lands covered by the railroad grant. After these veterans filed their claims they were notified that the land was not subject to entry and their entries were disallowed. They appealed the decision through Saville and Howard only to learn that the land had been certified to the state on October 7, 1859, for railroad purposes and that the land could not be open to homestead unless Congress acted.[21]

In July, 1867, Saville, now serving as bureau agent as well as locating agent, reported that about one hundred families of freedmen were preparing to move to the homestead lands in September. Requesting congressional action on the expired grant of the New Orleans, Opelousas, and Great Western Railroad, he estimated that if these lands were subject to entry, no less than five hundred freedmen's families would settle on homesteads that fall and winter.[22]

Initially, the resistance to settling the freedmen on home-

21. J. J. Saville to W. H. Sterling, January 28, 1867, Registers and Letters Received (BRFAL), in RG 105, NA, Microcopy 752, Roll 45, p. 610; J. Wilson to J. Tully, March 19, 1867, Letters of the Commissioner, Louisiana State Land Office; Endorsements on letter of O. McFadden to O. O. Howard, March 19, 1867, Selected Series of Records (BRFAL), in RG 105, NA, Microcopy 742, Roll 3, p. 440, endorsements sent April 19, 1867, to general land office; Wilson to Register and Receiver, April 27, 1867, Letters of the Commissioner, Louisiana State Land Office. Wilson sent the list of lands granted to the New Orleans, Opelousas, and Great Western Railroad; of the total, 571,391.75 acres fell within the lands formerly controlled by the Opelousas Land Office. J. Wilson to O. O. Howard, May 3, 1867, Registers and Letters Received (BRFAL), in RG 105, NA, Microcopy 752, Roll 42, p. 1122. Wilson explained to Howard that the railroad grant encompassed all odd numbered sections falling within fifteen miles on either side of the route of the proposed railroad. J. J. Saville to G. W. Julian, *Congressional Globe*, 40th Cong., 2nd Sess., 807, letter read in the House of Representatives, January 28, 1868.

22. J. J. Saville to W. H. Sterling, July 1, 1867, Registers and Letters Received (BRFAL) in RG 105, NA, Microcopy 752, Roll 47, p. 344; F. D. Sewall to J. S. Mower, September 14, 1867, Selected Series of Records (BRFAL), in RG 105, NA, Microcopy 742, Roll 3, p. 319, refers to appointment of Saville as bureau agent on May 25, 1867. Field Records of the Bureau of Refugees, Freedmen, and Abandoned Lands (BRFAL), in Records Group 105, National Archives, Louisiana records indicate that Saville served as agent at Carrollton, Louisiana, from May through August, 1867.

steads on the public lands came from southern whites. However, as Saville pressed his recommendation that Congress declare the railroad lands forfeited, opposition intensified but came from a different quarter. The New Orleans *Republican* on April 17, 1867, recommended that the government renew the grant to the New Orleans, Opelousas, and Great Western Railroad. Saville charged that the *Republican* was interested in railroad speculation and was therefore opposed to giving the land to the freedmen. There may have been some validity in the charge, since General J. S. Mower, the new assistant commissioner for Louisiana, revoked Saville's appointment as bureau agent on September 6, 1867.[23] Saville continued as locating agent and held several mass meetings in New Orleans to organize small colonies of freedmen for homesteading. He assisted ten families of blacks in settling on homestead lands in St. Landry Parish. About the same number settled in Winn Parish and while their families tended the fields they secured employment with neighboring farmers. In this fashion they provided for their families while preparing for their first harvest.

Saville's argument concerning the railroad grants was acknowledged, for in August, 1867, Congressman George W. Julian proposed a bill to declare forfeited to the United States all lands granted to southern states for the construction of railroads. This land was to be made subject to the Southern Homestead Act. However, the bill stipulated that those railroads which could demonstrate that they were controlled by loyal unionists would be exempt from forfeiture. A second provision of the bill authorized the Freedmen's Bureau to employ competent surveyors to resurvey the public lands of the South. This section would relieve the settlers of the necessity of hiring local survey-

23. F. D. Sewall to J. S. Mower, September 14, 1867, Selected Series of Records (BRFAL), in RG 105, NA, Microcopy 742, Roll 3, p. 319; J. J. Saville to G. W. Julian, *Congressional Globe*, 40th Cong., 2nd Sess., 807.

ors who were charging as high as thirty-two dollars for a survey.

Julian also proposed that all future sales of lands condemned either for non-payment of federal taxes or under the bankruptcy laws "shall be sold only in tracts of not less than twenty nor more than eighty acres." The final provision of the bill would declare forfeited to the United States the public lands in the South covered by the Swamp Lands Act. Since most of the states had violated the intent of the act by claiming all alluvial lands as swamp lands, the New Orleans *Republican* pointed out that this provision was just. The editor of the *Republican* commended Julian and urged that Congress, at its next session, enact this or similar legislation. He estimated that this act would give the "landless millions of the south an aggregate area of over two hundred millions of acres. The half of it would give a homestead of eighty acres each to 1,250,000 heads of families and homes and shelter to 6,250,000 persons, computing the families at an average of five persons."[24] It appears that the *Republican* was not the only New Orleans newspaper which supported the attempt to have the grant of the New Orleans, Opelousas, and Great Western Railroad reinstated. The New Orleans *Tribune*, in November, 1867, urged interested parties to visit its office to sign a petition to have the grant reinstated. Not only did the *Tribune* support the railroad company in its attempt to prevent the land grant from returning to the public domain and thereby becoming subject to the Southern Homestead Act, the editors also opposed the Freedmen's Bureau as unnecessary since "we no longer have freedmen among us, but citizens of the United States who have all the rights that others have, and who ought to be protected in enjoying them." The *Tribune* particularly objected to the paternalistic attitude of Assistant Commissioner Mower who urged the freedmen to remain on the plantations

24. New Orleans *Republican*, August 14, 1867.

and "desist from the course they have lately pursued to obtain their rights."[25]

Although the *Tribune*'s stand on the railroad grant was identical to that of the *Republican*, Saville, after his dismissal as bureau agent for Carrolton, joined with the *Tribune* in denouncing the bureau. He informed Congressman Julian that the bureau had outlived its usefulness in Louisiana and recommended that it be discontinued. He also reiterated his request for congressional action on the lands granted to the New Orleans, Opelousas, and Great Western Railroad. The most fertile land remaining in Louisiana was a belt of land about twenty miles wide within the railroad grant from Opelousas to the Mermenteau and Calcasieu rivers. He estimated that there were not more than one hundred thousand acres of government land fit for cultivation which lay outside the limits of the grant. Therefore, he recommended forfeiture of the grant as well as confiscation of all state lands. This would open approximately one million acres of fertile agricultural land to settlement by the freedmen.[26]

In December, 1867, Congressman Julian initiated a two-and-one-half-year fight to declare forfeited to the United States approximately five million acres of land granted to aid in the construction of railroads in the states of Alabama, Mississippi, Louisiana, and Florida. The New Orleans *Republican* and others requested that the bill be amended to exempt the New Orleans, Opelousas, and Great Western Railroad, but Julian successfully resisted their attempts. He secured passage of his bill in the House only to have the Senate Public Lands Committee, under the chairmanship of Samuel C. Pomeroy, refuse to report the bill, thus thwarting the effort to reopen these lands to homesteaders.[27] Senator Pomeroy presents an excellent example of

25. New Orleans *Tribune*, May 18, 1867, November 10, 1867.
26. J. J. Saville to G. W. Julian, *Congressional Globe*, 40th Cong., 2nd Sess., 807.
27. *Congressional Globe*, 40th Cong., 2nd Sess., 95, 694, 806, 985.

the inconsistency of the Radical Republicans. He represented the Congress in the Chiriqui colonization project and then in September, 1865, recommended that the freedmen be provided with homesteads from lands seized from southern planters. As chairman of the Senate Public Lands Committee he directed the efforts to pass the Southern Homestead Act, which he considered punitive legislation. However, when railroad grants were involved, he was careful not to report Julian's bill out of committee.

Republican officials in Louisiana also opposed the effort to declare the railroad lands confiscated. The register of the state land office informed Governor Henry Clay Warmoth in 1869, that the general land office had included in the grant to the New Orleans, Opelousas, and Great Western Railroad almost 47,000 acres which had been selected previously by the state under the Swamp Land Act. Since Congress could not give the same land twice, he pointed out to the governor that the state should attempt to retain the land as swamp land and thereby avoid losing it because the railroad had forfeited its claim. He reported that although the general land office had only approved and patented to the state a total of 8,391,903.71 acres, the state had a legitimate claim to an additional 1,573,876.90 acres of swamp land and railroad lands.[28]

Finally, by an act of July 14, 1870, the lands granted to Louisiana in aid of construction of the New Orleans, Opelousas, and Great Western Railroad were declared forfeited to the federal government. This land was opened for homesteading and the surveyor general for Louisiana indicated in 1871 that there was considerable interest in settling these lands. On March 15, 1873, due to increased efforts by railroad interests, the land was restored to the state of Louisiana for railroad purposes and on

28. W. B. Armstrong to H. C. Warmoth, December 1, 1869, in Louisiana State Land Office Records.

February 24, 1883, the governor conveyed the land to the New
Orleans and Pacific Railroad.[29]

While Congress debated the railroad grant, freedmen continued their efforts to secure homes. Many squatted on government land north of Shreveport, which had not yet been surveyed. It was not open for entry, and since the Southern
Homestead Act restricted entries to homestead for actual settlement, these squatters did not even have a preemption right to
the land and its improvements once the land was surveyed.[30]
From the records it is impossible to determine how many were
actually able to enter their homesteads when the Natchitoches
office began accepting entries in 1871, but under the prevailing
condition of white opposition it is doubtful that many succeeded.

The political climate in Louisiana in 1867 and 1868 was cer-
tainly not conducive to homesteading. Radical Reconstruction
began with the disfranchisement of white Democrats and the
election of Republican delegates to the constitutional convention. Rumors were rampant that the convention would seize the
estates of former rebels and parcel them into forty-acre tracts for
distribution to former slaves. There was even an attempt to
include in the constitution a section providing for the breakup of
large plantations by limiting purchase at distress sales to a
maximum of one hundred acres to any one person, firm, or
corporation. Another provision would have imposed double taxation on uncultivated land, thereby encouraging owners of such

29. U.S., *Statutes at Large*, XVI, 277. The disposition of these lands are recorded in
the various tract books for the townships involved. These tract books are located in
duplicate sets in the state land offices and in the general land office; *House Executive
Documents*, 42nd Cong., 2nd Sess., No. 1, p. 121. The New Orleans, Opelousas, and
Great Western was the only southern railroad to have its grant forfeited under this act.

30. White, *The Freedmen's Bureau in Louisiana*, 60–61; *House Executive Documents*, 42nd Cong., 2nd Sess., No. 1. Throughout this report the commissioner of the
general land office indicated that preemption rights were not transferable to homestead
entries but that since the homestead act was passed with the obvious intention of facilitat-
ing settlement of the public lands by the poor he was considering the possibility of
permitting preemptors to transfer their rights to homesteads.

tracts to parcel them out and sell them to the freedmen. Although neither of these provisions was approved in the form proposed, as long as the convention remained in session many freedmen anticipated a division of the land. Black delegates did achieve partial success in their efforts to break up large plantations because Article 132 of the constitution of 1868 stated: "All lands sold in pursuance of decrees of courts shall be divided into tracts of from ten to fifty acres."[31] Obviously, few freedmen would risk settling on uncleared land or on open prairie far from the nearest timber when they believed that all they had to do was wait for the convention to give them the cleared land of their former masters.

Assistant Commissioner W. H. Wood reported in December, 1867, that unless freedmen were provided with rations sufficient to sustain them until they could harvest their own crop, few indeed would risk homesteading. He therefore urged that such rations be guaranteed.[32] Unfortunately, Wood, who appeared to have a sincere concern for the freedmen, was replaced by General Robert Buchanan, who was more interested in assisting white planters to secure labor than he was in aiding freedmen to homestead.

Saville requested transportation and rations to assist those who still were willing to risk homesteading. When Buchanan refused his request, Saville informed Congressman Julian that Buchanan issued rations to whites but refused to issue rations to the freedmen to assist them in homesteading. Apparently Saville misunderstood the conditions under which Congress authorized the issuance of rations. Rations were to be issued to the employers of freedmen, who would sign a first lien on all crops and the equipment used to produce them. In other words, rations were not issued; employers were allowed to borrow from the

31. White, *The Freedmen's Bureau in Louisiana*, 58.
32. W. H. Wood to E. Whittlesey, December 31, 1867, Registers and Letters Received (BRFAL), in RG 105, NA, Microcopy 752, Roll 53, p. 977.

bureau only if the government was guaranteed that the loan would be repaid. Most planters could not employ laborers and produce a crop without borrowing the rations. Many, however, feared that the proffer of federal assistance was a scheme to deprive them of their land. Therefore, although $350,000 was allotted for loans in Louisiana, planters only borrowed $35,000.[33]

Although Saville had demonstrated true concern for the plight of the landless freedmen, he had committed the unpardonable sin of doubting the integrity and sincerity of an assistant commissioner. He had even recommended that the bureau be discontinued. Howard encouraged Buchanan to endeavor to settle as many freedmen as possible on the public lands and instructed him to appoint an agent for this purpose. Because of Saville's denunciation of the bureau, Howard doubted that he was the best man for the job. On April 23, 1868, Buchanan reported that Saville resigned as locating agent and had been replaced.

Howard called Buchanan's attention to the Louisiana Homestead Aid Association, which had been formed to assist loyal citizens in obtaining homesteads. He instructed Buchanan to cooperate with the association in settling freedmen. In late April Buchanan reported that he was unable to learn anything about the association; he could not even find a constitution. Since the constitution was printed in most of the Republican newspapers, it seems evident that Buchanan had little interest in securing homesteads for freedmen.

Apparently the freedmen continued to hope that either the state or the federal government would seize the land of their former masters. General Buchanan reported in April, 1868, that

33. White, *The Freedmen's Bureau in Louisiana*, 126–27; J. J. Saville to G. W. Julian, *Congressional Globe*, 40th Cong., 2nd Sess., p. 807; O. O. Howard to G. W. Julian, February 25, 1868, Selected Series of Records (BRFAL), in RG 105, NA, Microcopy 742, Roll 4, p. 207; E. Whittlesey for O. O. Howard to J. J. Saville, February 25, 1868, Roll 4, p. 209.

less than half of the freedmen were working. The remainder waited for the outcome of the election to determine whether the constitution was to be approved.[34] Republicans and Democrats vied for the support of the freedmen in the April election, but the Republicans swept the state, adopting the constitution and gaining an absolute majority in all branches of state government, even though in several parishes the Democrats retained control of local offices. Republicans were determined to build their strength in those parishes in preparation for the presidential election. They organized the blacks in these parishes, promising that if Grant were elected they would receive forty acres and a mule. They also warned that if Horatio Seymour was elected slavery would be reinstituted. The Democrats also attempted to win the black vote by organizing black Democratic clubs and by holding barbeques and parades. Although some die-hard Confederates resorted to violence and night riding to intimidate the black voters, the majority of whites in the rural parishes preferred to work within the law. This should not be surprising when one realizes that most local officers were conservative whites. As election day approached both parties increased their efforts to win the black vote. Incendiary remarks by leaders of both parties created a volatile situation which resulted in riots in New Orleans in August, in Bossier and St. Landry parishes in September, and in St. Mary and St. Bernard parishes in October.[35] Since most of the victims of the riots were black Republicans, this created an atmosphere of intimidation and fear which

34. O. O. Howard to R. C. Buchanan, March 18, 1868, Selected Series of Records (BRFAL), in RG 105, NA, Microcopy 742, Roll 4, p. 228; R. C. Buchanan to O. O. Howard, April 23, 1868, Registers and Letters Received (BRFAL), in RG 105, NA, Microcopy 752, Roll 53, pp. 1265–67; R. Buchanan to E. Whittlesey, February 29, 1868, Roll 53, p. 1237; April 30, 1868, Roll 59, p. 203.

35. For a more thorough analysis of this aspect of the problem, see Claude Oubre, "The Opelousas Riot of 1868," *Attakapas Gazette*, VIII (December, 1973), 139–52. *Senate Executive Documents*, 40th Cong., 3rd Sess., No. 15. The bureau report of these riots as well as a riot which occurred in Camilla, Georgia, may be found on Roll 59 of Registers and Letters Received (BRFAL), in RG 105, NA, Microcopy 752.

was not conducive to homesteading by freedmen. Yet, despite these impediments some did attempt to secure homesteads.

One black homesteader, Pierre Noire, may serve to illustrate the type of work required to succeed on the western prairies of Louisiana. Pierre and his family moved to St. Landry Parish, where he entered 160 acres of land under the Southern Homestead Act. He divided and fenced in his land in forty-acre tracts. Each year he systematically rotated the use of his land, running his cattle and horses on half the land and planting the other half. A former Confederate officer who toured the state in the late 1860s explained the effect of this system: "While this half is making an abundant supply of provisions for the family and winter food for the cattle, the other half in its turn is restored to fertility, and thus the land and animals are both kept in admirable order the year round. By this management M. Pierre has become famed far and wide as being the owner of the best stock in the prairie. He is reported to be worth some ten or twelve thousand dollars in hard cash, in addition to the large herd of horses, cows, and sheep he owns, and the fine farm he so successfully cultivates."[36]

When the New Orleans land office finally reopened for business in July of 1868, with both the register and receiver in attendance, many homesteaders filed their claims. They learned that the eighty-acre restriction had been lifted and they could enter 160 acres of land. However, they also learned that the two-year fee restrictions of the Southern Homestead Act had elapsed and therefore they had to pay the registration fee at the time of entry. They protested that they had settled upon their land while the fee restriction was in force and therefore they should not be compelled to pay their fees at the time of entry. The register and receiver were informed that the fees to be paid were those required by existing laws on the day that the entry

36. Lockett, *Louisiana As It Is*, 26.

was filed and could not "relate back to the operation of a pre-existing statute, the provisions of which are no longer in force."[37]

Fifteen months were apparently insufficient time for the register to familiarize himself thoroughly with the workings of his office. A survey of the letters of the commissioner of the general land office to the register and receiver of the New Orleans office indicated that the operation of that office was extremely inefficient. Many homestead entries were canceled, either because the affidavits were not in order or because either the applicant or the register forgot to sign the entry. Others were canceled because they were filed on land that had been certified to the state as swamp land. As previously stated, some entries which were made on the grant of the New Orleans, Opelousas, and Great Western Railroad were disallowed. Some conflicted with previous private entries and some conflicted with recent homestead entries. One can understand the register allowing entry on swamp land or on a railroad grant, or even on private land because of the lack of adequate township plats; but it is difficult to understand how the register could enter conflicting homestead claims on entries which he alone could have processed. The tragedy of it all was that the freedmen had settled on the land as long as a year before they could file their entry and had lived on the land for another year before the commissioner of the general land office disallowed their entries. In each case the register and receiver were instructed to "advise the respective parties that the cancellation is made without prejudice to their right to make other selections on tracts with which there are no interferences."[38] Unfortunately, the freedmen lost two years labor and all their improvements.

In some cases whites attempted to discourage blacks from

37. J. Wilson to Register and Receiver, August 1, 1868 and August 18, 1868, Letters of the Commissioner, Louisiana State Land Office.
38. J. Wilson to Register and Receiver, July 17, 1868, *ibid.*

settling on homestead lands by telling them that the land had already been entered. When they threatened to drive them from the land, many freedmen, who were too poor to resort to court action, applied to the register for protection of their claims. The register was instructed to assure himself of the legality of the claim and then write the homesteader an official letter stating that he had the only legal claim to the land. This action would give the homesteader legal protection which he could present in court. However, should the interference continue and parties trespass upon his land, the homesteader must have recourse to the legal authority since the land office lacked jurisdiction in such matters.[39] In those cases where the freedmen could not obtain justice in state court, the bureau courts offered some protection.

Unfortunately for the freedmen who required protection and assistance, after January 1, 1869, the Freedmen's Bureau activities were limited to the payment of soldier bounties and to education. As soon as the bureau phased out its land and labor contract functions, planters and landowners formed combinations pledged not to rent land to blacks. Most of the New Orleans newspapers disapproved this action of the planters but the *Tribune* was the most vocal in its opposition. The editor pointed out that "without homes, without any right in the soil, what freedom our people have, must be gradually reduced." He also pointed out that free blacks had owned large plantations prior to the war and that many still owned large plantations in the rural parishes, and asked: "Shall there be less liberty now that we are free? Has Emancipation restricted our rights?" The *Tribune* argued further that the sole purpose of these acts by the planters was to "keep the colored people in subjection, so that their wages, their votes, their movements may be controlled by the whites. This is a kind of slavery to which our people will not submit."[40]

39. J. Wilson to Register, September 27, 1867, *ibid*.
40. New Orleans *Tribune*, January 8, 1869.

In its struggle to find some ways for blacks to acquire land, the *Tribune* suddenly discovered the Homestead Act of 1862. Although the paper had published Saville's advertisements and Baird's directions concerning the Southern Homestead Act in every issue from September through December, 1866, there had been no editorial concerning the prospects of homesteading as long as the Freedmen's Bureau was active. Finally, in February, 1869, the *Tribune* published its first editorial on homesteading and encouraged freedmen to avail themselves of the benefit of the act.[41]

Despite the inefficiency of the land office and the many problems which beset those who attempted to homestead, 1,932 families filed homestead entries from January 17, 1867, to December 31, 1870. In St. Landry Parish, the area Saville seemed most interested in, homesteaders filed 437 entries, or 22.62 percent of the total. Of that number, 34 or 7.70 percent were black. Approximately 24.48 percent or 107 applicants in St. Landry Parish received final homestead certification. The figure for final certificates issued to blacks in the parish was six families, representing 17.65 percent. The record for the entire state indicates that 34 percent of all homesteaders under the Southern Homestead Act completed their entries. Assessing these figures one could safely estimate that in Louisiana approximately 200 black families actually filed homestead entries during this four-year period and that approximately fifty families carried their entries to completion.[42] Unfortunately, none of these figures takes into account the many who settled on land and were unable to enter their claims.

A study of the land records indicates that in general homesteading as a means of providing land to the poor of both races failed, not only in the South but throughout the nation. From

41. *Ibid.*, February 2, 1869.

42. Gates, *History of Public Land Law Development*, 414; Gates provided the 34 percent figure for the state completion ratio. The total number of state entries were derived from the receipt books of the land office for the four years in question. The homesteaders in St. Landry were derived from a section by section survey of the tract

1862 to 1890 approximately 400,000 final homestead certificates
were issued. However, if Louisiana can serve as an example of
what transpired, the various local courthouse records indicate
that many of those who received final homestead certificates
either sold, abandoned, or lost their land for non-payment of
taxes. It would therefore be impossible to determine how many
homesteaders actually benefited from the act either in Louisiana
or in the nation.

As a means of providing land for the freedmen, homesteading
proved relatively unsuccessful in Louisiana. This fact resulted
form a variety of causes. As long as the assistant commissioner of
the bureau was in sympathy with the homestead effort, freedmen received assistance in locating and settling their land.
When homesteading interfered with economic and party interests, loyal Republicans, including the assistant commissioner,
chose to aid railroad companies and white planters rather than
press the cause of Negro land ownership. This loss of interest on
the part of professed unionists, coupled with southern white
opposition, precluded success in homesteading. Some success
should have been achieved earlier, however, had it not been for
the chaotic condition of the land records and the gross inefficiency of the land officers. Unfortunately, these conditions were
not limited to Louisiana but prevailed in most of the states affected by the Southern Homestead Act. In contrast to Louisiana,
Florida was the scene of the most fervid, extensive, and relatively more successful homesteading activity.

---

books. Black homesteaders were identified through the unpublished census schedules
for St. Landry Parish in 1870. Unfortunately those who either abandoned their claims or
were driven from them do not appear in this census; therefore it is impossible to arrive at
the exact number of homesteaders in St. Landry in 1870. Furthermore, since no homesteaders by 1870 had received final certificates, the census taker did not identify them as
landowners. The census schedules also contain many inaccuracies, but they are among
the few records available which separate the population by race.

VII

Homesteading
in Florida

FLORIDA CONTAINED MORE public lands than any of the other states included in the Southern Homestead Act, and was more accessible to the South Atlantic states. For these reasons, Florida became the scene of the most feverish activity on the part of freedmen in search of homestead lands. As early as March, 1866, many freedmen squatted on government land.[1] The women cleared the land while the men earned wages at other jobs.

Upon notification of the passage of the Southern Homestead Act the assistant commissioner in Florida instructed his agents to give the matter the "greatest possible circulation, and furnish all the information and assistance in their power to all citizens who are entitled, and desire to avail themselves of the privileges of the Act of Congress referred to in the foregoing Circular." He instructed bureau agents to write to the register of the land office in order to obtain more extensive information concerning the Southern Homestead Act. He further authorized his officers to travel to Tallahassee to inspect the maps of their districts so that they would be familiar with the areas open to settlement in their respective districts.[2]

1. T. Leddy to J. G. Foster, March 31, 1866, Registers and Letters Received (BRFAL), in RG 105, NA, Microcopy 752, Roll 27, p. 325.
2. Circular No. 3, Headquarters, Department of Florida, July 20, 1866, Registers and Letters Received (BRFAL) in RG 105, NA, Microcopy 752, Roll 31, p. 859.

Although conditions in the Florida land office were somewhat better than in Louisiana, there was still some confusion. The register, although appointed earlier, did not open his office for business until August 25, 1866, when both he and the receiver were in attendance. Despite the assertion that the maps in the land office were too voluminous to be distributed, it appears that many plat maps were missing from the files of the office. The situation in Florida also resembled Louisiana in that over fourteen million acres of government land in the two states had not been surveyed by 1866 and were therefore not subject to immediate entry.[3]

The confusion in the land office did not deter the freedmen. By the end of July, actual homesteading under the Southern Homestead Act commenced. The sub-assistant commissioner for Lake City, Florida, received numerous requests for information from freedmen concerning land. Bewildered by the term "actual settlement and cultivation," he realized that if homesteaders had to reside upon and cultivate only the homestead land for five years, few whites and even fewer freedmen could hope to secure land. Since the soil in his district could not be made productive in less than two years, provisions for at least that amount of time were necessary; otherwise, the homesteaders would starve.[4]

Most of the land in the northern portion of the state had been open to unlimited purchase for many years; what remained was considered wild land. Under the graduation law the land was selling at 12.5 cents per acre, about the same as filing fees and registration for homesteads. Therefore, the Southern Homestead Act conferred very few favors on any except the freedmen who were forbidden to purchase land earlier. From a monetary

3. *Senate Executive Documents*, 39th Cong., 2nd Sess., No. 6, p. 45; Paul W. Gates, "Federal Land Policy in the South, 1866–1888," *Journal of Southern History*, VI (August, 1940), 309.

4. F. E. Grossman to S. L. McHenry, July 31, 1866, Registers and Letters Received (BRFAL) in RG 105, NA, Microcopy 752, Roll 37, p. 706.

point of view the assistant commissioner for Florida felt that the law offered little. In order to take advantage of the law, the freedmen needed at least one year's provisions, agricultural implements, and animals. From a political standpoint, however, he considered the law important since it would enable the freedmen to become landowners, and he informed Howard that he would extend all assistance possible to secure to freedmen the benefits of the law "even at the risk of having to support some that may utterly fail in their efforts to produce enough for their support."[5]

By September, the interest of the freedmen in homesteading increased so much that almost all of the sub-assistant commissioners in the state reported some activity.[6] Although he doubted that many freedmen would enter land due to their depressed financial condition, the assistant commissioner claimed that most were interested in trying to homestead anyway. He also received advance notice of colonies coming from South Carolina and some from other states.[7]

During September interest in homesteading increased to such a degree that the sub-assistant commissioners had to reassess their previous evaluations concerning the number who would attempt to settle on land of their own. The agent at Ocala reported that many had made their selections and depositions which he would forward to the land office. The agent at Lake City indicated that many freedmen had entered while others purchased land already cleared and still others intended to rent for the coming year. He pointed out that difficulty in ascertaining the location of public land hindered many who wanted to enter land. The bureau agent at Gainesville pointed out that in the absence of the plats of the public lands and his own igno-

5. J. G. Foster to O. O. Howard, August 10, 1866, *ibid.*, Roll 37, p. 706.

6. F. E. Grossman to S. L. McHenry, September 1, 1866, *ibid.*, Roll 37, p. 772; General Seymore to J. G. Foster, September 1, 1866; I. H. Durkee to J. G. Foster, September 3, 1866, p. 784; J. A. Remley to J. G. Foster, August 31, 1866, p. 776.

7. J. G. Foster to O. O. Howard, September 14, 1866, *ibid.*, Roll 37, p. 768.

rance of the location of such lands, he had difficulty assisting freedmen in locating and filing their entries. In spite of these difficulties freedmen entered approximately ten thousand acres of public land during September of 1866.[8]

As more freedmen became interested in homesteading, Florida whites began resisting. Many whites had purchased public lands from the Confederate government of Florida during the war; these purchases were now declared invalid. Consequently, they opposed any movement by the freedmen into the public lands and took every means at their disposal to stop them. Whites became so petty as to steal the compass needle and chains from a northern surveyor who was helping freedmen. They also threatened blacks with physical harm if they continued with their intention of homesteading. One party of ten blacks reported that they had attempted to locate land in Lafayette County. Although they were informed that whites had organized to prevent homesteading, they were determined to secure their own land. When one resident informed them that the bodies of three blacks had been found in the Suwannee River, however, they accepted this information as fact and abandoned their plans. Other blacks were more resolute and in spite of opposition, by the end of October, 1866, freedmen had entered over 32,000 acres in Florida.[9]

Before the freedmen could file their claims, it was necessary for them to secure the services of a surveyor. Florida whites,

8. J. A. Remley, Report for September, September 30, 1866, *ibid.*, Roll 37, p. 821; F. E. Grossman, Report for September, October 1, 1866, p. 818; I. H. Durkee, Report for September, October 3, 1866, p. 863; *Senate Executive Documents*, 39th Cong., 2nd Sess., No. 6, p. 45.

9. J. E. Quentin to J. G. Foster, November 1, 1866, Registers and Letters Received (BRFAL) in RG 105, NA, Microcopy 752, Roll 37, p. 866; J. Cory to O. O. Howard, October 20, 1866, p. 445; Foster's endorsement on Cory's Letter, November 4, 1866, p. 443; *Senate Executive Documents*, 39th Cong., 2nd Sess., No. 6, p. 45. Joe M. Richardson, *The Negro in the Reconstruction of Florida, 1865–1877* (Tallahassee: Florida State University Press, 1965), 74. For an extensive analysis of the activities of the bureau in Florida this source must be consulted.

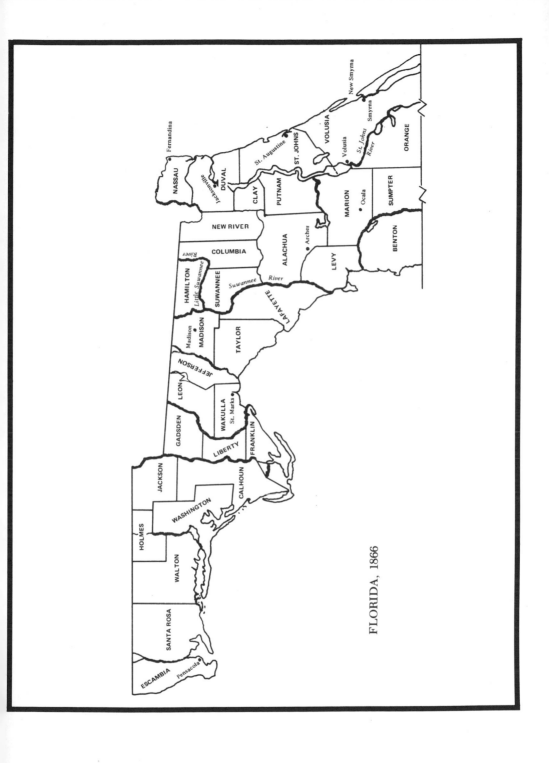

FLORIDA, 1866

feigning friendship, frequently deluded the freedmen into believing that they were acquiring good land. In some instances freedmen were directed to private land where they settled and made improvements. They were then forced to move or purchase at high prices. Consequently, the register of the land office required them to hire a northern surveyor to help them file their claims. In addition, the register requested that the bureau hire several surveyors in order to aid these people. Unless such action was taken, he feared that hundreds would abandon their claims and the intent of the homestead law would be frustrated. Most whites did not want the Negroes anywhere near their cattle ranges and plantations, and refused to permit them to tie in with existing fences when they did homestead. Many of the freedmen entered land already occupied illegally by whites who refused to give up possession. [10] Such factors caused serious difficulties for the blacks and increased the existing friction between the two races.

As the 1866 harvest season drew to a close, many freedmen began filing for government land with the little money they had accumulated. It was relatively easy for freedmen from those states bordering the Atlantic to go to St. Augustine and thence down the St. Johns River to the public lands of southern Florida. However, it was expensive for them to reach Tallahassee, where the only land office in the state was located. [11] In most cases, the trip to Tallahassee cost more than the purchase of land under the graduation law. Under that law, eighty acres cost ten dollars plus the two-dollar fee for registration. The trip to Tallahassee cost from twenty to forty dollars and then the prospective entrant obligated himself for the additional cost of surveying the land. Thus, he spent from forty to fifty dollars merely to file his claim.

10. A. B. Stonelake to O. O. Howard, January 5, 1867, Registers and Letters Received (BRFAL) in RG 105, NA, Microcopy 752, Roll 44, pp. 37–41; M. L. Stearns to J. G. Foster, December 31, 1866, Roll 42, p. 22; Richardson, *The Negro in the Reconstruction of Florida*, 74.

11. *House Executive Documents*, 40th Cong., 2nd Sess., No. 1, p. 677.

After five years and the payment of an additional seven dollars, he could finally receive the patent for his land. When bureau agents asked for legislation to relieve this condition, the commissioner of the general land office informed Howard that the freedmen could make the required affidavits before the clerk of court in the county in which they resided and then forward the affidavits together with the description of the land and the entry fees.[12] This step helped to reduce the cost for some later entrants.

By the end of December 1866, several groups of freedmen proposed moving to the homestead lands. From Pensacola, a group of about 200 families were transported to their land on the U.S.S. *Governor Marvin*. The bureau furnished transportation from Charleston, South Carolina, to Florida for 602 persons under the leadership of a freedman. The register of the Tallahassee land office notified Howard that several groups, with as many as 300 families per group, from different areas of the South had filed applications for homestead lands. Large numbers of freedmen were brought into the state, it was reported, by irresponsible persons who were unable to help settle the freedmen on their homesteads. Such actions led to a request for authority to assume general supervision over the settlement of public lands in Florida. Howard agreed and commanded bureau agents to actively assist all freedmen, whether they came individually or in groups, to locate land.[13]

One group of freedmen from South Carolina proposed to set-

12. J. Wilson to O. O. Howard, August 23, 1867, Registers and Letters Received (BRFAL), in RG 105, NA, Microcopy 752, Roll 46, p. 11.

13. J. T. Sprague to O. O. Howard, December 1, 1866, *ibid.*, Roll 42, p. 52; John T. Sprague, assistant commissioner for Florida, is not to be confused with John W. Sprague, who served as assistant commissioner for Arkansas; Endorsement on Communication of Moses Kelly, January 7, 1867, Selected Series of Records (BRFAL), in RG 105, NA, Microcopy 742, Roll 2, p. 468; A. B. Stonelake to O. O. Howard, January 5, 1867, Registers and Letters Received (BRFAL), in RG 105, NA, Microcopy 752, Roll 44, pp. 40–41; Endorsement on February 5, 1867, on Sprague's letter of January 19, 1867, Selected Series of Records (BRFAL), in RG 105, NA, Microcopy 742, Roll 2, p. 468.

tle near New Smyrna, about thirty miles south of St. Augustine. Although this colony failed, it illustrates the problems freedmen faced in homesteading the wilds of Florida. General Ralph Ely, civilian emigration agent for South Carolina, organized the New Smyrna colony, a group of about 1,200 people, and on December 13, 1866, registered 300 entries at a cost of six hundred dollars for them at the land office at Tallahassee. Investigators later discovered that Ely collected ten dollars from the head of each family, from widows, and anyone of age, for the entering and securing of their homesteads. Each of these people also paid Ely's clerk $0.75 in addition to $1.50 for the fare from Winsborough to Columbia.[14] Since registration was only $2.00 per entry and transportation was furnished by the government, the freedmen were fraudulently deprived of the little money they had saved to homestead.

Ely's communications with bureau agents led his readers to assume that the colony was well organized and that every care would be taken to provide for the needs of the freedmen. On December 16, 1866, he requested that a medical officer be appointed to accompany the colony to Florida. Since there were no medical officers in South Carolina or Florida who could be spared for this purpose, Howard dispatched a medical officer with medical supplies for the colony from New York. On January 1, 1867, Ely requested that the New Smyrna colonists be supplied with seed for planting. The assistant commissioner for South Carolina forwarded the request to Howard who approved it and sent it to the quartermaster general. Unfortunately, since Congress had made no appropriations for seed, the quartermaster did not fulfill the request.[15]

General Ely had served as a bureau agent in South Carolina

14. J. T. Sprague to O. O. Howard, February 28, 1867, Registers and Letters Received (BRFAL) in RG 105, NA, Microcopy 752, Roll 42, pp. 115–16; H. M. Whittlesey to A. P. Ketchum, December 22, 1866, Roll 40, p. 928.

15. Communications of Ralph Ely with all endorsements from December 16, 1866, to January 26, 1867, Selected Series of Records (BRFAL), in RG 105, NA, Microcopy 742, Roll 2, pp. 434–55.

immediately after the war but had been accused of misusing his office. Before official action could be taken on the accusation, however, his term of service ended and he was mustered out. Therefore, in order to protect the reputation of the bureau, Howard ordered the assignment of a bureau agent to accompany General Ely's colony. Making clear that Ely was not an agent of the bureau, Howard further directed the appointment of an agent to investigate the conduct and condition of the colony and to see that the freedmen were properly cared for and protected.[16]

The New Smyrna colonists left Charleston, South Carolina, in early January of 1867, with little but the clothes on their bodies. For some unaccountable reason the boat trip from Charleston to St. Augustine took thirty days. Due to the delay, on arrival at their destination they faced total destitution, having consumed their entire thirty-day rations furnished by the bureau. They found the land entered for them to be of the wildest sort possible. There was no settled community nearby, and their land had not even been surveyed. Faced with starvation, the vast majority of the colony hired out to the planters from Alachua and Marion counties who hastened there to engage them. Ely requested rations for some two hundred adults and one hundred children remaining. An investigation into the affairs of the colony later disclosed that even these rations were sold.

In March, 1867, all that remained at the site of the colony were thirty-eight families composed of 130 adults and 103 children. Twenty of these families lived on what they assumed to be their own land, but as yet none had received certificates from the land office at Tallahassee. The remaining eighteen squatted on private lands, waiting to be shown the location of their own land.

In spite of all handicaps, these thirty-eight families tried to

16. A. P. Ketchum for Howard to R. K. Scott, January 25, 1867, Selected Series of Records (BRFAL), in RG 105, NA, Microcopy 742, Roll 3, p. 73; A. P. Ketchum to J. T. Sprague for Howard, January 25, 1867, p. 74.

hold on to their land. They cleared the land with axes. With hoes, the only farm implements they possessed, they dug holes at regular intervals and planted corn. These men left their wives to tend the land they had cleared and walked from fifty to sixty miles in search of employment. They returned every few days with whatever meager provisions they could procure. The most common food of the colonists consisted of "comtee," a beetlike root which they grated into a tub and saturated with water. The mixture was left standing for a few days to permit the poison to evaporate, after which they strained it and retained the resultant milky liquid. This they permitted to set and then poured off the water. The paste dried until it became powdery and ready for baking into bread or biscuits.

The agents appointed to investigate concluded that the colonists were imbued with a strong desire to own homes of their own. "They have a point of pride, not to return, under any circumstances, to South Carolina, in case of the final failure of their colony." [17] All those who had anything to do with the investigation of the colony condemned Ely for his actions. They believed that only an unscrupulous person would have brought people to that area of Florida with only thirty days' subsistence and no tools. [18]

This assessment of Ely's moral character proved accurate. While his activities were being investigated, he went to the land office at Tallahassee, where he demanded that the register refund to him the six hundred dollars entry fee since the applications had not been acted upon. The receiver of the Tallahassee

17. W. J. Purman to W. C. Woodruff, March 20, 1867, Registers and Letters Received (BRFAL) in RG 105, NA, Microcopy 752, Roll 42, pp. 164–72.

18. Ralph Ely to W. C. Woodruff, January 3, 1867, *ibid.*, Roll 42, p. 6; J. T. Sprague to O. O. Howard, January 14, 1867, p. 2; R. Ely to O. O. Howard, February 5, 1867, Roll 41, p. 1040; J. T. Sprague to O. O. Howard, February 28, 1867, Roll 42, pp. 115–17; O. Morgan to J. Wilson, May 30, 1867, Roll 47, p. 78; J. T. Sprague to O. O. Howard, May 18, 1867, Roll 42, p. 195; Richardson, *The Negro in the Reconstruction of Florida*, 76.

land office reported that the register and Ely had arrived at a mutually satisfactory arrangement. Although the exact nature of the agreement was unknown, the receiver believed that the interests of the freedmen who had employed General Ely to assist them in the entry of lands were not consulted. He based his opinion on the fact that the register had returned every affidavit in his possession for correction except the three hundred which Ely had filed. Therefore the applicants had not filed corrected affidavits and were ignorant of the status of their entries.[19] A final report on the New Smyrna colony, issued in May, 1868, indicated that the colonists had finally abandoned the tracts of land selected by Ely and had scattered throughout the state. Many located homesteads elsewhere, while others found employment on plantations. The report's conclusion indicated that the colonists had proven themselves capable of taking care of themselves.[20]

Based on his experience with this colony, Assistant Commissioner J. T. Sprague concluded that the establishment of separate Negro colonies was impossible. Successful colonization required the active leadership of honest officers, along with sufficient rations, seed, and tools. Since Congress had not provided for these necessities, he recommended that the bureau homestead the freedmen near white settlers where the men could procure employment while the women cultivated their homesteads.[21]

In January, 1867, Sprague asked for two more land offices,

19. O. Morgan to J. Wilson, May 30, 1867, Registers and Letters Received (BRFAL) in RG 105, NA, Microcopy 752, Roll 47, pp. 7–8. While bureau agents investigated Ely's conduct he even had the audacity to request from the bureau reimbursement for expenses incurred and a monthly salary. Howard denied his request. Selected Series of Records (BRFAL), in RG 105, NA, Microcopy 742, Roll 3, p. 117.

20. F. D. Sewall, Inspection Report of Florida, South Carolina, and Texas, May 11, 1868, Registers and Letters Received (BRFAL) in RG 105, NA, Microcopy 752, Roll 55, p. 712.

21. J. T. Sprague to O. O. Howard, May 18, 1867, ibid., Roll 42, p. 195.

one at St. Augustine and one at Newnansville, in order to lower the cost of entering the land for many of the freedmen. He particularly wanted the one at St. Augustine because he believed that the most favorable lands for homesteading were in southern Florida along the Atlantic coast. He proposed that all land south of 28°31' be surveyed and laid out in forty-acre lots. Because this section had not been surveyed since 1833 and none of the corner posts remained, it was urgent that it be resurveyed. Detrimental to this plan was the infestation of bands of "renegades and desparadoes" [sic] who continually robbed and murdered the few whites in the area. However, Sprague felt that if sufficient numbers of freedmen settled in this area, he could justify sending in a regular detachment of troops to protect them until such time as they could constitute an auxiliary force and help protect the entire frontier.[22]

Along with the above recommendations, Sprague requested authority to appoint surveyors as locating agents to help settle the freedmen. Nothing decisive was done until late February, 1867, when he appointed four locating agents. By that time most of the freedmen who would have entered land that year had been forced to seek further employment; therefore, Sprague did not anticipate much homesteading activity until the end of the year.[23]

In June, 1867, Howard proposed to do away with the locating agents in the southern states. Sprauge argued that unless the freedman was placed on accurately surveyed land through the direction of a government agent, he would never be secure in

22. J. T. Sprague to O. O. Howard, January 31, 1867, Roll 42, pp. 88–89; March 31, 1867, p. 178; December 31, 1866, pp. 54–55; S. F. Halliday to J. G. Foster, September 4, 1867, Roll 49, pp. 622–23.

23. J. T. Sprague to O. O. Howard, January 31, 1867, ibid., Roll 42, p. 88; February 28, 1867, p. 117; endorsement on Sprague's request for locating agents, January 19, 1867, Selected Series of Records (BRFAL), in RG 105, NA, Microcopy 742, Roll 2, p. 268.

his claims and could easily be driven from his land. Sprague also pointed out that although the locating agents had settled relatively few freedmen since their appointment, they had prepared maps of the areas under their jurisdiction. When the freedmen were released from their labor contracts, therefore, they could settle land previously surveyed for that purpose.[24]

Probably the most discouraging aspect of homesteading for freedmen was the uncertainty of their being able to retain possession of the land. They incurred considerable expense traveling to the land and then waited as much as six or seven months before receiving certificates from the land office at Tallahassee. They registered many complaints with bureau agents against the register, A. B. Stonelake, concerning the delays.[25]

In October, 1866, J. E. Quentin, the sub-assistant commissioner for Madison County, charged that Stonelake was more interested in assisting whites than he was in helping the freedmen. He reported the case of Nat Goodman, a freedman who was deprived of his entry under the homestead law. During the war Dr. J. F. J. Mitchell, a Florida white, purchased land from the Confederate government. His slaves cleared the land, built a house, and planted crops. When the war ended Dr. Mitchell, realizing that his claim to the land was invalid, decided that his former slaves should have the benefit of the improvements and the crops which they had planted. He therefore sent Nat Goodman, one of his former slaves, to Tallahassee to enter claims for the eight families living on the land. Three days after he made the entries Stonelake accosted Goodman on the street and demanded the entry papers. Goodman complied and watched as

24. J. T. Sprague to F. D. Sewall, June 5, 1867, Registers and Letters Received (BRFAL), in RG 105, NA, Microcopy 752, Roll 46, pp. 787–89; J. A. Remley to J. T. Sprague, July 31, 1867, p. 984.

25. J. A. Remley to J. T. Sprague, February 28, 1867, *ibid.*, Roll 42, p. 120; T. Seymour to J. T. Sprague, April 19, 1867, Roll 47, pp. 955–56; J. A. Remley to J. T. Sprague, April 30, 1867, p. 204.

Stonelake destroyed the papers and stated that this was how he dealt with persons who deceived him.

Goodman reported the incident to Quentin, who, upon investigation, learned that Stonelake had entered the land in question for one Delilah Thomson, the widow of a Confederate soldier and paramour of Dr. Mitchell's overseer. Since she could not possibly take the required oath, Quentin concluded that Stonelake had exceeded his authority. Stonelake defended his actions by stating that since an error had been made on the entry papers, they were invalid and therefore should have been destroyed. He claimed that Goodman had attempted to enter land which had been entered in 1855, and pointed to the books of the land office to substantiate his statements. Unfortunately, since the entry papers had been destroyed Goodman could not prove that he actually had entered the land he claimed. Disappointed by the delay and convinced that he could not secure justice, Goodman decided to file entry on other land.[26]

Early in 1867, bureau agents reported that freedmen were charged as much as nine dollars to enter land. Stonelake explained that the discrepancies in fees resulted from the lack of adequate instructions from the general land office. He pointed out that 162 entrants under the homestead law paid seven dollars before the register and receiver were informed that under the law they should charge only two dollars. The commissioner of the general land office instructed the register and receiver to apply the additional five dollars toward the patent for the land which was to be issued five years later. This accounted for seven dollars, but some freedmen complained that they had paid nine dollars. Stonelake explained that in order to protect the freedmen he had established a survey fund to defray the expense of surveying the land. Although Stonelake's explanations appar-

26. J. E. Quentin to O. O. Howard, October 1, 1866, *ibid.*, Roll 74, pp. 484–88; J. G. Foster to J. E. Quentin, October 9, 1866, p. 491; J. G. Foster to O. O. Howard, December 3, 1866, Roll 37, p. 996.

ently convinced his readers of his honesty, the charges continued and finally an investigation commenced.[27]

One of the most serious charges brought against Stonelake was made by J. E. Quentin. He charged that Stonelake encouraged him to settle freedmen on land which whites had bought and cleared during the war but whose claims were invalid because the land was purchased from the Confederate government of Florida. Believing Stonelake to be sincere, Quentin settled freedmen on such land in order to give them the advantage of existing improvements. At this point, Stonelake showed his true colors by instructing the sheriff of Madison County to obtain all the information he could regarding squatters and any others who had entered land during the war but had been displaced by freedmen. Stonelake claimed the authority under the preemption law to restore the land to the former claimants. Quentin charged further that Stonelake had personally made several entries for freed people on occupied land. The sheriff threatened the freedmen with eviction and even told one freedman that he could get all his land back if he (the freedman) could raise enough money.

Quentin also stated that all the entries made in his district were for eighty acres; yet Stonelake claimed that the general land office had informed him of a law prohibiting entry of more than forty acres if the entry was within six miles of a railroad or navigable stream (double minimum land). Quentin was quite concerned since almost all of the entries in his district fell within this class of land. Stonelake proposed to take forty acres from each entry but not to let the freedmen decide which forty acres they wanted to keep. He had already written to Washington

27. J. Remley to J. T. Sprague, April 30, 1867, *ibid.*, Roll 42, p. 204; A. B. Stonelake to J. T. Sprague, March 11, 1867, Roll 44, pp. 405–408; A. B. Stonelake to O. O. Howard, March 11, 1867, p. 402; J. Wilson to O. O. Howard, June 10, 1867, Roll 47, p. 2. Howard sent Wilson's letter to Sprague on June 17, 1867; Sprague endorsed it on June 29, 1867, p. 5: O. Morgan to J. Wilson, May 30, 1867, pp. 7–8.

requesting permission to do just that. Quentin feared that Stonelake's request would be granted, since it did not include all the particulars. He therefore requested immediate action to thwart this move to deprive the freedmen of their land.[28]

During the month of July, 1867, S. F. Halliday, the locating agent at Ocala, Marion County, located forty-nine homesteads for freedmen. Based on the applications which he and the sub-assistant commissioner at Ocala had received, they estimated that at least five hundred homesteads would be entered in Marion County that season. On September 4, 1867, Halliday reported that he had located homesteads for twenty freedmen and transmitted their applications, with the required fees, to the land office at Tallahassee. He indicated that he had also made at least twenty locations for which the applicants were not prepared to pay the fees and consummate the entries. He pointed out further that the freedmen were "wild with excitement" at the prospect of securing homesteads and that in order to meet their demands a considerable number of surveyors would be necessary. He estimated that during that month he would only be able to complete the surveys for one hundred families because of the time required for each entry.[29]

By the end of September, 1867, freedmen throughout Florida were locating homesteads. They were planting on shares that year and anticipated having sufficient funds to homestead. The crop for the year proved to be a poor one, however, only one-fourth the normal yield, and as a result very few freedmen could afford to homestead. In spite of this, by the end of November,

28. J. E. Quentin to A. H. Jackson, July 22, 1867, *ibid.*, Roll 48, pp. 471–73; July 23, 1867, p. 473; J. E. Quentin to Robert Schenk, July 23, 1867, pp. 484–85. All land within six miles of a railroad or navigable stream was considered double minimum land valued at $2.50 per acre. Therefore, under the Southern Homestead Act, anyone who selected this type of land for entry could only claim forty acres; otherwise his entry would be disallowed.

29. Report of S. F. Halliday, locating agent at Ocala, September 4, 1867, Registers and Letters Received (BRFAL), in RG 105, NA, Microcopy 752, Roll 49, p. 622; September 18, 1867, pp. 639–40.

Sprague noted that all locating agents were having difficulty meeting the demand for assistance in homesteading. The number of entries far exceeded anything anticipated because there was a general scarcity of money throughout Florida. By December, 1, 1867, freedmen had entered 2,431 homesteads in Florida.[30]

Many freedmen who entered land possessed little more than one or two months' subsistence. Sprague realized that when this was exhausted they would be destitute. They had planted gardens but these would not have time to mature before their provisions ran out. Sprague believed that when the freedmen were faced with starvation they would take recourse to stealing the cattle and pigs running free in the swamps. This situation would inevitably lead to serious clashes with the whites who owned the animals. In order to avoid this, Sprague exceeded his authority and began issuing rations. In February, 1868, he instructed his agents to issue rations to any destitute freedmen owning ten acres of land under fence, and by the end of the month he recognized the move to be particularly beneficial to the homesteaders. Assured of rations, the freedmen busily engaged in building homes, making fences, and tilling the land. By the end of March, many were entering ten acres of land to become eligible for rations. In this manner many families secured homes for themselves, and the men were able to devote their time to the proper tillage of the land instead of having to work at other positions to provide food for their families.[31]

From January 1, 1868, to October 1, 1868, over 1,400 freedmen entered land, approximately 900 in Marion County alone.

30. J. T. Sprague to O. O. Howard, October 31, 1867, *ibid.*, Roll 49, p. 689; December 10, 1867, pp. 710–11; *House Executive Documents*, 40th Cong., 2nd Sess., No. 1, pp. 676–77; Richardson, *The Negro in the Reconstruction of Florida*, 73.

31. J. A. Remley to J. T. Sprague, February 27, 1866, Registers and Letters Received (BRFAL), in RG 105, NA, Microcopy 752, Roll 52, pp. 1020–24; J. T. Sprague to O. O. Howard, December 10, 1867, Roll 49, p. 710; January 10, 1868, Roll 52, pp. 934–45; March 31, 1868, pp. 1058–59; April 30, 1868, p. 1088.

Sprague indicated that locating agents could have accomplished more but there was no register at the land office for several months. Although the receiver accepted entries in the absence of the register, these entries were declared irregular and the agents were required to perform the work a second time. In spite of these difficulties and delays, Sprague estimated that the majority of the freedmen in Florida were settled on from ten to forty acres of land, and had produced sufficient corn and sweet potatoes to feed themselves for the following year. He concluded that the freedmen in Florida had established themselves as independent farmers and would henceforth require little assistance from the government. Since the activities of the bureau, except for education and soldier bounties, were to be discontinued on January 1, 1869, Sprague recommended that all agents be discharged except the locating agents. Their services were still required to assist those who had not yet homesteaded. The locating agents were retained and continued to supervise the location of freedmen at least until November, 1869.[32]

Since the holdings of individual freedmen were generally small, most observers believed that they would fail. Halliday pointed out that what the freedmen had done on their homesteads in 1868 was not a true index of their situation, since many had planted improved land in the vicinity of their homesteads while they cleared their own land and prepared it for the following year. Halliday gave some specific examples of successful homesteading by freedmen who received rations under Circular No. 3. James McCartin, in 1866, entered eighty acres near Newnansville. By September, 1868, he had fenced forty acres, which was under cultivation. He had built a comfortable house, stables, and a cowbarn and had dug a well. In the latter year he

---

32. F. D. Sewall, Inspection Report for Florida, South Carolina, and Texas, May 11, 1868, *ibid.*, Roll 55, p. 712; J. T. Sprague to O. O. Howard, July 25, 1868, Roll 57, p. 947; June 30, 1868, p. 936; July 31, 1868, pp. 958–59; August 31, 1868, p. 966, October 1, 1868, pp. 973–93; G. W. Gile to E. Whittlesey, November 1869, Roll 65, pp. 505–557.

harvested an abundance of corn and potatoes and at least two bales of sea island cotton. Charles Williams, his son Samuel, and daughter Nancy entered individual homesteads adjoining each other in 1867 near the town of Archer. In 1868 they harvested five hundred bushels of corn and three bales of sea island cotton. Their cotton crop had been estimated at six bales before it was attacked by the caterpillars. William Drayton, another freedman, settled on a homestead of eighty acres near Newnansville, where he built a home and other buildings. He planted twenty acres of his own land and rented other land. During the year he produced sufficient provisions for another year. Cyrus Jackson settled on a homestead of eighty acres near Morrison Mills, where he made an excellent crop of corn and cotton and became independent and comfortable. Robert Marshall, who was entirely destitute of provisions, settled a homestead near Newnansville and through the aid of Circular No. 3 was able to maintain his settlement and produce an abundance of necessities for the next year.

Halliday pointed out that the provisions of Circular No. 3 benefited not only homesteaders but also those who rented land. James Evans, with the help of three of his children, produced 1,500 bushels of corn and other provisions in proportion on rented land. After retaining sufficient provisions and seed for the following year, he sold his crop and from the proceeds purchased a farm. Halliday indicated that these were only a few of the families who had come under his immediate observation and that he could mention many more names and case histories if necessary. He concluded that the freedmen homesteading in Florida would compare in their success at retaining their land with the old settlers who had received bounty lands earlier and had faced similar circumstances.[33]

Homesteading in the wilds of Florida was dangerous at best.

33. S. F. Halliday, Annual Report of Locating Agent, September 15, 1868, *ibid.*, Roll 57, p. 979; Richardson, *The Negro in the Reconstruction of Florida*, 79–80.

The hardships these settlers faced and overcame proved how strong their desire for land must have been. By the time the bureau discontinued most of its activities on January 1, 1869, approximately four thousand freedmen in Florida had entered homesteads. Unfortunately, by November, 1874, many of these farms reverted to the government. Of the 6,492 homestead entries made at Tallahassee by both whites and Negroes between 1866 and 1873, only 577 final homestead certificates were issued. This indicates a completion ratio of only 8.9 percent. On the basis of these figures one can safely estimate that at least 356 freedmen actually carried their entries to completion.[34]

These facts demonstrate that at least in Florida many of the bureau agents were concerned about homesteading and did everything in their power to help the freedmen. Their efforts were hindered by some of their fellow agents, by white southerners, and by the register of the land office at Tallahassee. Yet in spite of all these hindrances, bureau agents persisted in their endeavors and for a brief time they assisted the majority of the freedmen in Florida in settling on land of their own choosing, either through homestead or purchase. Unfortunately, after the bureau became inoperative on January 1, 1869, many freedmen lost their homes. Although many factors contributed to the failure of the freedmen to retain possession of their land, probably the prime factor was the actual condition of the land available to settlers. The homesteaders faced virtually impenetrable palmetto swamp land, which required twentieth-century construction equipment to clear and drain. Much of the land in Florida that was available under the Southern Homestead Act remained unsettled even after the collapse of the Florida land boom of the mid-1920s. It is therefore evident that those freedmen who

34. Harry P. Yoshpe and Philip P. Brower (comps.), *Preliminary Inventory of the Land Entry Papers of the General Land Office: Preliminary Inventory No. 22* (Washington: National Archives, 1948), 27; Richardson, *The Negro in the Reconstruction of Florida*, 78.

succeeded in clearing their land and retaining possession of it did so against virtually insurmountable odds. So uncertain was the future and so great were the dangers involved in homesteading in Florida that many freedmen who accumulated sufficient finances preferred to purchase land in their home states in familiar surroundings rather than travel to homestead lands.

VIII

A Stake in
the Land

WHEN OLIVER OTIS HOWARD accepted the position as commissioner of the Freedmen's Bureau, he made quite clear, both by word and by deed, his belief that only through acquiring land and education could the freedmen become truly free. He chose as his subordinates men who shared this conviction. They believed that the freedmen should have land, but they also believed that they must pay for their land. The role of the government was limited to providing the opportunity to acquire land. This philosophy is well illustrated in Howard's reply to freedmen who objected that President Johnson's restoration of abandoned and confiscated property in 1865 deprived them of their homes. He indicated that he could protect them only in the possession of land which they actually purchased.[1] The Southern Homestead Act made land available and, since the cost of registering land was approximately equal to the cost of purchase

---

1. *House Executive Documents*, 39th Cong., 1st Sess., No. 70, p. 103; Instructions to the freedmen at Orangeburg, South Carolina, from Captain Charles Soule, sent to Howard June 12, 1865, Registers and Letters Received (BRFAL) in RG 105, NA, Microcopy 752, Roll 17, p. 54; A. P. Ketchum to John Alvord, July 26, 1865, Roll 74, p. 47; O. O. Howard to the Committee of Colored People of Edisto Island, October 22, 1865, Selected Series of Records (BRFAL), in RG 105, NA, Microcopy 742, Roll 1, p. 243; *Senate Executive Documents*, 39th Cong., 1st Sess., No. 27, pp. 4–5; E. Knowlton to W. P. Fessenden, May 20, 1865, in William P. Fessenden Papers, Library of Congress.

under the graduation law, Howard and his subordinates frequently equated homesteading with purchase.

In accord with Howard's philosophy of self-help, assistant commissioners encouraged those with sufficient financial resources to rent or purchase land. They advised others to contract their labor and save their earnings until they could purchase and successfully cultivate their own land. Whenever rumors of land distribution by the government arose, bureau agents did everything in their power to dispel these rumors and convince the freedmen that the government had no land to give them and would not take land from their former masters.

On the day that Congress created the Freedmen's Bureau it also chartered the Freedmen's Savings and Trust Company. The Freedmen's Bank, as it soon became known, was not under the actual jurisdiction of the bureau, but the two institutions were closely associated and tended to function together. Howard encouraged the freedmen to learn the value of thrift and savings, while the bank offered them the facilities to save their money and earn a dividend of 5 percent per annum.

Freedmen availed themselves of the services of the bank, for within a year of its creation it had expanded to nineteen branch offices in which freedmen deposited over $600,000. The *Nation* reported in April, 1866, that freedmen had withdrawn $96,000, which they invested in land and homesteads. By July 1, 1866, depositors had withdrawn over $380,000. One European observer reported that by 1868 over two hundred blacks had purchased buildings in Macon, Georgia. He reported also that freedmen had deposited over $1.5 million in the Freedmen's Savings Bank. With a portion of these funds they purchased homes. In 1868, 180 blacks bought places around Augusta; 220 built houses in Atlanta; "at Columbia, where one black mechanic has already amassed a fortune of $50,000, forty heads of families purchased city property for homes, at from $500 to $1,200 each, within six months." Bureau agents reported that freedmen were generally depositing their savings. Assistant Commissioner Sprague reported that in Florida alone, from October, 1867, to October, 1868, freedmen deposited $251,383.41.[2]

One method whereby the Freedmen's Bank assisted freedmen was through its loan and real estate department. During a six month period from May 6 to November 1, 1870, this department made loans totaling $423,630.77. Ninety percent of the loans ranged from one hundred to four hundred dollars and were secured by a mortgage on the property purchased. The incidence of default on these loans was less than 10 percent.[3]

Many freedmen who opened accounts had already acquired property. During the period from February 20, 1871, to May 2, 1874, freedmen opened 1,170 accounts in the Shreveport, Louisiana, branch of the Freedmen's Bank. Of these depositors, 201 indicated that they were farming, 113 farmed land for someone else, and 88 owned their own farms. The records indicate that several who were farming for others in 1872 were not only working their own land by 1874, but had hired others to work for them.[4]

Reports from bureau agents gave the general impression that almost all funds withdrawn from the Freedmen's Bank were invested in lands. However, George Williams, in 1880, indicated that 70 percent of the funds withdrawn prior to July 1, 1870, were invested in real estate.[5]

2. *Nation,* II (March 15, 1866), 325; II (April 5, 1866), 420; III (September 27, 1866), 243; David Macrae, *The Americans at Home: Pen and Ink Sketches of American Men, Manners, and Institutions* (Edinburgh, Edmonston, and Douglas, 1870), II, 55.

3. Records of the Freedmen's Savings and Trust Company, Loan and Real Estate Ledgers, in Record Group 101, National Archives.

4. Registers of Signatures of Depositors in Branches of the Freedmen's Savings and Trust Company, 1865–1874, in Record Group 101, National Archives, Microcopy 818, Roll 12, New Orleans Branch; Roll 16, Shreveport Branch.

5. George W. Williams, *History of the Negro Race in America from 1619 to 1880* (New York: G. P. Putnam's Sons, 1883), II, 408.

Unfortunately, not all transactions of the Freedmen's Bank were in the best interest of the freedmen. One account in particular appeared to be of questionable legality. Tucked away behind the leather jacket of the loan and real estate ledger, was a letter dated April 19, 1875, from the commissioners assigned to manage the affairs of the bank after its collapse, to R. M. Pomeroy, the president of the central branch of the Union Pacific Railroad. The letter indicates that the railroad company had received in 1871 an interest-free loan of $150,000.00. By April 19, 1875, Pomeroy had repaid $124,456.84, "leaving a balance of $50,543.16." In other words, during the time in question, the bank did not collect any interest on the loan, yet had to pay depositors 5 percent or approximately $7,500.00 per year. It is impossible to determine how many other loans of this nature were granted by the bank. On the other hand, although the transactions of the bank during its last two years of existence were questionable, if not dishonest, the bank was operated on a sound financial basis at least until 1870. By July 1, 1870, freedmen had deposited $16,960,336.00, of which slightly over $2 million remained on deposit. If one accepts Williams' claim that approximately 70 percent of the money withdrawn was invested in real estate, it appears that freedmen expended at least $9,800,000.00 for land from their savings during the time that the bureau actively supervised the labor system of the South. Two years later the Freedmen's Bank reported that Negro laborers in the southern states had deposited $31,260,499.00. When the bank collapsed in the wake of the Panic of 1873, it had deposits totaling $3,299,201.00. Ignoring all deposits made after 1872, it is evident that freedmen withdrew at least $28 million. If they continued their alleged practice of investing 70 percent in real estate, then one can assume that approximately $19,600,000.00 was used to secure homes. Much of this represented town property for which freedmen paid from $150.00 to

$1,200.00 per lot, but there can be no doubt that many freed-men purchased farms with the money they saved.[6]

When the bureau commenced its activities, many southern landowners lacked the resources to hire the freedmen. Although the planters could not utilize all their land, they were often unwilling to sell or rent to the freedmen. Concerned that the unemployed freedmen would become a burden to the government, Howard encouraged northerners to either purchase or lease farms in the South in order to provide work for the freedmen. He encouraged bureau agents to invest their own funds in leasing farms for the benefit of freedmen and to cooperate with northern men seeking such investments. He suggested that farms be subdivided and homes built for the freedmen who would contract to work for wages and rations. In this way he hoped to prove that free labor would succeed. Unfortunately, such activities left the bureau open to charges of conflict of interest.[7]

When Congress debated whether to extend the life of the bureau in April of 1866, President Johnson, who had already vetoed one bureau extension bill, decided to appeal to the public. In order to sway public opinion away from the bureau, he sent Generals Steedman and Fullerton on an inspection tour of the South. Rather than attack the bureau itself, Steedman and Fullerton charged corruption on the part of some bureau

6. William S. McFeely, *Yankee Stepfather: General O. O. Howard and the Freedmen* (New Haven: Yale University Press, 1968), 322–27; John A. Carpenter, *Sword and Olive Branch* (Pittsburgh: University of Pittsburgh Press, 1964), 188–91; Walter L. Fleming, *The Freedmen's Savings Bank* (Chapel Hill: University of North Carolina Press, 1927); Williams, *History of the Negro Race in America*, II, 408; Harriet Elizabeth (Beecher) Stowe, *Palmetto-Leaves* (Boston: J. R. Osgood and Company, 1873), 316; J. Alvord to O. O. Howard, January 1, 1866, Registers and Letters Received (BRFAL), in RG 105, NA, Microcopy 752, Roll 74, p. 297; J. T. Sprague to O. O. Howard, October 1, 1868, Roll 57, p. 987; J. Langston to O. O. Howard, September 17, 1870, Roll 70, p. 647; J. Cook to O. O. Howard, October 10, 1871, Roll 72, p. 593.

7. O. Brown to O. O. Howard, July 28, 1865, Registers and Letters Received (BRFAL) in RG 105, NA, Microcopy 752, Roll 13, p. 864; S. Thomas to O. O. Howard,

agents. Their strongest attacks were leveled against Eliphalet Whittlesey, the assistant commissioner in North Carolina, who had invested in a farm to provide labor for the freedmen. Although Whittlesey was later acquitted of all charges brought against him in general court-martial, the Steedman-Fullerton report succeeded in creating the impression that bureau agents who leased plantations were operating with a conflict of interest.[8] These attacks caused Howard to withdraw his earlier recommendations and to become more cautious in projects that might draw criticism.

Howard continued to encourage private assistance to blacks but exercised more caution in making his recommendations. When a citizen of South Carolina offered to sell the government a 2,000-acre farm at three dollars per acre, Howard cautioned General Scott, the assistant commissioner for South Carolina, not to purchase the land for the government. He suggested, however, that Scott attempt to find a purchaser or a joint stock company which could purchase the land and either rent or sell small farms to the freedmen.[9]

One unionist offered to purchase a large tract of land in Florida which he would subdivide and sell to freedmen in lots of from twenty-five to one hundred acres. He estimated that he could provide land for approximately fifty families, most of whom would need no assistance. However, approximately 80 persons would require rations. He suggested that the bureau supply the rations, which the freedmen would pay for out of the

---

September 21, 1865, Roll 22, p. 52; O. O. Howard to all assistant commissioners, Selected Series of Records (BRFAL), in RG 105, NA, Microcopy 742, Roll 2, p. 59; S. Barns to O. Brown, May 28, 1866, Registers and Letters Received (BRFAL), in RG 105, NA, Microcopy 752, Roll 30, p. 792; *Senate Executive Documents*, 39th Cong., 1st Sess., No. 6, p. 54.

8. McFeely, *Yankee Stepfather*, 247–58; Carpenter, *Sword and Olive Branch*, 118–20.

9. O. O. Howard to R. K. Scott, February 19, 1867, Selected Series of Records (BRFAL), in RG 105, NA, Microcopy 742, Roll 3, p. 90.

proceeds of their first crop. Howard responded that there was no practical way of supplying government aid to such a scheme without incurring the charge of corruption and speculation. Therefore, although he favored the project, Howard did not authorize the advance of rations to these settlers. He recommended that the price of the land should include the cost of supplies needed to produce the first crop. Then the freedmen would repay the land and supplies in monthly installments. In this way the government need not be involved and the freedmen would have provisions. Howard expressed his own philosophy by pointing out that "If two thousand capitalists would do this, they would thoroughly reconstruct the South and wrest that whole country from the hands of the rebel land aristocrats."[10]

The bounties paid to Negro soldiers enabled many to secure land. Bounties paid to black soldiers were either one hundred or three hundred dollars, depending upon the veteran's date of enlistment. In addition to the bounty payments many blacks who had been free prior to April 19, 1861, received back pay of six dollars per month—"the difference between the monthly pay actually received by them prior to the 1st of January 1864, and the monthly pay allowed during that period to white officers." In order to facilitate payment to these veterans, Howard in 1866 established a claims division in the bureau to protect these ex-soldiers from fraud. Then in 1867, Congress assigned the bureau full responsibility for paying all bounty claims. The law specified that the Treasury Department pay the bounty money to Howard, who would then pay the rightful claimant in cash. Howard utilized the facilities of the Freedmen's Savings Bank to pay the bounties. The New Orleans *Tribune* reported that in a seven day period in February of 1869 the New Orleans branch alone paid bounties amounting to $27,000. Howard estimated that the

10. J. O. Matthews to H. Wilson, June 29, 1868, Registers and Letters Received (BRFAL) in RG 105, NA, Microcopy 752, Roll 61, pp. 500–508; E. Whittlesey for O. O. Howard to H. Wilson, July 14, 1868, Selected Series of Records (BRFAL) in RG 105, NA, Microcopy 742, Roll 4, p. 293.

bureau processed claims for over $8 million, of which only $39,000 represented fraudulent claims.[11]

The bureau received numerous requests from groups of black soldiers proposing to use their bounty claims to purchase entire plantations which they wanted to divide among themselves. One such proposal was made by a group of 260 soldiers in Mississippi who wished to purchase the 10,690-acre A. K. Farrar farm, which the owner offered to sell at ten dollars an acre. The freedmen formed a joint stock company, Jacobs, Williams, Wood and Company, for the express purpose of collecting subscriptions to purchase the farm. They elected George Hichen to serve as secretary and treasurer, as well as to advise them and manage their affairs. Hichen wrote to Howard and Senator Charles Sumner, requesting that Congress assure payment to Farrar from the bounties of the men who subscribed for his land. With such assurance Farrar would give the freedmen possession of the land and execute a bond to issue deeds to the lots purchased in this manner. Howard approved the plan and instructed the Treasury Department to retain the bounties. He proposed to process all the bounties together and then send a special agent with the money to assist Hichen in completing the contract with Farrar.[12]

In the meantime, however, General F. D. Sewall, Howard's special inspector, arrived in Mississippi and learned of the proposal. He investigated the case and reported that Hichen was irresponsible and that his reputation among the best friends of the freedmen in Natchez was bad. He informed Howard that

11. New Orleans *Tribune*, October 20, 1866; July 21, 1867, February 19, 1869; Oliver O. Howard, *Autobiography of Oliver Otis Howard* (New York: The Baker and Taylor Comapny, 1907), 452; George R. Bentley, *A History of the Freedmen's Bureau* (Philadelphia: University of Pennsylvania Press, 1955), 87, 201–202.

12. G. Hichen to O. O. Howard, January 4, 1868, Registers and Letters Received (BRFAL) in RG 105, NA, Microcopy 752, Roll 53, pp. 409–419; C. Sumner to O. O. Howard, January 22, 1868, p. 422; O. O. Howard to G. Hichen, January 21, 1868, Roll 55, p. 211; G. Hichen to C. Sumner, p. 211. Hichen identifies himself as black but Sewall refers to him as a white man whose reputation with the friends of the freedmen in Mississippi was poor.

Hichen "should not be entrusted with the management or connected with a scheme so important to the colored men, who are likely to be deceived and imposed upon."[13] His investigation revealed that G. D. Allen, a white man, claimed verbal authority to receive the subscriptions either in cash or bounties and transfer them to Hichen, who was directed to deposit the cash to the credit of Jacobs, Williams, Wood and Company, and to keep a record of the subscription. Since the directors did not know how much had been paid in subscriptions except what Hichen told them, Sewall inspected the bank records and learned that $448 had been deposited and $50 withdrawn. When questioned, Hichen replied that he had withdrawn the funds to pay expenses. However, neither the depositors nor the subscribers had authorized such withdrawals.

Sewall also questioned the directors of the company and discovered that they really did not know what they were purchasing and how much it would cost them. They had formulated no plan for the division of land among the shareholders, nor had they considered how they were to subsist until their crop was harvested. Sewall concluded that the entire plan was impractical since the freedmen would exhaust their finances in purchasing the land and would therefore be unable to support themselves. Moreover, Farrar wanted to sell the entire plantation at ten dollars an acre; yet, there were other landowners who offered to sell in lots of one to fifty acres to individuals at prices of five to ten dollars an acre.

Nevertheless, some of the freedmen who paid their subscription to G. D. Allen moved to the farm and commenced planting. When Farrar questioned them they informed him that they had bought the land and had their subscriptions to prove it. The bureau agent in Natchez investigated the matter to protect the freedmen from fraud.[14]

Farrar, who appears to have been sincere, suggested a plan

13. F. D. Sewall to O. O. Howard, January 29, 1868, *ibid.*, Roll 55, p. 189.
14. *Ibid.*, 189, 198–99.

whereby he, the freedmen, and the government could be protected from fraud. He proposed the assignment of a bureau
agent to become the legal proprietor of the land, farming implements, stock, and supplies for one year. The bureau would
assign a civilian manager to supervise the plantation until the
government was repaid. Immediately upon payment of his debts
each freedman would receive title to his land.[15] Howard was
advised that the plan proposed by Farrar was excellent but that
Hichen and Allen were untrustworthy. If the plan was basically
acceptable, it should be entirely under the control of the
bureau. Furthermore, no freedman should be allowed to subscribe with insufficient resources to support himself. Already
conscious of charges of corruption and conflict of interest against
the bureau and its agents, Howard cautiously charted a new
course for aiding the freedmen in securing land. Based on his
agents' recommendations of the Farrar proposal, Howard withdrew his earlier instructions to the Treasury Department to withhold all such bounties until they could be processed together
and exchanged for land. Instead he instructed bureau agents
to encourage the freedmen to use their bounty money as subsistence while homesteading the public lands in Mississippi.[16]

Land ownership came slowly to the freedmen in the first years
of freedom but there were many blacks who did acquire land
through the help of the bureau and its agents. John W. Alvord,
on an inspection tour of South Carolina in 1865, reported to
Howard that blacks had secured many small farms and that
where the fields were large they had joined together into joint
stock companies in order to derive the greatest benefit from the
land. One plantation near Georgetown, South Carolina, was operated by 160 families in this manner.

15. A. K. Farrar to J. Biddel, February 10, 1868, *ibid.*, Roll 54, pp. 264–66; February
19, 1868, pp. 270–74.

16. Biddel endorsement on A. K. Farrar letter, February 27, 1868, Registers and
Letters Received (BRFAL) in RG 105, NA, Microcopy 752, Roll 54, pp. 261–63; G.
Hichen to C. Sumner, January 31, 1868, Roll 55, pp. 215–16; C. Sumner to O. O.
Howard, January 30, 1868, pp. 174–79.

About three hundred black families on the island of St. Helena purchased small farms of ten to fifteen acres at the tax sale in 1864 and built homes. They planted on their own that year and from all appearances were independent after the harvest. One freedman, Henry McMillen, a full black who could neither read nor write, purchased and subsequently paid for 315 acres. He proudly showed Alvord the cotton gin and ginhouse which he erected. He had also acquired twelve cows, four horses, twenty pigs, and a flock of chickens. He employed twenty freedmen and provided their families with comfortable quarters on the farm. That year they had planted sixty acres of sea island cotton, fifty-two acres of corn, as well as crops of sweet potatoes and melons. Alvord concluded his report by stating that an additional seven hundred families along the coast of South Carolina had purchased homes.[17]

Davis Bend in Mississippi provided another example of successful black proprietorship initiated by the bureau. In 1865, Benjamin Montgomery, a former slave of Joseph Davis, farmed rent-free land provided by the bureau at Davis Bend. He also managed a store on the plantation from which he netted a profit of $2,500.00. After the restoration of the property to its former owner, Montgomery leased two plantations from Davis. He advertised in the Vicksburg *Times* that he wished to plant a colony of freedmen and invited blacks to join him under certain rules as tenants. General Wood, the assistant commissioner of the bureau in Mississippi, approved the project and promised full protection to Montgomery and his colonists. By 1874, Montgomery had purchased the land from Davis and paid an annual property tax of $2,447.09. Montgomery and his heirs eventually sold some of the property to the colonists. However, because of the annual flooding of the Mississippi the Davis Bend colonists moved to Bolivar County, where they created the all-Negro com-

17. J. Alvord to O. O. Howard, September 1, 1865, Registers and Letters Received (BRFAL), in RG 105, NA, Microcopy 752, Roll 74, p. 102.

munity of Mound Bayou, Mississippi.[18] From the Davis Bend experiment, therefore, came an independent Negro community which is still in existence.

One unionist, Henry Warren, participated in the reconstruction of Mississippi and assisted freedmen in a variety of ways. In 1866, he and his brothers purchased a 1,280-acre plantation. As soon as the freedmen who worked the plantation could afford it, they purchased mules and implements and then contracted with the Warrens to purchase from forty to eighty acres of uncleared land. By 1875 practically the entire plantation was either owned by freedmen or under contract to sell to freedmen. Warren indicated that the freedmen were industrious and efficient. He pointed out that by 1874 over three hundred freedmen in Yazoo County, Mississippi, owned real estate valued at not less than $1.5 million. This property varied from town lots to cotton plantations of over two thousand acres.[19] Freedmen in other states also prospered.

During his inspection tour in 1870, John Alvord, the bureau inspector of schools, cited numerous examples of freedmen who had purchased land and were prospering. He summarized the efforts of the freedmen to secure land: "I find the following history of Freedmen's labor: The first year, they worked for subsistence; second year, they bought stock—mules, implements, etc.; third year, many rented land; and now, the fourth year, large numbers are prepared to buy."[20] In one day Alvord observed seventeen freedmen withdraw their money from the Charleston branch of the Freedmen's Bank to pay for land they

18. Report of Board of Investigation on Davis Bend to S. Thomas, November 24, 1865, *ibid.*, Roll 20, p. 52; Vernon Lane Wharton, *The Negro in Mississippi, 1865–1890* (New York: Harper Torchbooks, 1965), 42; Hinds County (Miss.) *Gazette*, citing the Vicksburg *Times*, November 23, 1866, January 22, 1874, in Vernon Lane Wharton Collection, Box 8, University of Southwestern Louisiana Archives.

19. Notes for *The Negro in Mississippi*, in Vernon Lane Wharton Collection, University of Southwestern Louisiana Archives, Box 9.

20. John W. Alvord, *Letters from the South Relating to the Condition of the Freedmen* (Washington: Howard University Press, 1870), 19.

were buying, generally forty to fifty acres at about ten dollars per acre. One group of ten men purchased a seven-hundred-acre plantation, which they paid for out of the proceeds of their crop for the previous year. Several freedmen in Houston County, Georgia, purchased one hundred to six hundred acres each.[21] By 1870 most southern landowners recognized the value of Negro labor and any program to keep them in the South rather than drive them out. Blacks were affected by this changed attitude toward the value of the labor, particularly in the diminishing white opposition to Negro land ownership. This attitudinal change, however, in no way indicated an increased interest in the economic plight of the freedmen.

Fully convinced that freedmen would not be truly free unless they were secure from the demands of landlords, whether on farms or in city tenements, Howard decided that the bureau must set the example and prove that freedmen not only wanted lands and homes but were capable of paying for them. With this in mind, in April, 1867, he established a trust fund capitalized at $52,000, to be used to purchase land for resale as homesites to freedmen. The money thus invested was derived from the rentals collected from abandoned and confiscated property. Since whites were opposed to Negro land ownership in the nation's capital, John R. Elvans, a local merchant and trustee of the fund, was selected to purchase the land, thereby disguising the eventual ownership by freedmen. He purchased the Barry farm, a tract of land on the outskirts of Washington containing approximately 375 acres. The bureau surveyed the land and, after marking off the streets, subdivided it into 359 lots of one acre each. The lots were then offered for sale at prices ranging from $125 to $300, depending on the location. The average price for a lot and sufficient lumber to build a house was $225. The freedmen agreed to pay regular monthly installments of ten dollars, ap-

21. *Ibid.*, 15, 19, 24; J. W. Alvord to O. O. Howard, January 15, 1870, Registers and Letters Received (BRFAL), in RG 105, NA, Microcopy 752, Roll 67, p. 50.

proximately the same amount they paid for rent in the crowded tenements of Washington. At the end of two years most of the freedmen completed their payments and were given titles in fee simple for the land thus purchased. In order to protect the bureau and the trust fund's investment, the contract of sale stipulated that failure to pay as agreed would result in repossession of the property.

The avidity with which the freedmen purchased the lots and their fidelity to their contracts demonstrated the extent of their desire for homes. By October, 1868, Charles Howard reported that of the three hundred lots sold to freedmen only forty had reverted to the bureau. He pointed out that lumber had been issued for 185 houses and that the supply was exhausted. In March, 1869, he requested lumber for 107 houses, at a cost of $75.58 per house. Lots had been sold with the promise of this amount of rough lumber. When the project ended almost three hundred freedmen owned one-acre lots with houses.[22]

The bureau also initiated other projects similar to the Barry farm. In Americus, Georgia, freedmen purchased one hundred houses and lots, paying for them from wages ranging from $159 to $175 per year. Near Augusta, Georgia, blacks, with the assistance of the bureau, established a settlement of about one hundred families. The freedmen purchased small lots with houses ranging in value from one hundred to five hundred dollars, which they paid for in monthly installments.[23]

Howard used his position as commissioner of the bureau to urge northern liberals to invest in land for resale to freedmen. He accepted the position as treasurer of "The National Land Agency for Providing Homesteads and Normal Training for

22. Howard, *Autobiography*, 419–20; C. H. Howard to O. O. Howard, October 10, 1868, Registers and Letters Received (BRFAL), in RG 105, NA, Microcopy 752, Roll 74, p. 727; October 27, Roll 57, p. 724; D. Swaine to O. O. Howard, November 10, 1868, Roll 57, p. 753; L. E. Sleigh to C. H. Howard, Roll 62, pp. 897–98.

23. J. Alvord to O. O. Howard, Registers and Letters Received (BRFAL) in RG 105, NA, Microcopy 752, Roll 67, p. 50.

Freedmen," but informed its founder Yardley Warner, a Pennsylvania Quaker, that his duties would prevent his active participation. Since Howard was an officer, however, contributors were assured of the honesty of the association. The association successfully established small colonies of freedmen at Greensboro, Hillsboro, Salisbury, and Chapel Hill, North Carolina. However, when Warner solicited subscribers to purchase land in Virginia in 1869, he experienced difficulty. He reported that the interest of prospective investors in real estate for freedmen was waning and that he was compelled to depend entirely on "some few earnest souls that stick to principles and have their eyes on the landmarks of the great transition which we have lived to witness."[24]

Black abolitionist Frederick Douglass also proposed a plan for reconstructing the nation by helping the freedmen to acquire land. He wanted to establish a national land and labor company, capitalized at one million dollars, to buy land for resale on easy terms to blacks. Like Yardley Warner, Douglass also experienced disappointment, since few of the industrialists and philanthropists who supported the Radical Republicans were willing to establish the freedmen as small landowners. They considered such a move unwise since it would make the blacks potential allies of western agrarian and democratic interests.[25]

Charles Stearns, a northerner who moved to the South during Reconstruction, also reported a lack of interest on the part of northerners in the economic welfare of the former slaves. His observations in the South had convinced him that the most pressing need of the freedmen was land. He pointed out that

24. Y. Warner to O. O. Howard, September 24, 1869, Registers and Letters Received (BRFAL), in RG 105, NA, Roll 66, p. 667; R. Townsend to O. O. Howard, June 10, 1869, Roll 64, pp. 119–22; Y. Warner to O. O. Howard, September 5, 1869, Roll 66, p. 635; S. McKensie to O. O. Howard, September 10, 1869, Roll 65, pp. 903, 905, 912, 914; Y. Warner to O. O. Howard, September 16, 1869, pp. 669–71; Y. Warner to O. O. Howard, September 29, 1869, Roll 66, p. 674.

25. Benjamin Quarles, *Frederick Douglass* (New York: Atheneum, 1970), 243.

without the bureau to protect them the freedmen would be left to the mercy of their former masters. In 1869, Stearns visited the North in order to solicit aid in securing homes for the freed-men. He managed to obtain sufficient funds to provide land for twenty families, but since they lacked the means to cultivate the land, they experienced difficulty retaining it. Stearns concluded that "the great northern public was not sufficiently awake on this subject. While many admit that the colored man should have land, very few are willing to aid him in obtaining it; and still fewer, in furnishing means for its cultivation."[26]

John Edmonds, a northern writer, in 1867 summarized the prevailing attitude among northern whites toward southern Negroes. "Their emancipation is already fully secured, and that by the strongest obligations known to our institutions. Their present relief and protection are already provided for through the Freedmen's Bureau and the military governments. Their ultimate enjoyment of the right of suffrage already devised, will afford them the same means of self-protection that we enjoy." In other words, everything that can be done for the ex-slave has been done; now he must succeed or fail through his own ef-forts.[27]

By 1870, therefore, it appears that northern concern for the plight of the landless freedmen had diminished. Mrs. Henry Ward Beecher provides an excellent example of the changing attitude of the self-styled friends of the freedmen. In a series of letters she suggested that northerners come to Florida to take advantage of the opportunities afforded in that frontier state. She recommended that northern philanthropists set aside one hundred dollars a year to send deserving poor white families from the North to Florida. With one hundred dollars a family

26. Charles Stearns, *The Black Man of the South, and the Rebels: or, The Charac-teristics of the Former and the Recent Outrages of the Latter* (New York: American News Company, 1872), 515.

27. John Edmonds, *Reconstruction of the Union* (New York: American News Com-pany, 1867), 77.

could secure a homestead on the public lands and provide for themselves until they harvested their first crop.[28] Apparently, the conviction that land made a man free persisted, but northerners henceforth would provide aid to northern whites rather than to southern blacks.

In spite of this loss of interest, the freedmen continued their efforts to secure land. Black delegates to the 1867–1868 constitutional conventions in several southern states attempted to institute land reforms which would provide land for the freedmen and protect them in their possession. In Louisiana, two blacks from Caddo Parish, Ingraham and Antoine, proposed to protect landowners from forfeiture of land for non-payment of debt. Their article stipulated that "every homestead of eighty acres of land and the dwelling houses thereon, and the appurtenances to be selected by the owner thereof... not exceeding in value one thousand dollars, shall be exempt from forced sale on execution or any other final process from a court for any debt contracted after the adoption of this constitution."[29] As mentioned above, black delegates to the Louisiana convention attempted, though with only partial success, to break up the great plantations.

In South Carolina, 76 of the 124 delegates to the constitutional convention of 1868 were Negroes. Richard Cain, the leading black spokesman for land reform, called for a resolution petitioning Congress for a loan of one million dollars from the Freedmen's Bureau fund to purchase land. Proponents of Cain's resolution pointed out that if the bureau had spent most of its funds to purchase lands for the poor, rather than expending it on salaries and temporary relief, some permanent relief might have

28. Eunice White (Bullard) Beecher, *Letters from Florida* (New York: D. Appleton and Company, 1879), 15.

29. New Orleans *Republican*, December 22, 1867, *Official Journal of the Proceedings of the Convention for Framing a Constitution for the State of Louisiana, 1867–1868* (New Orleans: N.p., 1868), November 30, 1867. For an analysis of the role played by blacks in the Louisiana Constitutional Convention of 1867–1868 and in the legislature, see Charles Vincent, *Black Legislators in Louisiana During Reconstruction* (Baton Rouge: Louisiana State University Press, 1976).

been assured. The convention adopted Cain's resolution by a vote of 101 to 5. Of the five dissenting votes three were cast by blacks: Robert Smalls, Stephen A. Swails, and William J. Whipper. Smalls was a native of South Carolina and a former slave who had become a hero during the Civil War by escaping to federal lines in the Confederate steamer *Planter*. Swails and Whipper were ex-soldiers who were employed by the Freedmen's Bureau in South Carolina. They opposed the resolution because they feared that Congress would simply ignore it. They realized, furthermore, that although Congress might ignore the resolution it would raise "the hopes of the entire poor people of the country, and the freedmen would leave their contracts, run to land offices where three quarters will go away with shattered hopes."[30]

Since neither Congress nor the bureau was willing to commit one million dollars to purchase land in South Carolina, the convention delegates directed the South Carolina general assembly to provide for a board of land commissioners to purchase land for resale to freedmen. After a delay of one year, on March 27, 1869, the legislature established an advisory board, composed of the five most important state officials, who would appoint a land commissioner. The act specified that the land commissioner would purchase plantations to be subdivided into lots of not less than twenty-five or more than one hundred acres. During the first three years the settlers would pay all taxes on their land plus 6 percent interest on the value of their land. After three years, those settlers who could prove continuous residence and provide evidence that they were cultivating the land, would receive certificates of purchase. They then had eight years to pay out the principal and 6 percent interest.[31]

30. Carol Bleser, *The Promised Land: The History of the South Carolina Land Commission, 1869–1890* (Columbia: University of South Carolina Press, 1969), 19–22. For a thorough coverage of the South Carolina Land Commission this source must be consulted. Alrutheus A. Taylor, *The Negro in South Carolina During Reconstruction* (Washington: Association for the Study of Negro Life and History, 1924), 134.

31. Bleser, *The Promised Land*, 28.

During the first year of operation the legislature appropriated $200,000 for the purchase of large estates. The land commission divided the estates and sold approximately forty thousand acres. The following year the legislature appropriated an additional $500,000. Unfortunately, South Carolina governor Robert Scott, a leading member of the land commission, together with several others, purchased worthless land which they sold to the land commission at exorbitant rates, thereby defeating the intent of the legislature and defrauding the state of over $200,000. Prior to becoming governor Scott had served as bureau assistant commissioner for South Carolina. After his election he offered to serve as assistant commissioner without pay. One of his subordinates informed Howard that while Scott was assistant commissioner he had defrauded the government of over $100,000. He also charged that Scott's offer to serve without pay was prompted by his need to prevent an investigation into his affairs. [32]

In spite of the fraud involved in most of the land commission's activities prior to 1870, the state acquired title to some 112,404.6 acres by 1872. By February, 1871, some 1,992 small farms had been created out of 97 plantations. Fortunately for the blacks of South Carolina, Francis L. Cordozo, the only black member and the only honest member of the land commission, assumed control of the commission in March, 1872. By the fall of 1872 Cordozo increased the number of families settled on commission lands to 5,008. These farms ranged in size from seven and one-half acres to one hundred acres. The determination of South Carolina blacks to retain their land against all odds is amply demonstrated by the land commission records. As late as 1890 blacks retained posses-

32. *Ibid.*, 28–29, 54–56; Taylor, *The Negro in South Carolina*, 54, 164–65. All accusations by Scott's subordinate were signed "a Union Soldier." Information on this case may be found in Registers and Letters Received (BRFAL) in RG 105, NA, Microcopy 752, Roll 61, pp. 668–783. For an analysis of Scott's character see Martin Abbott, *The Freedmen's Bureau in South Carolina, 1865–1872* (Chapel Hill: University of North Carolina Press, 1967), and Bleser, *The Promised Land*.

sion of 44,579 acres of land purchased from the land commission. Therefore, despite the graft and corruption involved in the activities of members of the land commission, some blacks benefited from the only attempt by any southern state to apply the principles of the homestead laws to lands purchased by the state.[33]

Fortunately, not all who came South to work with the freedmen participated in the graft and corruption which swept the nation. One of Howard's associates, George Whipple, representing the American Missionary Association, purchased 175 acres on the Hampton River. In 1872 Whipple and the association transferred 121 acres, together with buildings which had been paid for by the Freedmen's Bureau, to Hampton Institute. Between 1867, when he first acquired the property, and 1872, when he transferred ownership, Whipple sold forty-four lots to freedmen.[34]

The friends of the freedmen, such as the Freedmen's Aid Associations, the American Missionary Association, and the Freedmen's Bureau, realized that any effort to help the freedmen must be in accord with the economic concepts of the time. The Freedmen's Aid Association of New Orleans offered premiums to freedmen "to promote labor, reward industry and good order, and thus prove to the world they are as good tillers of the land, law-abiding citizens, and worthy of the title of American Citizens, as they have proved themselves good soldiers on many hard battlefields."[35] The bureau encouraged thrift and hard work and actively assisted freedmen in settling land under the Southern Homestead Act. The American Missionary Association and other religious groups strove to educate the freedmen in order that they would be able to protect their investments. These actions helped lay the foundations upon which the freedmen themselves could build.

33. Bleser, *The Promised Land*, 83, 90, 157–59.
34. Edward H. Bonekemper, "Negro Ownership of Real Property," *Journal of Negro History*, LV (July, 1970), 176–77.
35. New Orleans *Tribune*, al issues from June 13, 1865, to December 31, 1865.

Although it is difficult to determine with exactness the amount of land purchased by freedmen during the latter part of the nineteenth century, Georgia provides a model. Georgia was the only southern state which separated its tax list between blacks and whites and therefore provides the only continuing statistics of Negro land ownership between 1865 and 1900. In 1866, blacks in Georgia owned approximately ten thousand acres of land, valued at $22,500. By 1876, they had increased the amount to 457,635 acres having a tax value of $1,234,104. Over the next ten years they doubled the amount of land in their possession and owned 802,939 acres with an assessed value of $2,508,198. By 1900, 9,547 black farmers in Georgia owned all the land they farmed and an additional 1,828 owned a portion of the land they farmed. The average holding of these 11,375 farmers was 27 acres owned and 23 additional acres rented. The improved land of the 9,547 who farmed only land which they owned was valued at $3,571,540 and the buildings thereon were valued at $1,173,990.[36]

The census figures for 1900 indicate that black farm owners in Georgia represented only 13.7 percent of the black farmers in the state. This is the lowest percent of black farm ownership in any of the southern states. Therefore, one can assume that the record for securing land in the other southern states either paralleled or surpassed that of Georgia. In fact, throughout the entire South in 1900, 25.2 percent of the black farmers owned their own farms. The corresponding figure for white farm owners is 62.9 percent.[37] When one considers that there were relatively few black land owners in 1865, this represents a considerable increase in thirty-five years of freedom.

36. Booker T. Washington, *The Story of the Negro: The Rise of the Race from Slavery* (New York: Doubleday, Page, and Company, 1909), II, 40–41; *Twelfth Census of the United States: 1900*, Vol. V., Agriculture, Pt. I, p. lxxxiv, Table LXXXIII, 174–83, Table 14.

37. Department of Commerce and Labor, Bureau of the Census, *Negroes in the United States, Bulletin 8* (Washington: Government Printing Office, 1904), 81.

Table 2
COMPARISON BY RACE OF FARM OPERATORS IN SEVEN SELECTED STATES OF THE DEEP SOUTH, 1900*

	Percentage of Farms operated by whites			Percentage of Farms operated by blacks		
	Owner	Manager	Tenant	Owner	Manager	Tenant
Alabama	61.5	0.9	37.9	15.0	0.1	84.9
Arkansas	64.4	0.6	35.0	25.4	0.2	74.4
Georgia	54.4	1.0	44.6	13.7	0.3	86.0
Louisiana	66.2	1.7	32.1	16.2	0.1	83.7
Mississippi	66.2	0.9	32.9	16.3	0.1	83.6
S. Carolina	57.9	1.2	40.9	22.2	0.2	77.6
Texas	53.8	0.9	45.3	30.8	0.1	69.1
Seven states	58.9	0.9	40.2	19.1	0.1	80.8

*U.S. Department of Commerce and Labor. Bureau of the Census. *Twelfth Census of the United States, 1900:* Agriculture, Vol. V. p. cxi, Table CIX.

Table 3
FARMS OF MIXED TENURE OPERATED BY BLACKS IN 1900*

Regions	Number of farms	Acres		Average number of acres	
		owned	rented	owned	rented
South Atlantic	14,302	390,252	331,719	27.3	23.2
South Central	13,895	670,057	454,232	48.2	32.7

*The South Atlantic Region comprises the following states: Delaware, Maryland, District of Columbia, Virginia, West Virginia, North Carolina, South Carolina, Georgia, and Florida.

The South Central Region comprises the following states: Kentucky, Tennessee, Alabama, Mississippi, Louisiana, Texas, Oklahoma, Indian Territory, and Arkansas.

U.S. Department of Commerce and Labor, Bureau of the Census, *Twelfth Census of the United States, 1900:* Agriculture, Vol. V., p. lxxxiv, Table LXXXIII.

Table 4

NEGRO FARMERS WHO OWNED THEIR OWN FARMS
IN THE SOUTH, 1900

State	Number of black farm owners	Percent of total black farmers
West Virginia	534	72.0
Virginia	26,566	59.2
Florida	6,552	48.0
Kentucky	5,402	48.0
Delaware	332	40.5
North Carolina	17,520	31.2
Texas	20,139	30.7
District of Columbia	5	29.4
Tennessee	9,426	27.8
Arkansas	11,941	25.4
South Carolina	18,970	22.2
Mississippi	21,973	16.3
Louisiana	9,378	16.1
Alabama	14,110	15.0
Georgia	11,375	13.7

*U.S. Department of Commerce and Labor, Bureau of the Census, *Negroes in the United States* (Washington, D.C.: Government Printing Office, 1904), Bulletin No. 8, pp. 80–83.

IX

Conclusions

ONE OF THE MOST persistent myths in American history, that which surrounds the slogan "forty acres and a mule," remains unexplained. Some historians have argued that Congress never promised the freedmen that they would receive land, others that the origin of the slogan would probably never be known. Although this latter conclusion is probably correct, it is possible to trace the events which led freedmen to believe that they would indeed receive "forty acres and a mule."

It appears that the concept of land distribution may have originated within the abolitionist camp. Less than one month after the war began, abolitionist William Goodell demanded that Congress confiscate land belonging to rebels and redistribute it among freed slaves.[1] By enacting the first confiscation act in August, 1861, Congress provided freedom for some slaves and, at the same time, confiscated their masters' lands. The second confiscation act included a provision to colonize the slaves freed by the act. The most publicized colonization proposal involved the Chiriqui Improvement Company's grant in the district of Panama. Prospective colonists were promised forty acres and employment in the company's coal mines.

Although President Lincoln proposed the Chiriqui project

1. James M. McPherson, *Struggle for Equality: Abolitionists and the Negro in the Civil War and Reconstruction* (Princeton: Princeton University Press, 1964), 247.

and actively supported it, he did not limit his efforts to colonization as a means of providing economic security for the newly
freed slaves. In September, 1863, he reserved twenty thousand
acres of land in South Carolina which had been condemned for
non-payment of the federal direct tax. He ordered the land subdivided into twenty-acre plots and sold to freedmen at not less
than $1.25 per acre. Believing that twenty acres was insufficient,
General Saxton and abolitionist Mansfield French convinced Secretary of the Treasury Salmon P. Chase that he should permit
preemption of up to forty acres of land at the rate of $1.25 per
acre.

After Lincoln's Emancipation Proclamation became effective
January 1, 1863, rumors of confiscation and land distribution
spread throughout the South. Evidence suggests that as early as
1863 slaves in Mississippi and Alabama believed that if the South
lost they would receive their masters' lands, for when federal
soldiers raided the countryside near Jackson, Mississippi, they
told the slaves they were free. The blacks "measured off the land
with a plowline, making a fair apportionment among themselves, and also divided the cotton and farm implements."[2] Although these blacks were soon driven from the land by the
returning Confederates, the rumor that land was actually being
seized and distributed spread wherever Union troops were
victorious.

As General Sherman's soldiers marched across Georgia and
South Carolina in 1864 they told blacks that they were free and
could have the land they had made productive. General Sherman's Special Field Order No. 15, issued in January, 1865, with
the approval of Secretary of War Stanton, appeared to substantiate what the soldiers had been saying. The order created a

2. *Clark County Journal* (Alabama), June 11, 1863; Notes for *The Negro in Mississippi*, in Vernon Lane Wharton Collection, University of Southwestern Louisiana Archives, Box 9; Vernon Lane Wharton, *The Negro in Mississippi, 1865–1890* (New York:
Harper Torchbooks, 1965), 58; *Colored Tennessean*, August 12, 1865.

reservation for the exclusive use of the freedmen, with each family to receive forty acres of land. Sherman's decision to lend the freedmen horses and mules probably accounted for the inclusion of the animal in the slogan. As General Saxton settled freedmen on the Sherman Reservation, Congress created the Freedmen's Bureau and gave it control of the confiscated and abandoned lands with the stipulation that the land be leased in forty-acre tracts to the freedmen. They also were given the option to buy and receive such title as the government could convey.

The initial circulars and orders issued by the bureau convinced freedmen that they would receive land. Assistant Commissioner Clinton B. Fisk even told a Negro convention in Tennessee that "they must not only have freedom, but homes of their own, thirty or forty acres, with mules, cottages, and school houses."[3]

By October, 1865, however, President Johnson's amnesty and land restoration program convinced some bureau agents that an alternative must be provided if the freedmen were to have land. Assistant Commissioner Brown in Virginia recommended that the government set aside in Florida sufficient land to provide forty acres to each family who was willing to settle there. Brown's proposal was included in a bill, sponsored by Lyman Trumbull in December, 1865, to provide approximately three million acres for allotment to freedmen in parcels not exceeding forty acres. Each settler would be furnished a house and the necessary provisions for farming, such as mules, seed, and tools. When this bill was vetoed by President Johnson in 1866, Congress enacted the Southern Homestead Act, which provided that all remaining public lands in five southern states could be acquired only by homesteading. Until 1868, no entry could exceed forty acres of double minimum or eighty acres of minimum land.

3. Theodore Wilson, *The Black Codes of the South* (University, Ala.: University of Alabama Press, 1965), 49–53.

From the above it is rather evident that some freedmen had reason to believe that the benevolent government which had freed them would also provide forty acres and a mule. Even the attempts by the bureau to dissuade them of their false premise only reinforced their conviction that they would receive land. Moreover, after the passage of the Radical Reconstruction Act of 1867, and the subsequent constitutional conventions and reorganization of state governments in the South, rumors became more rampant throughout the South that the lands of their former masters would be divided among the former slaves. General Scott, in February, 1868, reported that the freedmen believed that the South Carolina constitutional convention would provide them with rations, land, and mules: "A report of this kind upon reaching any locality spreads like 'wild fire' among the colored people, enlarging as it goes until it almost sets them wild with excitement."[4] Assistant commissioners in Mississippi and Georgia also reported that the freedmen were convinced that the lands of their former masters would be confiscated and divided among them. A Republican mass meeting in Webster County, Georgia, in September, 1868, demanded "Division now; don't wait until Christmas; we want it now!"[5]

In Louisiana, when the constitutional convention failed to provide the freedmen with land, Republican politicians promised them that the election of Grant would ensure their forty acres and a mule. Although the majority of congressmen never really intended to give the freedmen land, the action of high-ranking military and political officials convinced freedmen that there was substance to all the land rumors they had heard. This belief, unfortunately, by creating a false hope, deprived many freedmen of the incentive to acquire land through their own efforts.

4. R. K. Scott to O. O. Howard, March 26, 1869, Registers and Letters Received (BRFAL), in RG 105, NA, Microcopy 752, Roll 55, p. 454.
5. Moulton (Alabama) *Advertiser*, September 11, 1868; Notes for *The Negro in Mississippi*, in Wharton Collection.

The reasons for the failure to establish the freedmen as land owners by 1870 are varied, yet the responsibility must be shared by Congress, the president, the military, the federal land offices, white apathy and opposition, the Freedmen's Bureau, and the freedmen themselves.

The Freedmen's Bureau resulted from wartime efforts by the Congress, the president, and military commanders to resolve the problems arising from emancipation. Congress enacted confiscation legislation primarily as a punitive measure, but discovered as a result that it also incurred the humanitarian responsibility of caring for the former slaves on confiscated plantations. President Lincoln and Congress attempted several colonization plans but quickly recognized the impracticality of colonizing four million people. Military commanders, on the other hand, were more directly concerned with the problem because fugitive slaves flocked to the military camps seeking protection and subsistence.

Any plan to provide for the ex-slaves had to be self-supporting since it was secondary to the war effort. Congress assigned to the military control of both confiscated land and slaves, thereby assuming that the blacks could provide for themselves at no cost to the government. As military costs increased, Congress assigned the land to the Treasury Department. Unfortunately, this cast the entire burden of maintaining the ex-slaves on the Freedmen's Department of the Army. The problems resulting from the transfer of land convinced congressional leaders that any institution which they created must control both land and blacks. Many congressmen, believing that the confiscated and abandoned lands should be sold, attempted to repeal the joint amendatory resolution to the Confiscation Act of 1862, which prohibited the permanent seizure of property. Only by repealing this resolution could the government acquire full title to confiscated land. The Senate refused to act on the measure,[6] thereby inducing the House to pass the Freedmen's Bureau bill

6. Edward McPherson, *The Political History of the United States of America, During the Great Rebellion* (3rd ed.; Washington: Solomans and Chapman, 1876), 202-203.

with the stipulation that the bureau could sell the land to the freedmen and issue such titles as the government could convey.

During the first six crucial months of freedom Congress was not in session. However, southern white resistance to Negro land ownership and President Johnson's restoration program convinced some congressmen that additional legislation was necessary if the freedmen were to be provided with land and protected in their possession of it. Although Thaddeus Stevens and Charles Sumner requested enforcement of confiscation legislation and confirmation of the Sherman land titles, Congress agreed only to confirm the holders of Sherman warrants in their possession for three years from the date of the special field order.[7] When President Johnson vetoed this bill, Congress failed to muster enough votes to override the veto.

By July, 1866, Congress was sufficiently united to extend the life of the Freedmen's Bureau and to pass the Southern Homestead Act. Although this legislation promised much, it failed to provide for the needs of most freedmen. At the time the freedmen were already under contract to work until the end of the year. The bill stipulated that freedmen would have the right to enter the land without competition from "disloyal" whites until January 1, 1867, yet most labor contracts did not expire until that date.[8] Consequently, the bureau's contract labor policy, although necessary for the protection of the uneducated freedmen, proved detrimental to initial homesteading efforts. In order to alleviate this situation, Congress should have extended the time for exclusive entry by freedmen and loyal whites at least one full year.

The Southern Homestead Act failed to provide freedmen with needed implements, seed, and rations. Although it had been

7. *Congressional Globe*, 39th Cong., 1st Sess., 16–17; James S. Allen, *Reconstruction: The Battle for Democracy, 1865–1876* (New York: International Publishers, 1937); Vernon Lane Wharton Collection, Box 9; New York *Times*, March 20, 1867.

8. U.S. *Statutes at Large*, XIV, 66.

their labor which had made the soil of the South productive, when they received their freedom they had nothing to show for a lifetime of toil. As free laborers, their wages provided them with little more than the necessities of life. Therefore, any plan to homestead the freedmen could succeed only with additional assistance. Since Congress made no provisions to render this assistance, most were unable to consider homesteading and many of those who did actually enter land were forced to give up the attempt in order to avoid starvation.[9] Only those who received rations from the bureau or had sufficient financial resources actually succeeded.

Apparently most congressmen were unaware of the chaotic conditions which prevailed in the federal land offices and hindered homesteading efforts. Most of the local offices were not reopened until several years after the war and those which did reopen lacked the necessary records to facilitate filing homestead entries. Although the general land office utilized all its personnel in duplicating the missing records, the task had not been completed by 1869 when the Freedmen's Bureau discontinued most of its activities. Homesteading was also hindered by the temporary absence of land officers, sometimes lasting several months, as well as the dishonesty of at least one land officer.

Another factor that Congress ignored was the quality of the land included in the Southern Homestead Act. Most of the land had been open to unrestricted purchase for at least thirty years. Therefore, the more accessible lands had already been taken and the remaining land available for homesteading was refuse land, either heavily overgrown woods, swamp, or treeless prairie. Since this land had been revalued under the graduation law to as low as 12.5 cents per acre, and therefore cost approximately the same as filing fees under the Southern Homestead Act, it would have been better to permit the freedmen to buy the land they

9. Oliver O. Howard, *Autobiography of Oliver Otis Howard* (New York: The Baker and Taylor Company, 1907), 243.

wanted, up to eighty acres, instead of forcing them to homestead for five years before they could receive their patents. Under the earlier public land laws, the land would have belonged to them free and clear as soon as they paid the cost of the land, but under the homestead law they were uncertain of their possession until five years after they filed their claims. Between 1866 and 1870 approximately 6,500 freedmen entered land; yet, probably less than 1,000 of these entrants received final certificates. This indicates that at least 5,500 families expended as much or more than they would have under the earlier laws, but still did not secure ownership of their land.[10] Therefore, what Congressman Julian intended as a land reform measure rendered the the acquisition of land by freedmen more difficult.

By mid-1867, congressional debates seldom mentioned the economic plight of the freedmen and instead played upon the theme of southern rejection of the Fourteenth Amendment to prove that the South was still recalcitrant. Also, by June, 1867, Republicans had gained control of most southern state governments and in order to retain this control concentrated on voting rights rather than on land. Hence, when Thaddeus Stevens proposed his confiscation plan, he could not muster the backing of even the Radical Republicans and introduced the bill as his own. Congress apparently was not committed to the idea that the former slaves could not be truly free until they were economically independent of their former masters.

Although Congress failed to provide adequately for the eco-

10. Paul W. Gates, *History of Public Land Law Development* (Washington: Government Printing Office, 1970), 413; *House Reports*, 40th Cong., 2nd Sess., No. 30, p. 16; Harry P. Yoshpe and Philip P. Brower (comps.), *Preliminary Inventory of the Land Entry Papers of the General Land Office: Preliminary Inventory No. 22* (Washington: National Archives, 1948), 14–15, 27, 45–46. McFeely, in *Yankee Stepfather*, 215, using Howard's estimates of 1870 erroneously concluded that 4,000 freedmen obtained patents for homestead lands. Since no final certificates could possibly have been issued prior to June 16, 1871, Howard's figures represent only attempted homesteads, not final certificates.

nomic security of the freed people, one must admit that their meager efforts were hindered by not being in session during the critical period from April to December of 1865. However, President Johnson cannot escape blame for his failure during this time. He was the one person who controlled the actual destiny of the freedmen. Had he enforced the confiscation legislation and supported the land program of the Freedmen's Bureau, the history of Negro land ownership could have been drastically changed. Instead of making land available for freedmen to purchase, he chose to ingratiate himself with southerners by restoring their property, regardless of all the promises made to the freedmen.

Johnson admitted that the government had a responsibility to the freedmen, but he did not view this responsibility as one which required establishing the freedmen on land of their own. He seemed concerned only with providing the Negroes with the opportunity to work and earn money. Then they would be able to purchase land and not be a burden on the taxpayers. He apparently felt that by restoring the land to the former owners he would assure that those who had capital could provide work for their former slaves.

When abolitionists asked the president to preserve for the freedmen all the land promised to them, he refused to act. When asked to provide transportation and subsistence to those who wished to move to the homestead lands of the West, he merely replied that since the freedmen were "wards" of the government they would be provided for. Although he signed the Southern Homestead Act, he took no positive action to ensure that all land offices were properly staffed. Through his appointive power, he actually controlled the federal land offices in the South. Furthermore he decided not to reopen several important offices until after the time for exclusive entry by freedmen and loyal whites had elapsed. According to Howard, instead of assisting freedmen to secure land, Johnson tried to remove every prominent officer who attempted to help the blacks.[11]

Rather than support the bureau when Congress attempted to extend its life in February, 1866, Johnson justified his veto of the measure by stating that an extension of the bureau would make the freedmen dependent on the government. He further pointed out that by extending the life of the bureau and appropriating funds for its operation Congress would encourage the freedmen to believe that the government would provide for them.

Johnson's selection of Generals James B. Steedman and J. Scott Fullerton as his special investigators provides evidence that, regardless of his pronouncements to the contrary, he really was not concerned about the welfare of the freedmen. He had sent Fullerton to Louisiana earlier to replace Conway, who was opposed to restoring to the planters the land which had been promised to the freedmen. As interim assistant commissioner for Louisiana in 1865, Fullerton directed the chief of police of the city of New Orleans to arrest all vagrant or idle blacks and turn them over to the provost marshal of the bureau. He directed the provost marshal to secure employment for all such vagrants or idlers. He ordered the orphanages closed and provided that Negro minors be apprenticed to white masters. Instead of retaining land for the use of the freedmen, he restored the land to its former owners. In one of his final actions as assistant commissioner he ended the collection of taxes to support Negro schools. The New Orleans *Tribune* compared Fullerton's vagrant order to the Opelousas Ordinance, one of the most infamous of the municipal black codes issued in 1865. The *Tribune* later referred to Steedman as "the public scavenger of Andrew Johnson doing all the dirty work that his master called upon him to perform."[12] Evidently the black press, at least in

11. Howard, *Autobiography*, 282.
12. New Orleans *Tribune*, October 27, 1865, April 19, 1867.

Louisiana, was convinced that neither Steedman nor Fullerton was concerned about the welfare of the freedmen. Their sole responsibilty was to discredit the bureau and thus hinder congressional action on the second bureau extension bill. This is evident from Fullerton's charge that the bureau's provost marshal in New Orleans had converted his office into a slave pen. It must be remembered that the provost marshal had merely carried out orders issued by Fullerton as assistant commissioner.[13] Since Steedman and Fullerton were Johnson's personal investigators, one can only assume that they acted in accord with his instructions. Apparently Johnson was not committed to the principle that true freedom required land ownership. Had he been so committed, he would have supported the bureau, permitted it to retain control of the abandoned and confiscated land in its possession, and would have taken positive action under the Southern Homestead Act. Congress and President Johnson attempted to follow different plans for reconstructing the South and in their efforts they ignored the idea of justice to four million freedmen.

Southern white opposition to Negro land ownership was also a decisive factor in the failure of blacks to acquire land in the first few years of freedom. Beginning as early as July 3, 1865, southern communities and, later that year, state legislatures enacted black codes which, for all intents and purposes, relegated the former slaves to a position of virtual slavery.[14] Although the

13. James E. Sefton, *The United States Army and Reconstruction, 1865–1877* (Baton Rouge: Louisiana State University Press, 1967), 26; George R. Bentley, *A History of the Freedmen's Bureau* (Philadelphia: University of Pennsylvania Press, 1955), 71; New Orleans *Tribune*, October 27, 1865; New York *Times*, August 10, 1866; *House Executive Documents*, 39th Cong., 1st Sess., No. 120, p. 68.

14. *Senate Executive Documents*, 39th Cong., 1st Sess., No. 2, pp. 92–94, 96; Hinds County (Miss.) *Gazette*, November 25, 1865; Vernon Lane Wharton Collection, Box 9; S. Thomas to O. O. Howard, October 12, 1865, Registers and Letters Received (BRFAL), in RG 105, NA, Microcopy 752, Roll 22, p. 193; G. Pillsbury to O. O. Howard, August 8, 1865, Roll 16, p. 646; R. S. Donaldson to O. O. Howard, forwarding statement of W. Head, Negro, concerning threats made by citizens, November 28, 1865,

bureau immediately invalidated the black codes, enforcement of bureau directives depended entirely on the military force available. Unfortunately, the rapid demobilization of the Union army left vast areas of the South unoccupied and therefore under southern control. As late as February, 1866, bureau agents in Nashville, Tennessee, reported that many Negroes were still being held as slaves despite all bureau efforts to free and protect them.[15]

In view of the above, one might well wonder why the bureau even attempted to help the freedmen. Bureau agents knew that their own lives were in danger (some actually were murdered); yet, many faced this danger and tried to assist those blacks brave enough to face the hardships involved in clearing new land and earning a living from it.[16] Men like Howard, Brown, Thomas, Sprague, Fisk, Ord, and Granger were apparently interested in seeing the Negro as a land owner. However, their orders were of little value when their subordinates failed to carry them out in the right spirit; and in too many cases their subordinates were not interested in the economic security of the blacks. Those blacks who received some assistance from the bureau probably could not have succeeded without this aid. But the fact remains that the majority of the minor bureau agents were white northerners who felt no moral obligation to the freedmen. Indeed, many were dishonest and used their positions for personal and

---

Roll 22, pp. 533–34; D. Tillson to O. O. Howard, March 5, 1866, Roll 27; A. H. Galloway to O. O. Howard, June 16, 1866, Roll 32, pp. 373–77. Rolls 30 through 35 convey the general impression that there was considerable resistance to civil rights by southern whites and contain voluminous accounts of atrocities perpetrated upon the freedmen. Roll 59 contains reports of riots in New Orleans, St. Bernard and St. Landry parishes, Louisiana, and Camilla, Georgia, in 1868, during the presidential campaign. These attacks on the political rights of the freedmen also affected their attempts to secure land at that time.

15. *House Executive Documents*, 39th Cong., 1st Sess., No. 70, p. 236.

16. *Nation*, I (September 21, 1865), 356; II (February 15, 1866), 196; III (August 9, 1866), 103; D. Tillson to O. O. Howard, Registers and Letters Received (BRFAL), in RG 105, NA, Microcopy 752, Roll 32, p. 285.

political gain. When the assistant commissioner for Louisiana prepared to discontinue most bureau activities in early 1869, his examination of the affairs of the bureau convinced him that "many of its agents in this state are thoroughly dishonest." One agent in Louisiana even boasted openly "I am on the make, my pockets are open." [17]

During 1865, since no funds had been allocated for the bureau, Howard had to depend on the military for agents. In some cases military post commanders were assigned the additional responsibility of caring for the freedmen. Some officers resented this additional duty.[18] Consequently, proper assistance was rendered only in those areas where the agents were personally honest and dedicated to the idea that if the freedmen were to be truly free they must also be economically independent. Only in these circumstances would they not be subject to the legal and extra-legal pressures which white southerners might employ in order to force them into a position of subservience.

The conditions of natural disaster compounding the distressed state of the freedmen could have been taken as a golden opportunity to settle freedmen on homesteads with guaranteed rations. In 1866, 1867, and 1868, many areas of the South suffered from flooding which destroyed the crops. Those who saved their cotton crop from the flood waters lost most of it to the army worm. The resulting destitution could be alleviated only by issuing 32,662 whites and 24,283 blacks needed food until they could harvest their crop for that year. Congress authorized the issue of such rations. In addition, Congress ordered the bureau to transfer fifty thousand dollars to the Department of Agriculture. The

17. Howard Ashley White, *The Freedmen's Bureau in Lousiana* (Baton Rouge: Louisiana State University Press, 1970), 34–38; Louisiana Field Records (BRFAL) in RG 105, NA.

18. *Nation*, I (December 21, 1865), 779; E. Hatch to General Whipple, June 22, 1865, Registers and Letters Received (BRFAL), in RG 105, NA, Microcopy 752, Roll 15, p. 470; S. Thomas to O. O. Howard, August 7, 1865, pp. 477–79.

funds were to be used to purchase seed to replace that lost through flooding.[19] However, since the freedmen had already entered labor contracts for the year they could not leave to settle land of their own. Thus the bureau's contract labor policy again hindered homesteading efforts.

The bureau's limited policy of transporting freedmen to homestead lands and to states where they could secure employment proved helpful and also increased the value of the labor of those who remained where they were. In Virginia, South Carolina, and Georgia particularly, migration to homestead lands and to other states forced land owners to offer higher wages. This enabled many to save money and purchase land.

Restricted in their activities as bureau agents were by lack of adequate legislation and military power, they could only hope that some of their recommendations would be acted upon. Unfortunately, Congress limited itself to such short-term measures as rations for the destitute rather than long-term objectives such as economic security. Consequently the bureau strengthened its contract labor policies to ensure that freedmen would receive fair wages, while the Freedmen's Bank encouraged blacks to save money to purchase land.

When the bureau ceased its land activities it had established a foundation based on the economic principles of thrift and hard work. In Beaufort County, South Carolina, over 1,900 families

19. *House Executive Documents*, 40th Cong., 2nd Sess., No. 1, pp. 642–43; *House Executive Documents*, 41st Cong., 2nd Sess., No. 1, p. 501, J. T. Sprague to O. O. Howard, May 25, 1866, Registers and Letters Received (BRFAL), in RG 105, NA, Microcopy 752, Roll 34, pp. 111–12; A. Baird to O. O. Howard, May 15, 1866, Roll 33, p. 704; T. Ruger to O. O. Howard, June 2, 1866, Roll 35, pp. 2–3; E. D. Townsend to O. O. Howard, December 29, 1866, Roll 37, p. 297; T. J. Wood to O. O. Howard, October 9, 1866, Roll 38, p. 679; E. M. Stanton to O. O. Howard, Roll 40, p. 823; A. Gillem to O. O. Howard, April 17, 1867, Roll 43, p. 230; Rations issued in 1866 and 1867, Roll 49, p.345; R. K. Scott to O. O. Howard, Report for April, 1868, Roll 55, p. 700; New Orleans *Tribune*, April 17, 1867.

purchased 19,040 acres from the government through the tax sales and under the Sherman land provision of the second bureau bill. In St. Landry Parish, Louisiana, where there were only 126 free Negro farmers in 1860, by 1870 there were 431 farming land which they had purchased. Blacks constituted 10 percent of the 10,000 farm owners in Florida in 1870 and at least 6,500 black families filed homestead entries in all five southern states with public land. In all the southern states, through their own efforts and with the aid of the bureau and other concerned whites, freedmen did obtain land.[20] However, by and large, those who secured land during the first years of freedom were the exception rather than the rule, probably less than 5 percent of the total Negro population.

Nevertheless, by 1870, the bureau's economic policies succeeded in encouraging freedmen to save money and purchase land. Since this land represented hard work and sacrifice, the freedmen continued working to ensure against loss of the land. European observers pointed out that those who acquired land in the first years of freedom were generally those who had refused to be broken by slavery but rather had forced that system to recognize and reward their ability with positions of authority.[21] As freedmen increased their savings they also increased their

20. *House Executive Documents*, 40th Cong., 2nd Sess., No. 1, p. 672; U.S. Bureau of the Census, *Ninth Census of the United States, 1870*, unpublished population schedules for Louisiana and Florida; *House Executive Documents*, 41st Cong., 2nd Sess., No. 1, p. 505; Gates, *History of Public Land Law Development*, 414; Vernon Lane Wharton Collection, Box 9; Joe M. Richardson, in *The Negro in the Reconstruction of Florida*, 78–79, indicates that by 1868, 3,000 freedmen in Florida had homesteaded, but only 1,000 controlled land in 1870. He pointed out further that in Marion County freedmen entered 900 homesteads in 1868, but only 163 had land in 1870. He based his conclusions on the unpublished census schedules for Florida in 1870. However, if the census enumerators in Florida followed the same instructions as did those in Louisiana, none of the homesteaders were listed as landowners since they did not yet have title to the land. Therefore the control of land by Florida blacks in 1870 was probably greater than Professor Richardson estimated.

21. Philip Bruce, *The Plantation Negro as a Freedman: Observations on His Character, Condition, and Prospects in Virginia* (New York: G. P. Putnam's Sons, 1889), 211.

land ownership. Unfortunately, the failure of the Freedmen's Bank in 1874 destroyed much of the work of the bureau. Freedmen who lost money were reluctant to trust banks again. As a result, although freedmen continued to purchase land throughout the remainder of the century, land ownership did not increase as rapidly as it would have under a system of regular savings.

By 1900, 25 percent of the black farmers in the South owned their own land. In the south Atlantic region they owned an average of twenty-seven acres of land, whereas in the south central region the average landholding was forty-eight acres. Although the bureau cannot be assigned credit for land ownership in 1900, one must admit that without the bureau freedmen would have experienced considerably more opposition in their efforts to acquire land.

Historians generally have indicated that Congress failed to enact adequate legislation; President Johnson restored the land to former owners; the military and the Freedmen's Bureau failed to provide adequate protection; and southern whites opposed Negro land ownership. All these allegations are quite valid. However, in developing the negative aspects of failure, historians have frequently ignored the positive gains made during Reconstruction.

Although congressional actions were inadequate, Congress did in fact enact legislation which was both prejudicial and beneficial to the freedmen. President Johnson's action in restoring the land, while depriving the freedmen of land which they believed had been promised to them, was necessitated by the economic concepts of the time; any other action would have constituted a threat to property rights and would have further antagonized southern whites and thereby aggravated the existing racial tensions. Northern demand for demobilization negated any long-range military occupation policy. Soldiers who were compelled to remain in service to protect the freedmen resented this involuntary extension of their enlistment. Consequently, the protection they afforded their charges was less than enthusiastic. On the other hand the military did provide some protection and the bureau courts did afford the freedmen some measure of justice before the law.

Although many southern whites opposed Negro land ownership because land carried status, some southerners assisted blacks in their efforts to acquire land. By 1871 even Mississippi whites recognized the need to retain their labor supply. A convention of planters enacted a resolution recommending the division of large tracts into parcels of forty or eighty acres for sale "upon the most favorable terms to the colored people that they may soon become better citizens, and have more interest in the welfare of the state." [22]

Unfortunately, slavery had served as a conditioning agent which deprived many freedmen of the knowledge or ability to take advantage of the opportunities thus provided. This factor, combined with the depressed economic conditions of the South, and with the ravages of war and nature, forced many freedmen to join some former planters in becoming tenant farmers, share croppers, or renters.

Efforts to assist the freedmen to become landowners must therefore be judged a failure. The only land the nation was willing to offer was the homestead lands of the South. Nostrums which failed to make land owners of whites who had never experienced slavery could hardly be expected to succeed for freedmen. The tragedy of Reconstruction is the failure of the black masses to acquire land, since without the economic security provided by land ownership the freedmen were soon deprived of the political and civil rights which they had won.

Yet, despite the failure of the masses, freedmen did achieve considerable success. During the first thirty-five years of free-

22. Hinds County (Miss.) *Gazette*, February 8, 1871; Vernon Lane Wharton Collection, Box 8.

dom 25 percent of the black farmers of the South acquired land. Since the assistance provided by the bureau only helped to counteract the negative aspects of slavery and in no way altered the prevailing racial attitude, their success represents a personal triumph against overwhelming odds.

Selected Bibliography

I. Primary Sources

A. Manuscript Collections

LIBRARY OF CONGRESS

Zachariah Chandler Papers
James R. Doolittle Papers
William P. Fessenden Papers
Ulysses S. Grant Papers
Andrew Johnson Papers
Benjamin Wade Papers

LOUISIANA STATE LAND OFFICE

Letters of the Commissioner of the General Land Office to the Register
and Receiver, 1866–1876
Letters of the Commissioner of the State Land Office, 1868–1871

NATIONAL ARCHIVES

Record Group 101
    Records of the Freedmen's Savings and Trust Company
    Registers of Signatures of Depositors in Branches of the Freedmen's
        Savings and Trust Company, Microcopy 818
Record Group 105
    Records of the Assistant Commissioner for the State of Alabama
        Bureau of Refugees, Freedmen and Abandoned Lands (BRFAL),
        1865–1870, Microcopy 809
    Records of the Assistant Commissioner for the State of Georgia

Bureau of Refugees, Freedmen and Abandoned Lands (BRFAL), 1865–1870, Microcopy 798

Records of the Assistant Commissioner for the State of Mississippi Bureau of Refugees, Freedmen, and Abandoned Lands (BRFAL), 1865–1869, Microcopy 826

Records of the Assistant Commissioner for the State of North Carolina Bureau of Refugees, Freedmen and Abandoned Lands (BRFAL), 1865–1870, Microcopy 843

Records of the Assistant Commissioner for the State of South Carolina Bureau of Refugees, Freedmen and Abandoned Lands (BRFAL), 1865–1870, Microcopy 869

Records of the Field Offices of the Bureau of Refugees, Freedmen and Abandoned Lands (BRFAL)

Records of the Land Division of the Bureau of Refugees, Freedmen and Abandoned Lands (BRFAL)

Registers and Letters Received by the Bureau of Refugees, Freedmen and Abandoned Lands (BRFAL), Microcopy 752

Selected Series of Records Issued by the Commissioner of the Bureau of Refugees, Freedmen and Abandoned Lands (BRFAL), Microcopy 742

UNIVERSITY OF SOUTHWESTERN LOUISIANA ARCHIVES

Alexandre Mouton Collection
Dalton Watson Collection
Vernon L. Wharton Collection

B. OFFICIAL DOCUMENTS AND PUBLICATIONS

Congressional Globe. 37th Congress through the 41st Congress.

Official Journal of the Proceedings of the Convention for Framing a Constitution for the State of Louisiana 1867–1868. New Orleans: N.p., 1868.

Richardson, J. D., ed. *Compilation of the Messages and Papers of the Presidents, 1789–1902.* 10 vols. (53rd Cong., 2nd Sess., House Miscellaneous Document No. 210, pts. 1–10). Washington, D.C.: Government Printing Office, 1907.

U.S. Congress. *House Executive Documents.* 39th Cong., 1st Sess., No. 11 and No. 70; 39th Cong., 2nd Sess., No. 1; 40th Cong., 2nd Sess., No. 1; 40th Cong., 3rd Sess., No. 1; 41st Cong., 2nd Sess., No. 1; 42nd Cong., 2nd Sess., No. 1.

——. *House Reports.* 40th Cong., 2nd Sess., No. 30.

————. *Senate Executive Documents.* 39th Cong., 1st Sess., No. 2, No. 6, and No. 27; 40th Cong., 3rd Sess., No. 15.

U.S. Department of Commerce and Labor. Bureau of the Census. *Ninth Census of the United States, 1870.* Unpublished population schedules for Louisiana and Florida.

————. *Twelfth Census of the United States, 1900.* Agriculture, Vol. V.

————. *Negroes in the United States.* Bulletin No. 8. Washington, D.C.: Government Printing Office, 1904.

U.S., *Statutes at Large.* Vols. XII, XIII, XIV, XVI.

C. Contemporary Newspapers and Periodicals

Clark County (Alabama) *Journal.* 1863
Cincinnati (Ohio) *Colored Citizen.* 1865
Hinds County (Mississippi) *Gazette.* 1865–1870
Moulton (Alabama) *Advertiser.* 1868
Nashville *Colored Tennessean.* 1865
Nation. 1865–1870
New Orleans *Daily Picayune.* 1865–1870
New Orleans *Era.* 1864
New Orleans *Republican.* 1865–1868
New Orleans *Times.* 1865–1867
New Orleans *Tribune.* 1864–1867
New York *Times.* 1862–1870
Opelousas (Louisiana) *Courier.* 1865–1868
Opelousas (Louisiana) *Journal.* 1866–1868
Vicksburg (Mississippi) *Times.* 1866

D. Printed Travel Accounts, Letters, Memoirs, Reminiscences, and other Contemporary Sources

Alvord, John W. *Letters from the South Relating to the Condition of the Freedmen.* Washington, D.C.: Howard University Press, 1870.

Basler, Roy P., ed. *The Collected Works of Abraham Lincoln.* 8 vols. New Brunswick, New Jersey: Rutgers University Press, 1953.

Bayne, Thomas, and John Brown. *An Address from the Colored Citizens of Norfolk, Virginia, to the People of the United States.* New Bedford, Mass.: E. Anthony and Sons, Printers, 1865.

Beecher, Eunice White (Mrs. Henry Ward Beecher). *Letters from Florida.* New York: D. Appleton and Company, 1879.

Bruce, Phillip A. *The Plantation Negro as a Freedman: Observations on His Character, Condition, and Prospects in Virginia*. New York: G. P. Putman's Sons, 1889.

Douglass, Frederick. "The Future of the Negro People in the Slave States." *Douglass' Monthly* (March, 1862).

Eaton, John, Jr. *Grant, Lincoln, and the Freedmen: Reminiscences of the Civil War*. New York: Longman, Green and Company, 1907.

Edmonds, John. *Reconstruction of the Union*. New York: American News Company, 1867.

Frazier, Thomas R., ed. *Afro-American History: Primary Sources*. New York: Harcourt Brace Jovanovich, Inc., 1970.

Howard, Oliver O. *Autobiography of Oliver Otis Howard*. New York: The Baker and Taylor Company, 1907.

Leigh, Frances (Butler). *Ten Years on a Georgia Plantation since the War*. London: R. Bentley and Son, 1883.

Lockett, Samuel H. *Louisiana As It Is: A Geographical and Topographical Description of the State*. Lauren Post, ed. Baton Rouge: Louisiana State University Press, 1969.

McPherson, Edward. *The Political History of the United States of America, During the Great Rebellion*. 3d ed. Washington, D.C.: Solomons and Chapman, 1876.

Macrae, David. *The Americans at Home: Pen and Ink Sketches of American Men, Manners, and Institutions*. Edinburgh, Edmonston, and Douglas, 1870. 2 vols.

Pickett, William P. *The Negro Problem: Abraham Lincoln's Solution*. New York: G. P. Putnam's Sons, 1909.

Sherman, William T. *Memoirs of General William T. Sherman*. Bloomington: Indiana University Press, 1957.

Stearns, Charles. *The Black Man of the South and the Rebels; or, The Characteristics of the Former and the Recent Outrages of the Latter*. New York: American News Company, 1872.

Stowe, Harriet (Beecher). *Palmetto-Leaves*. Boston: J. R. Osgood and Company, 1873.

Trowbridge, John T. *The Desolate South, 1865–1866: A Picture of the Battlefields of the Devastated Confederacy*. Hartford: L. Stebbins, 1866.

U.S. Department of War. *The War of the Rebellion: A Compilation of the Official Records of the Union and Confederate Armies*. 104 Vols. Washington, D.C.: Government Printing Office, 1880–1900.

Williams, George W. *History of the Negro Race in America from 1619 to 1880*. 2 vols. New York: G. P. Putnam's Sons, 1883.

Yoshpe, Harry P., and Philip P. Brower, comps. *Preliminary Inventory of the Land Entry Papers of the General Land Office: Preliminary Inventory No. 22.* Washington, D.C.: National Archives, 1949.

II. Secondary Sources

A. ARTICLES

Abbott, Martin. "Free Land, Free Labor, and the Freedmen's Bureau." *Agricultural History*, XXX (October, 1956), 150–56.

Bethel, Elizabeth. "The Freedmen's Bureau in Alabama." *Journal of Southern History*, XIV (February, 1948), 49–92.

Bonekemper, Edward H. "Negro Ownership of Real Property." *Journal of Negro History*, LV (July 1970), 165–81.

Cox, John, and La Wanda Cox. "General O. O. Howard and the 'Misrepresented Bureau." *Journal of Southern History*, XIX (November, 1953), 427–56.

Cox, La Wanda. "The Promise of Land for the Freedmen." *Mississippi Valley Historical Review*, XLV (December, 1958), 413–40.

Gates, Paul W. "Federal Land Policy in the South, 1866–1888." *Journal of Southern History*, VI (August, 1940), 303–360.

Hoffman, Edwin D. "From Slavery to Self Reliance." *Journal of Negro History*, XLI (January, 1956), 8–42.

Oubre, Claude F. "The Opelousas Riot of 1868." *Attakapas Gazette*, VIII (December, 1973), 139–52.

B. BOOKS

Abbott, Martin. *The Freedmen's Bureau in South Carolina, 1865–1872.* Chapel Hill: University of North Carolina Press, 1967.

Allen, James S. *Reconstruction: The Battle for Democracy, 1865–1876.* New York: International Publishers, 1937.

Bentley, George R. *A History of the Freedmen's Bureau.* Philadelphia: University of Pennsylvania Press, 1955.

Bleser, Carol. *The Promised Land: The History of the South Carolina Land Commission.* Columbia: University of South Carolina Press, 1969.

Carpenter, John A. *Sword and Olive Branch: Oliver Otis Howard.* Pittsburgh: University of Pittsburgh Press, 1964.

Fleming, Walter L. *The Freedmen's Savings Bank.* Chapel Hill: University of North Carolina Press, 1927.

Gates, Paul W. *History of the Public Land Law Development*. Washington, D.C.: Government Printing Office, 1969.

Korngold, Ralph. *Thaddeus Stevens: A Being Darkly Wise and Rudely Great*. New York: Harcourt Brace and World, 1955.

McFeely, William S. *Yankee Stepfather: General O. O. Howard and the Freedmen*. New Haven: Yale University Press, 1968.

McPherson, James M. *The Struggle for Equality: Abolitionists and the Negro in the Civil War and Reconstruction*.Princeton: Princeton University Press, 1964.

Pease, Jane H., and William H. Pease. *Bound with Them in Chains: A Biographical History of the Antislavery Movement*. Westport, Conn.: Greenwood Press, Inc., 1972.

Peirce, Paul Skeels. *The Freedmen's Bureau*. Iowa City: University of Iowa Press, 1904.

Quarles, Benjamin. *Frederick Douglass*. New York: Atheneum, 1970.

Richardson, Joe M. *The Negro in the Reconstruction of Florida: 1865–1877*. Tallahassee: Florida State University Press, 1965.

Ripley, C. Peter. *Slaves and Freedmen in Civil War Louisiana*. Baton Rouge: Louisiana State University Press, 1976.

Robbins, Roy M. *Our Landed Heritage: The Public Domain, 1776–1936*. Lincoln: University of Nebraska Press, 1962.

Rose, Willie Lee. *Rehearsal for Reconstruction: The Port Royal Experiment*. New York: The Bobbs Merrill Company, 1964.

Sefton, James E. *The United States Army and Reconstruction, 1865–1877*. Baton Rouge: Louisiana State University Press, 1967.

Taylor, Alrutheus A. *The Negro in South Carolina During the Reconstruction*. Washington D.C.: Association for the Study of Negro Life and History, 1924.

Taylor, Joe Gray. *Louisiana Reconstructed: 1863–1877*. Baton Rouge: Louisiana State University Press, 1974.

Vincent, Charles. *Black Legislators in Louisiana During Reconstruction*. Baton Rouge: Louisiana State University Press, 1976.

Washington, Booker T. *The Story of the Negro: The Rise of the Race from Slavery*. 2 vols. New York: Doubleday, Page and Company, 1909.

Wharton, Vernon Lane. *The Negro in Mississippi, 1865–1890*. New York: Harper Torchbooks, 1965.

White, Howard Ashley. *The Freedmen's Bureau in Louisiana*. Baton Rouge: Louisiana State University Press, 1970.

Williamson, Joel. *After Slavery: The Negro in South Carolina During*

Reconstruction, 1861–1877. Chapel Hill: University of North Carolina Press, 1965.

Wilson, Theodore. *The Black Codes of the South*. University, Ala.: University of Alabama Press, 1965.

C. UNPUBLISHED SOURCES

Boyd, Willis. "Negro Colonization in the National Crisis." Ph. D. dissertation, University of California at Los Angeles, 1953.

Index